# Lecture Notes in Computer Science 12921

El Kindi Rezig · Vijay Gadepally ·
Timothy Mattson · Michael Stonebraker ·
Tim Kraska · Fusheng Wang · Gang Luo ·
Jun Kong · Alevtina Dubovitskaya (Eds.)

# Heterogeneous Data Management, Polystores, and Analytics for Healthcare

VLDB Workshops, Poly 2021 and DMAH 2021
Virtual Event, August 20, 2021
Revised Selected Papers

*Editors*
El Kindi Rezig
Massachusetts Institute of Technology
Cambridge, MA, USA

Timothy Mattson
Intel Corporation
Portland, ME, USA

Tim Kraska
Massachusetts Institute of Technology
Cambridge, MA, USA

Gang Luo
University of Utah
Salt Lake City, UT, USA

Alevtina Dubovitskaya
Lucerne Unviersity of Applied Sciences
Rotkreuz, Zug, Switzerland

Vijay Gadepally
Lincoln Laboratory
Massachusetts Institute of Technology
Lexington, MA, USA

Michael Stonebraker
Massachusetts Institute of Technology
Cambridge, MA, USA

Fusheng Wang ⓘ
Stonybrook University
Lake Grove, NY, USA

Jun Kong
Georgia State University
Atlanta, GA, USA

ISSN 0302-9743        ISSN 1611-3349  (electronic)
Lecture Notes in Computer Science
ISBN 978-3-030-93662-4       ISBN 978-3-030-93663-1  (eBook)
https://doi.org/10.1007/978-3-030-93663-1

LNCS Sublibrary: SL4 – Security and Cryptology

This Springer imprint is published by the registered company Springer Nature Switzerland AG
The registered company address is: Gewerbestrasse 11, 6330 Cham, Switzerland

# Preface

In this volume we present the accepted contributions for the VLDB 2021 workshops entitled "Polystore systems for heterogeneous data in multiple databases with privacy and security assurances" (Poly 2021) and the "Seventh International Workshop on Data Management and Analytics for Medicine and Healthcare" (DMAH 2021). The workshops were held virtually in conjunction with the 47th International Conference on Very Large Data Bases (VLDB 2021) on August 20, 2021.

Poly 2021 aimed to focus on the broader real-world polystore problem, which includes data management, data integration, data curation, privacy, and security. Enterprises are routinely divided into independent business units to support agile operations. However, this leads to "siloed" information systems which generate a host of problems, such as the following:

- Discovery of data relevant to the problem at hand. For example, Merck has approximately 4000 Oracle databases, a data lake, large numbers of files, and an interest in public data from the web. Finding relevant data in this sea of information is a challenge.
- Integrating the discovered data. Independently constructed schemas are never compatible.
- Cleaning the resulting data. A good figure of merit is that 10% of all data is missing or wrong.
- Ensuring efficient access to the resulting data. At scale, operations must be performed "in situ", and a good polystore system is a requirement.

It is often said that data scientists spend 80% (or more) of their time on these tasks, and it is crucial to have better solutions. In addition, the EU has recently enacted the General Data Protection Regulation (GDPR) that will force enterprises to assuredly delete personal data on request. This "right to be forgotten" is one of several requirements of GDPR, and it is likely that GDPR-like requirements will spread to other locations, for example, California. In addition, privacy and security issues are increasingly an issue for large internet platforms. In enterprises, these issues will be front and center in the distributed information systems in place today. Lastly, enterprise access to data in practice will require queries constructed from a variety of programming models. A "one size fits all" model just won't work in these cases.

All submissions for Poly 2021 were reviewed in a single-blind manner, and the acceptance was determined by the aggregated scores from all reviewers.

The goal of the DMAH workshop is to bring together people in the field crosscutting information management and medical informatics to discuss innovative data management and analytics technologies highlighting end-to-end applications, systems, and methods to address problems in healthcare, public health, and everyday wellness, with clinical, physiological, imaging, behavioral, environmental, and omics data, along with data from social media and the Web.

DMAH 2021 provided a unique opportunity for interaction between information management researchers and biomedical researchers in this interdisciplinary field. All submitted papers were rigorously reviewed by three reviewers and the acceptance was determined by the aggregated scores.

We are grateful to everyone involved in the organization of these workshops, including all authors for submitting their work and the workshop participants. We hope that you enjoy reading the papers included in this volume.

El Kindi Rezig
Vijay Gadepally
Michael Stonebraker
Tim Kraska
Fusheng Wang
Gang Luo
Jun Kong
Alevtina Dubovitskaya

# Organization

## Poly 2021

### Workshop Chairs

| | |
|---|---|
| El Kindi Rezig | MIT CSAIL, USA |
| Vijay Gadepally | MIT Lincoln Laboratory, USA |
| Tim Kraska | MIT CSAIL, USA |
| Timothy Mattson | Intel Corporation, USA |
| Michael Stonebraker | MIT CSAIL, USA |

### Program Committee

| | |
|---|---|
| Vijay Gadepally | MIT Lincoln Laboratory, USA |
| El Kindi Rezig | MIT CSAIL, USA |
| Danny Weitzner | MIT Internet Policy Research Initiative, USA |
| Michael Gubanov | Florida State University, USA |
| Edmon Begoli | Oak Ridge National Laboratory, USA |
| Dimitris Kolovos | University of York, UK |
| Amarnath Gupta | University of California, San Diego, USA |
| Ratnesh Sahay | AstraZeneca, UK |
| Rada Chirkova | North Carolina State University, USA |
| Sam Madden | MIT, USA |
| Tim Kraska | MIT, USA |
| Pedro Pedreira | Facebook Inc., USA |
| Timothy Mattson | Intel Corporation, USA |
| Michael Stonebraker | MIT CSAIL, USA |
| Mourad Ouzzani | Qatar Computing Research Institute, Qatar |
| Makoto Onizuka | University of Osaka, Japan |
| Ahmed Abdelhamid | Purdue University, USA |
| Ismail Oukid | Snowflake, USA |

## DMAH 2021

### Workshop Chairs

| | |
|---|---|
| Fusheng Wang | Stony Brook University, USA |
| Gang Luo | University of Washington, USA |

Alevtina Dubovitskaya          Lucerne University of Applied Sciences and
                                  Arts/Swisscom, Switzerland
Jun Kong                       Georgia State University, USA

## Program Committee

Yang Cao                       Kyoto University, Japan
Dejun Teng                     Stony Brook University, USA
Blair Christian                Oak Ridge National Laboratory, USA
Vagelis Hristidis              University of California, Riverside, USA
Tahsin Kurc                    Stony Brook University, USA
Peter Elkin                    University at Buffalo, USA
Jerome Carter                  Informatics Squared, Inc., USA
Ye Ye                          University of Pittsburgh, USA
Yanhui Liang                   Google Inc., USA
Peter Dolog                    Aalborg University, Denmark
Halil Kilicoglu                University of Illinois Urbana-Champaign, USA
Chunjie Zhou                   Ludong University, China
Xiaxia Yu                      Shenzhen University, China

# Friends Don't Let Friends Deploy Black-Box Models: the Importance of Intelligibility and Explanation for Machine Learning in Healthcare (Keynote Talk)

Rich Caruana

Microsoft Research, Redmond, Washington, USA

rcaruana@microsoft.com

**Abstract.** In machine learning sometimes a tradeoff must be made between accuracy and intelligibility: the most accurate models usually are often not very intelligible, and the most intelligible models usually are less accurate. This can limit the accuracy of models that can safely be deployed in mission-critical applications such as healthcare where being able to understand, validate, edit, and ultimately trust a model is important. We have developed a learning method based on generalized additive models (GAMs) that is as accurate as full complexity models such as boosted trees and random forests, but even more intelligible than linear models. This makes it easy to understand what models have learned and to edit models when they learn inappropriate things. Making it possible for medical experts to understand and repair a model is critical because most clinical data is complex and has unanticipated problems. I'll present a number of healthcare case studies where these high-accuracy GAMs discover surprising patterns in the data that would have made deploying black-box models risky. The case studies include surprising findings in pregnancy, pneumonia, ICU and COVID-19 risk prediction.

**Bio.** Rich Caruana is a Senior Principal Researcher at Microsoft. His research focus is on intelligible/transparent modeling and machine learning for medical decision making. Before joining Microsoft, Rich was on the faculty at Cornell, at UCLA's Medical School, and at CMU's Center for Learning and Discovery. Rich's Ph.D. is from CMU, and his thesis on Multitask Learning helped create interest in the new subfield of Transfer Learning. Rich has received a number of best paper awards, an NSF CAREER Award in 2004 for Meta Clustering, and chaired KDD in 2007.

# Contents

# Privacy, Security and/or Policy Issues
# for Heterogenous Data

# Data Virtual Machines: Enabling Data Virtualization

Damianos Chatziantoniou[1](✉) and Verena Kantere[2]

[1] Department of Management Science and Technology,
Athens University of Economics and Business, Athens, Greece
`damianos@aueb.gr`
[2] School of Electrical and Computer Engineering,
National Technical University of Athens, Athens, Greece
`verena@mail.ntua.gr`

**Abstract.** Modern analytics environments are characterized by a data infrastructure that comprises a great variety of datasets, data formats, data management and processing systems. Such environments are dynamic and data analysis needs to be performed in a flexible and agile manner via data virtualization techniques. Towards this end, we have proposed the Data Virtual Machine (DVM), a graph-based conceptual model based on entities and attributes. The basic idea of the DVM is that the relations of entities and attributes are based and expressed as the output of data processing tasks. In this paper we discuss the notion of data virtualization and propose a set of goals for relevant techniques in terms of modeling capabilities, query formulation and schema flexibility. We also place DVMs with respect to these goals.

**Keywords:** Data virtualization · Data virtual machines

## 1 Introduction

Modern analytics environments in research and industry aim at the analysis of diverse datasets. The latter may be produced by a variety of applications or collected by autonomous agents and stored in dispersed locations. Therefore, such datasets are expected to be inherently heterogeneous in both the semantics that they encapsulate as well as the data structures that hold them and relevant systems that manage and process them. This heterogeneity extends from the data to the analysis itself, since various users of analytics environment – most probably data scientists, but also data engineers, simple end-users, data regulation officers etc. – want to deploy different analysis projects, related to traditional BI, data exploration, data mining, prediction etc.

Coping with this diversity in the data management landscape is a well-known research mandate [1,6]. Multiple big data systems and analysis platforms need to coexist, integrated and federated. While data warehousing is the usual approach, it is rigid for a rapidly changing data environment. In addition, [1] discusses the need for techniques that can create *late-bound schemas* on data that

E. K. Rezig et al. (Eds.): Poly 2021/DMAH 2021, LNCS 12921, pp. 3–13, 2021.
https://doi.org/10.1007/978-3-030-93663-1_1

may be persisted but are processed seldomly, if ever. In the analytics environment as described above, this need is more prevalent, since the whole data infrastructure is dynamic and analysis purposes change agilely. For such environments, producing full-fledged classical integrated schemas on structured, semi-structured and unstructured data is not only extremely expensive in terms of time and resources, but it may also be impossible to achieve in the time-window of the analysis.

To tackle the above challenges, we have proposed the Data Virtual Machine (DVM), which was briefly introduced in [3], a graph-based conceptual model based on entities and attributes - concepts that users understand well. A DVM is a graph where nodes represent attribute domains and edges represent mappings between these domains. These mappings are expressed by the output of data processing tasks (e.g. a query or a program.) This output must be provided as $(v_1, v_2)$ value pairs. The argument is that these data processing tasks can be easily defined, in an on-demand and visual manner. The schema is *then* generated. Furthermore, this graph is appropriate for visual query formulation (emphasis is given on dataframes). We have developed a research prototype, called DataMingler [5] that demonstrates the DVM and its potential.

A DVM is a *data virtualization* technique, a significant enterprise trend [9]. The goal is to allow an application to retrieve and manipulate data without requiring technical details about the data, i.e. abstracting data out of its form and manipulating it regardless of the way it is stored or structured [11]. It also provides a single customer view (or single view of *any other entity*) of the overall data [14]. All major DB vendors offer products in this field, e.g. [7,10,12,13]. Data virtualization is closely related to mediators and federated databases [8], concepts that the research community has dealt with decades ago, when systems heterogeneity was also an issue. The focus of data virtualization however is on availing common database features, such as data modeling, querying and data extraction to DB-naive users [2,11].

In this paper we propose a set of goals for dynamic and efficient data virtualization environments (Sect. 2) in terms of modeling capabilities, query formulation and schema flexibility. We then discuss data virtual machines with respect to these challenges (Sects. 3 and 4).

## 2    Data Virtualization

The research question is how a db-literate person can create quickly, *agilely* a virtual data layer on top of an organization's data infrastructure that can be easily and *intuitively* used by db-illiterate people (usually data scientists) for data exploration and query formulation.

### 2.1    Analytics Environments

The term *data infrastructure* encompasses much more than data persistently stored in data management systems, SQL, NoSQL, or otherwise. It also involves flat files, spreadsheets and transient data handled by stream engines. Last but not least, it includes processes (e.g. queries, scripts, models, web services, programs in general) that produce output that could be perceived as data and exploited in the analysis phase, for instance a Python program that computes the social influence or the churn category of each customer. These are also attributes of the customer and it is important to easily and agilely represent them at the conceptual data layer (think: derived attributes in ER model).

We identify four distinct roles of data stakeholders in an analytics environment. *Data engineers* are technical people whose main duty is to extract, transform and integrate data from multiple sources. They would like to have a formalism where they can easily and quickly map data and programs' output onto it. They also create/prepare data structures appropriate for input to data analysis tasks, for example dataframes. They would like to delegate this task to data scientists. *Data scientists*, not necessarily DB-literate people, usually build a model for an entity, using the features (attributes) of that entity. They would like to have at their disposal a simple model that identifies entities and attributes, so they can easily select/experiment with those of interest. Ideally, they would like to create/manage themselves the data inputs to their algorithms. *Data subjects or contributors*, such as customers, suppliers, users, will soon be involved in the data supply chain due to the EU GDPR's data portability requirement – data markets have already emerged in various domains. They have to be provided with a high-level model, easy to understand and manage, and possibly link to data from other organizations. Some "self-service" data integration and data portfolios management will be necessary. In addition, data subjects should be enabled to export selected data to the logical model of their choice (e.g. XML, JSON, relational.) Finally, *data protection officers* whose primary role is to ensure that their organization processes personal data according to applicable data protection laws. They want to easily see data provenance and consent of data at a fine granular level.

## 2.2 Goals of Data Virtualization Systems

A data virtualization layer should serve appropriately all data stakeholders of an analytics environment. This layer should exhibit the properties mentioned below. As a running example, assume the following – very simple – collection of data sources.

*Example 1.* Assume a data setting with the following data sources:

- *S1*: A relational table Customers(custID,Age,Gender,City),
- *S2*: An excel spreadsheet called Transactions having columns 1 to 4 labeled as: transactionID, custID, Amount, Date,
- *S3*: A text file keeping the customers' comments as (custID, comment) lines,
- *S4*: A java program implementing a churn prediction model which outputs when executed the customer's ID and her churn category for all customers. □

**Model Simplicity, Plasticity and Agility.** The data virtualization model should be simple, based on concepts that people understand well, for example entities and attributes. It should represent these in a graphical manner and should be amenable to visual manipulations, both in terms of schema management and query formulation. Data sources become rapidly available and unavailable in modern analytics environments. Data engineers should be able to easily and quickly, in an ad hoc manner, incorporate parts of these in a virtual schema without significant semantic effort. It should also be easy to modify the virtual schema with no major implications to the rest of it. In Example 1, the question is how can one *quickly* represent the `customer` entity along with his `transactions`, `age`, `gender`, `city`, `comments`, `churn category` attributes. At the same time, a `transaction` is an entity itself with its own attributes `customer`, `date`, `amount`.

**Intuitive Data Exploration/Query Formulation.** Data exploration and query formulation should be facilitated by non-DB experts (e.g. statisticians, data subjects) in a simple and intuitive, visual, manner. One should easily select attributes, express conditions and define transformations, using built-in or plug-in functions in some programming language of his/her choice to form a query. Query evaluation should be efficient and based on a theoretical framework, possibly similar to relational algebra. For example, one should easily ask for each `customer` his `age` and `gender`, the average sentiment of his `comments` containing the keyword "google", the actual list of her `comments` and the total amount of her `transactions` on May 2019.

**Data Sharing:** Data sharing has been identified as a key element of the big data era. Data sharing is related to many different research topics, such as ontologies, common vocabularies, vertical and horizontal sharing, etc. In real-life analytics environments, people need to share parts of spreadsheets, flat files, json documents or relations. In most cases this is done manually, in an ad hoc manner, by exporting data to a text file and moving this file around. There is no principled way to describe what someone shares in an intermediate representation, unless if imported to a data warehouse. A data virtualization model should make this process easy, quick and semantically clear. It should serve as the medium for data sharing in a standardized, collaborative, distributed manner.

**Support for "Any Entity View":** This is not a known term in conceptual modeling, yet it is an important, practical requirement in analytics applications of an organization. Traditionally refers to the *customer* entity ("single customer view"), which means structuring/representing attributes from several sources around the customer entity (e.g. think of a JSON document rooted on customer's id). However, data scientists want to study features of other entities as well, such as *suppliers, employees, products, transactions*, etc. Going one step further, they want to convert entities' attributes, such as the *age* of a customer, the *churn category* of a customer, or the *date* of a transaction, to entities and study them individually. For example, think of a JSON document rooted on *age* or *churn category* or *date*. To do so, all model's constructs should be conceived as an attribute and an entity at the same time, i.e. they have to be symmetric in a way. The ER model does not exhibit this property, since it represents entities and attributes with different constructs. It should be easy to "reorient" the schema around any entity.

**Model Polymorphism:** One size does not fit all and a virtual schema has to be easily concretized to different logical models. While in a traditional database design the data model is predefined and determines storage models, in a conceptual design one can create database instances in different logical models (e.g. relational, semi-structured, multi-dimensional). These instances can then be queried by data scientists via the native query language of the model (e.g. SQL, Mongo queries, MDX).

**Linkability and Crawlability:** Data exploration requires a "connected" model, where the schema can be navigated. In addition, feature selection is a well-known topic in statistics: the data scientist selects appropriate features for a model. For this, a model that supports crawling is needed, i.e. starting from an entity, an algorithm collects or defines relevant attributes. This property also plays an important role in GDPR's data portability requirement. Data subjects could build their own data models from multiple domains.

## 3  Data Virtual Machines

A Data Virtual Machine (DVM) is a graph-based representation of a collection of Data Manipulation Tasks (DMT) defined over the data infrastructure of an organization. For example, consider the SQL query: ``SELECT custID, Age from Customers''. The *output* of this query provides two mappings between two attribute domains, custID and Age. These mappings can be represented by two key-list structures, as shown in Fig. 1. Attribute domains become nodes in the DVM graph and edges represent mappings between them, as manifested by the output of DMTs. The motivation of the main idea lies on multi-valued, derived attributes in Entity-Relationship theory: each node in a DVM is a derived, multi-valued attribute for any other attribute that is related to (which plays the role of the primary key of an entity) and vice versa. More details can be found in [4].

**Definition 1.** *[Key-List Structure] A key-list structure (KL-structure) $K$ is a set of (key, list) pairs, $K = \{(k, L_k)\}$, where $L_k$ is a list of elements or the empty list and $\forall\ (k_1, L_{k_1}), (k_2, L_{k_2}) \in K$, $k_1 \neq k_2$. Both keys and elements of the lists are strings. The set of keys of KL-structure $K$ is denoted as $keys(K)$; the list of key $k$ of KL-structure $K$ is denoted as $list(k, K)$. If $k \notin keys(K)$, the value of $list(k, K)$ is null. The schema of a KL-structure $K$, denoted as $K(A, B)$ consists of two labels, $A$ and $B$. $A$ is the role of the key and $B$ is the role of the list in the key-list pairs.* □

A key-list structure is essentially a multi-map data structure, where mapped values to a key are organized as a list. There are many key-value stores (e.g. Redis) that efficiently handle key-list structures.

**Definition 2.** *[Data Virtual Machines] Assume a collection $\mathcal{A}$ of $n$ domains $A_1, A_2, \ldots, A_n$, called attributes. Assume a collection $\mathcal{S}$ of $m$ multisets, $S_1, S_2, \ldots, S_m$, where each multiset $S$ has the form: $S = \{(u, v) : u \in A_i, v \in A_j, i, j \in \{1, 2, \ldots, n\}\}$, called data manipulation tasks. For each such $S \in \{S_1, S_2, \ldots, S_m\}$ we define two key-list structures, $K_{ij}^S$ and $K_{ji}^S$ as:*

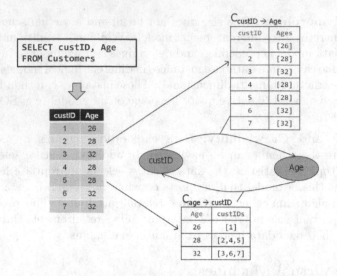

**Fig. 1.** A data manipulation task as a mapping between attributes

$K_{ij}^S$: *for each $u$ in the set $\{u : (u, v) \in S\}$ we define the list $L_u = \{v : (u, v) \in S\}$ and $(u, L_u)$ is appended to $K_{ij}^S$.*
$K_{ji}^S$ *is similarly defined.*

*The data virtual machine corresponding to these attributes and data manipulation tasks is a multi-graph $G = \{\mathcal{A}, \mathcal{S}\}$ constructed as follows:*

- *each attribute becomes a node in $G$*
- *for each data manipulation task $S$ we draw two edges $A_i \rightarrow A_j$ and $A_j \rightarrow A_i$, labeled with $K_{ij}^S$ and $K_{ji}^S$ respectively.*

*The key-list structure that corresponds to an edge $e : A_i \rightarrow A_j$ is denoted as $KL(e)$, with schema $(A_i, A_j)$.*                                                 □

The term "data manipulation task" refers to its output. The terms "attribute" and "node" are used interchangeably in the remaining of the paper.

Note that DVM modeling is somehow the inverse process of traditional data modeling. While in the latter one *first* designs the schema and *then* creates the DMTs to accommodate (fit) this schema, in DVM modeling one first defines the DMTs and a schema is produced according to the DMTs.

## 4    Data Virtualization and DVMs

In this section, we revisit the goals of data virtualization, as presented in Sect. 2.2, in the context of DVMs.

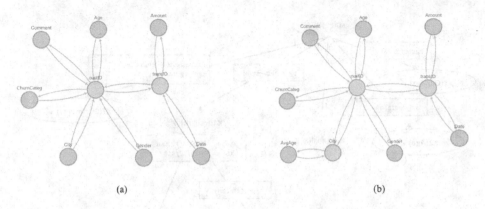

(a)                                    (b)

**Fig. 2.** A DVM generated according to a collection of DMTs

## 4.1 Agile Schema Modeling

Let us consider Example 1 and define the following data manipulation tasks over it – with the obvious semantics for each one:

- *DMT1:* SELECT custID, Age From Customers using S1
- *DMT2:* SELECT custID, Gender From Customers using S1
- *DMT3:* SELECT custID, City From Customers using S1
- *DMT4:* SpreadsheetReader(S2,1,2,'transID','custID')
- *DMT5:* SpreadsheetReader(S2,1,3,'transID','Amount')
- *DMT6:* SpreadsheetReader(S2,1,4,'transID','Date')
- *DMT7:* TextReader(S3,1,2,'custID','Comment')
- *DMT8:* ExecEnv(S4,1,2,'custID','ChurnCateg')

The generated DVM is shown in Fig. 2(a), as generated by the DataMingler tool [5]. Nodes having degree >1 are painted blue for visualization purposes and one could think of them as "entities", although all nodes have the same status in the graph. Assume now that one wants to relate each city with the average age of city's customers. s/he could do this by defining the following DMT.

- *DMT9:* SELECT City, CAST(avg(Age) AS int) as AvgAge FROM Customers GROUP BY City using S1

The generated DVM is shown in Fig. 2(b). Note that the City attribute is painted blue now. We reiterate here that *DMT9* provides not only an average age per city, but also a list of cities per age.

## 4.2 Simple and Efficient Dataframing

What kind of queries can we have on top of DVMs? Defining a complete query language over DVMs is work in progress. We focus on what data scientists/ statisticians usually do, since this is the primary target group of this work. They

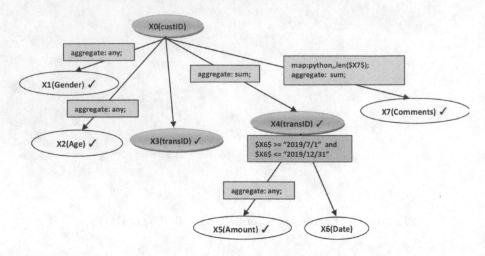

**Fig. 3.** A dataframe query example

usually form dataframes in Python, R or Spark. A dataframe is a table built incrementally, column-by-column, around an entity. The first column(s) is usually the key of the entity (e.g. customer ID) and the remaining ones are related attributes. An attribute can be processed (aggregated, filtered or transformed via a user-defined function in Python or R) before added as a column to the dataframe. The latter often serves as input to learning algorithms or for ad hoc reporting. It is important to facilitate this process in a simple and intuitive, visual manner. One should easily select (possibly along a path) attributes, express conditions and define transformations, using built-in methods or plug-in functions in a programming language of her choice (polyglotism) to form a dataframe.

A dataframe query over a DVM is defined as a tree, consisting of nodes and edges of the DVM [5] - *not necessarily* a subtree of the DVM. The same node/edge could appear multiple times in a dataframe query. For example, the query: "for each customer (custID), show his/her Gender and Age, the list of his/her transactions, the total amount of these transactions in the second semester of 2019 and the total number of characters of his/her comments" is shown in Fig. 3. To evaluate a dataframe query, the transformations on the edges have to be applied and the edges have to be combined, either along a path or across the same level. This evaluation (as well as optimization) take place within an algebraic framework equipped with operators that take as input one or more edges (i.e. key-list structures) and have as output an edge (another key-list structure).

### 4.3  Any-Entity View, Model Polymorphism

One of the goals of data virtualization is to provide a single view of any entity of the overall data. Traditional logical models, such as the relational or semi-structured ones fall through this goal because they provide a single-angle view of a schema, built with a specific entity in mind. Moreover, traditional conceptual models, such as the ER or UML, build a diagram in which metadata about the data are encapsulated in schematic objects of the model in a absolute manner, e.g. as entity sets, as relationship sets (ER) or as attributes, with absolute relation to other such schematic objects (e.g. an attribute belongs to a specific entity set or two entity sets or more are connected semantically in specific way via a relationship set. As a result, it is difficult to reorient a schema (or diagram) adhering to traditional models, in a way that all metadata can be viewed with respect and in relation to a specific schematic object, essentially giving different conceptual angles of the encapsulated world. Such schema reorientation can be a very useful tool in the hands of data scientists, enabling them to define very easily and using always the same schema different views of the overall data with respect to different entities in the data.

As an example, let us consider the nodes custID, transID, Date and ChurnCateg in Fig. 2(b). custID and transID are blue nodes, i.e. are considered as entities with attributes. In a respective ER diagram, these would correspond to two entity sets (with their respective attributes) connected with a relationship set. The produced relational schema would encode only this specific conceptual view, in which, for example, Dates are referenced with respect to transIDs and not to custIDs. In order to view Datess with respect to custIDs (i.e. the dates in which customers have made transactions) one would need to query the data and produce new relations (not encapsulated in the original conceptual schema). Moreover, Dates, which correspond to an attribute in the respective ER and relational schema, can be viewed only in reference to transIDs, whereas it may be useful to a user to view transIDs and even, furthermore, custIDs, with respect to Datess (i.e. what are the transactions made on a date and which customers made these transactions). As in the previous case, this can be done only via querying the data to produce a new relation that does not adhere to the original conceptual schema, but, in this case, the query is also quite complex, as it attempts to turn around the relationship of entity-attribute between transID and Dates. The same holds if one wants to view the data of customers and their transactions with respect to ChurnCateg.

The DVM is a model that achieves the goal of 'any-entity view' by simplifying all conceptual objects to graph nodes and all conceptual relations to graph edges. The exact conceptual relations between two nodes are determined by the data itself via the corresponding data processing tasks. Therefore, the exact conceptual objects are also defined by the data itself, i.e. if a node is an entity or an attribute. In the DVM, we define the notion of *entity's view* with respect to some node $N$ as a graph consisting of the node $N$ and a collection of DVM's paths that originate from $N$ and end on a node $M$ different than $N$.

The simplest structure of the DVM together with the fact that it is the data and the data processing tasks that form the entities, attributes and relations between entities and entities as well as entities and attributes, make it possible for a DVM to represent multiple different conceptual and logical schemas. The latter certainly necessitate different representations in all traditional conceptual

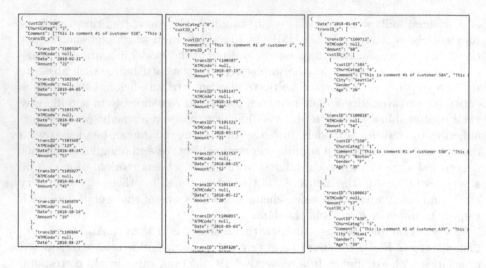

**Fig. 4.** Creating JSON documents for different DVM's nodes, conceived as entities

and logical models. For example, we would need two different ER schemas to represent `transID` as an entity set and `Date` as an attribute and the opposite. Furthermore, we would need schema mappings between logical schemas that are derived from the conceptual schemas. The DVM not only alleviates all this complexity, but enables the extraction of multiple schemas in traditional structured and semi-structured models, via the implementation of the notion 'entity view', achieving in this way, polyglotism. For example, based on a given graph for a specific 'entity view', a relational (work in progress) or semi-structured database can be materialized.

Using DataMingler [5], a user can selects a node in the DVM and a breadth-first-search tree rooted on that node is defined and the system generates a collection of JSON documents corresponding to the tree defined. It implements attributes as lists or strings, depending on the cardinality of lists (whether they contain multiple or single elements.) Fig. 4 shows the output when (a) `custID` is selected, (b) `ChurnCateg` is selected, and (c) `Date` is selected. This way one may define any node as an entity and analyze data based on that entity.

## 5   Conclusions

We discuss the notion of data virtualization as the enabler of agile, efficient and effective data processing in modern analytics environments. We focus on the fact that such environments are characterized on one hand by tremendous heterogeneity of data, formats, systems etc. and on the other by dynamicity and different analysis needs by users with multifarious roles that may not have data management expertise. We set goals of data virtualization and we briefly present DVM, a graph-based data virtualization model that we have proposed.

# References

1. Abadi, D., et al.: The Beckman report on database research. Commun. ACM **59**, 692–699 (2016)
2. Alagiannis, I., Borovica-Gajic, R., Branco, M., Idreos, S., Ailamaki, A.: Nodb: efficient query execution on raw data files. Commun. ACM **58**(12), 112–121 (2015)
3. Chatziantoniou, D., Kantere, V.: Data virtual machines: data-driven conceptual modeling of big data infrastructures. In: Workshops of EDBT 2020 (2020)
4. Chatziantoniou, D., Kantere, V.: Data virtual machines: a novel approach to data virtualization (2021, submitted for publication)
5. Chatziantoniou, D., Kantere, V.: Datamingler: a novel approach to data virtualization. In: Li, G., Li, Z., Idreos, S., Srivastava, D. (eds.) SIGMOD 2021: International Conference on Management of Data, Virtual Event, China, 20–25 June 2021, pp. 2681–2685. ACM (2021). https://doi.org/10.1145/3448016.3452752, https://doi.org/10.1145/3448016.3452752
6. Chatziantoniou, D., Tselai, F.: Introducing data connectivity in a big data web. In: Proceedings of the Third Workshop on Data analytics in the Cloud, DanaC 2014, pp. 7:1–7:4 (2014). http://doi.acm.org/10.1145/2627770.2627773
7. Denodo: Data virtualization: the modern data integration solution (2019). https://www.denodo.com/en/document/whitepaper/data-virtualization-modern-data-integration-solution
8. Doan, A., Halevy, A.Y., Ives, Z.G.: Principles of Data Integration. Morgan Kaufmann, San Francisco (2012)
9. Gartner: Market Guide for Data Virtualization (2018). https://www.gartner.com/en/documents/3893219/market-guide-for-data-virtualization
10. IBM: IBM's data virtualization tool: Cloud Pak for data (2021). https://www.ibm.com/analytics/data-virtualization
11. Karpathiotakis, M., Alagiannis, I., Heinis, T., Branco, M., Ailamaki, A.: Just-in-time data virtualization: lightweight data management with ViDa. In: CIDR 2015 (2015)
12. Microsoft: Introducing data virtualization with polybase (2021). https://docs.microsoft.com/en-us/sql/relational-databases/polybase/polybase-guide?view=sql-server-ver15
13. Oracle Corp.: Oracle Data Service Integrator (2020). https://www.oracle.com/middleware/technologies/data-service-integrator.html
14. Data virtualization and data warehousing (2020). https://en.wikipedia.org/wiki/Data_virtualization

# A Formal Category Theoretical Framework for Multi-model Data Transformations

Valter Uotila[✉] and Jiaheng Lu

Unified Database Management Systems, University of Helsinki, Helsinki, Finland
{valter.uotila,jiaheng.lu}@helsinki.fi

**Abstract.** Data integration and migration processes in polystores and multi-model database management systems highly benefit from data and schema transformations. Rigorous modeling of transformations is a complex problem. The data and schema transformation field is scattered with multiple different transformation frameworks, tools, and mappings. These are usually domain-specific and lack solid theoretical foundations. Our first goal is to define category theoretical foundations for relational, graph, and hierarchical data models and instances. Each data instance is represented as a category theoretical mapping called a functor. We formalize data and schema transformations as Kan lifts utilizing the functorial representation for the instances. A Kan lift is a category theoretical construction consisting of two mappings satisfying the certain universal property. In this work, the two mappings correspond to schema transformation and data transformation.

**Keywords:** Polystores · Multi-model databases · Data and schema transformations · Database theory · Category theory

## 1 Introduction

The biggest success stories in database theory are the relational model and relational algebra. Codd's theory [3] on relational databases has had an incomprehensible huge impact on database theory and applications. More formal and theoretical treatment of polystores and multi-model databases would make it possible us to repeat this success story in polystores and multi-model databases. A solid mathematical foundation would highly benefit their research and industry. Besides, to standardize the existing techniques and systems, a rigorous formulation is crucial.

Polystores and multi-model databases are a solution to the problem of handling a variety of data [12,14,20]. Native graph, document, key-value, and column databases have reached the point where they are competitive alternatives for relational databases especially in the cases when we perform a lot of read- and write-operations and heavy data analysis tasks. Since ML and AI are relying on massive amounts of data, NoSQL databases have gained attention.

Undoubtedly, polystores and multi-model databases are more complicated systems than ordinary relational databases since they subsume relational

© Springer Nature Switzerland AG 2021
E. K. Rezig et al. (Eds.): Poly 2021/DMAH 2021, LNCS 12921, pp. 14–28, 2021.
https://doi.org/10.1007/978-3-030-93663-1_2

databases. The theory and language describing the systems have to evolve along with the systems which are gradually becoming more complex. But this should not mean that the theory and languages become more complex for end-users or even for database administrators and architects. Different databases have their own theoretical foundations and query languages that are not automatically compatible at a practical or theoretical level. This creates a huge challenge that we are tackling from the theoretical perspective.

Data and schema transformations form a significant part of the data integration and migration problems [10]. For example, the transformations might be needed at any point during the development of ML and AI solutions where databases are a part of the process. Initially, importing data requires transformations. Data integration between the databases can require multiple transformation-based views between the participating databases. Sometimes the most efficient solution is to materialize the transformed data. When the amount of data grows, the transformation systems need to be able to adapt for the growth. Thus monotonicity and temporality aspects of transformations are important to take into account. Eventually, the data require transformations before it can fit ML and AI models. For example, ML and AI models can use a knowledge graph approach but the data is stored in a relational database. The same transformation problems are also apparent for polystores and multi-model databases.

Often these transformations lack formal treatment. Daimler et al. [7] argue that informal data transformations are harmful. This is one of the challenges we are addressing in this work. The language, which is proved to be capable of capturing highly complex structures with a compact notation, is category theory. Liu et al. [19] visioned that the foundations of multi-model databases could be built on category theory because relational algebra's expressiveness is not powerful enough. We argue that the same applies to polystores. Our contributions include

- continuing previous research connecting category theory and database theory,
- formalizing graph and hierarchical models and instances in terms of category theory, and
- formalizing data transformations in polystores and multi-model databases as a solution to a category theoretical lifting problem.

Informally category can be thought of as a graph or a network with a certain additional structure. The additional structure is usually easy to find from computer science and database applications. If our goal is to express database theory precisely, it does not make sense to use only graphs because we can do modeling much better with categories.

In this work, we are often mentioning "schema". By schema, we do not only mean the conventional relational schema but a larger piece of information that contains any constraint related to a model. Also, the information about the model is part of the schema. Although modern NoSQL data is often referred to as schemaless, the data always have some constraints which we include in a schema in this context.

## 1.1  Related Work

There are influential transformation frameworks but only a few of them are developed formally. SQLGraph [27] is a system, which translates graph databases to relational databases. It utilizes hashing and the fact that the modern relational databases natively support JSON. A framework of converting relational databases to graph databases by Virgilio et al. [9] utilizes schema paths. Das et al. [8] have developed a framework that creates RDF-view for property graph data in Oracle databases. All of these transformations are considered from a domain-specific and practical perspective although we identify that they have characteristical features which could be theoretically modeled and unified.

Jananthan et al. [15] propose associative algebra as a mathematical foundation for polystores. Leclercq et al. [18] built foundations of polystores on the tensor-based data model. Liu et al. [19] visioned that the foundations of multi-model databases could be built on category theory and we continue this work for polystores and multi-model databases.

There has been relatively much research on applying category theory to database theory. Our approach is highly influenced by David Spivak [25,26]. As he points out in [25], the category theoretical database research can be divided into two schools: category-based [24] and sketch-based [16]. A sketch [28] is a category with certain limit objects. Our position is category-based.

Besides work on database theory, category theory has been applied widely in computer science. Some of the most interesting and recent applications are programming languages (foundations of many functional programming languages), machine learning [6,11], automata learning [13], natural language processing (DisCoCat [5]), and quantum computing and mechanics [1,4]. Applied category theory has its annually organized conference called ACT (Applied Category Theory).

## 2  Prerequisites

### 2.1  Categories

Category theory is a relatively new field of mathematics. Saunders MacLane and Samuel Eilenberg introduced categories, functors, and natural transformations in the mid-1940s as a "meta-mathematical" tool to study algebraic topology. MacLane [17] is the standard introduction to the topic. Other good introduction from mathematical perspective is [22] and from computer science perspective [26,28].

**Definition 1 (Category).** *A category $C$ consists of a collection of objects denoted by $Obj(C)$ and a collection of morphisms denoted by $Hom(C)$. For each morphism $f \in Hom(C)$ there exists an object $A \in Obj(C)$ that is a domain of $f$ and an object $B \in Obj(C)$ that is a target of $f$. In this case we denote $f : A \to B$. We require that all the defined compositions of morphisms are included in $C$: if $f : A \to B \in Hom(C)$ and $g : B \to C \in Hom(C)$ are morphisms, then the composition $g \circ f \in Hom(C)$ is defined and $g \circ f : A \to C$ is a morphism.*

*Also, we assume that the composition operation is associative and that for every object $A \in Obj(\mathsf{C})$ there exists an identity morphism $id_A \colon A \to A$ so that $f \circ id_A = f$ and $id_A \circ f = f$ whenever the composition is defined.*

See Fig. 1 as a simple example of a category. In this work sans serif font always indicates a category. We follow the standard notation of category theory literature that is used, for example, in [22]. One of the most important categories

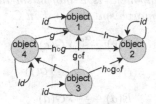

**Fig. 1.** A simple four object category with three non-trivial morphisms $f$, $g$ and $h$ and identities. In this case all the compositions of morphisms are drawn.

is the category Set whose objects are sets and morphisms are functions between the sets. The composition operation of the morphisms is the composition of functions.

## 2.2 Functors

In science and mathematics, we often have functions or mappings which respect the underlying structures. Next, we define a structure-preserving mapping for categories. The mapping is called a functor.

**Definition 2 (Functor).** *Assume $\mathsf{C}, \mathsf{D}$ are categories. A functor $F \colon \mathsf{C} \to \mathsf{D}$ is defined so that*

- *for every object $c$ in the category $\mathsf{C}$, $F(c)$ is an object in the category $\mathsf{D}$ and*
- *for every morphism $f \colon c \to d$ in $\mathsf{C}$, it holds that $F(f) \colon F(c) \to F(d)$ is a morphism in $\mathsf{D}$.*

*Besides, we assume that following axioms hold:*

- *For every object $c \in \mathsf{C}$ it holds that $F(id_c) = id_{F(c)}$ and*
- *if the composition $f \circ g$ is defined, then $F(f \circ g) = F(f) \circ F(g)$.*

*If every morphism in the category $\mathsf{D}$ has a preimage in the category $\mathsf{C}$, we call the functor $F$ full.*

See Fig. 2(a) as an example of functor between two simple categories. The fact that a functor preserves the structure of a category is apparent in the example.

## 2.3 Natural Transformations

The idea behind structure-preserving mappings is so fundamental that we can study what it means to preserve a structure of structure-preserving mappings.

The category theoretical notion for this is called a natural transformation. We follow a convention from category theory and denote a natural transformation by "$\Rightarrow$"-arrow.

**Definition 3 (Natural Transformation).** *Assume $F, G\colon \mathsf{C} \Rightarrow \mathsf{D}$ are functors. A natural transformation $\alpha\colon F \Rightarrow G$ contains the following information: For each $c \in \mathsf{C}$ is associated a component of the natural transformation $\alpha_c\colon F(c) \to G(c)$. This component is a morphism in $\mathsf{D}$ so that the following diagram commutes for any morphism $f\colon c \to d$ in $\mathsf{C}$*

$$
\begin{array}{ccc}
F(c) & \xrightarrow{\ \alpha_c\ } & G(c) \\
{\scriptstyle F(f)}\big\downarrow & & \big\downarrow{\scriptstyle G(f)} \\
F(d) & \xrightarrow[\ \alpha_d\ ]{} & G(d)
\end{array}
$$

*In equational format commuting means that $G(f) \circ \alpha_c = \alpha_d \circ F(f)$.*

See Fig. 2(b) as an example of a natural transformation.

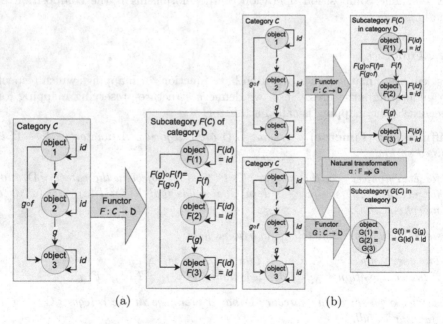

(a)                                                  (b)

**Fig. 2.** (a) An example of a simple functor. (b) An example of a simple natural transformation $\alpha\colon F \Rightarrow G$. The component morphisms $\alpha_i\colon F(i) \to G(i)$ are defined so that they map everything to the single object in D.

## 2.4    Kan Lifts

We discuss Kan lifts [21] shortly. Kan lift is a pair consisting of a functor and a natural transformation. The problem can be expressed as a diagram

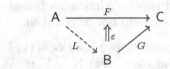

where all the arrows represent functors and a natural transformation $\varepsilon\colon G \circ L \Rightarrow F$. The category theoretical problem is to find a suitable functor $L\colon \mathsf{A} \to \mathsf{B}$ and a natural transformation $\varepsilon\colon G \circ L \Rightarrow F$ which make the construction universal i.e. the natural transformation $\varepsilon$ is universal among all the suitable natural transformations which satisfy the diagram. The problem is called a *lifting problem*.

**Definition 4 (Kan Lift).**    *Let $F\colon \mathsf{A} \to \mathsf{C}$ and $G\colon \mathsf{B} \to \mathsf{C}$ be functors. A right Kan lift of $F$ through $G$ consists of a functor $\mathrm{Rift}_G F\colon \mathsf{A} \to \mathsf{B}$ and a natural transformation $\varepsilon\colon G \circ \mathrm{Rift}_G F \Rightarrow F$ so that they satisfy the following universal property: given any other pair of a functor and a natural transformation $(H\colon \mathsf{A} \to \mathsf{B}, \eta\colon G \circ H \Rightarrow F)$ then there exists a unique natural transformation $\gamma\colon H \Rightarrow \mathrm{Rift}_G F$ so that $\eta$ factors through $\varepsilon$ i.e. $\eta = \varepsilon \circ (G \circ \gamma)$. Diagrammatically if*

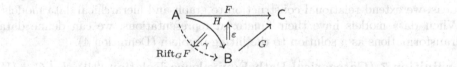

*then*

$$\begin{array}{c}\mathsf{A} \xrightarrow{\;\;F\;\;} \mathsf{C}\\ \text{with } H, \gamma, \varepsilon, \mathrm{Rift}_G F, G \to \mathsf{B}\end{array}$$

The problem of finding the pair $\mathrm{Rift}_G F\colon \mathsf{A} \to \mathsf{B}$ and $\varepsilon\colon G \circ \mathrm{Rift}_G F \Rightarrow F$ is called a *lifting problem*. The intuition behind Kan lifts is that we find a functor $\mathrm{Rift}_G F$ that is the best approximation which makes the triangle "commute". The notion of Kan lift grabs a larger collection of data transformations since we do not require that the triangle necessarily commutes in strict sense. Although the definition is abstract, we believe that is suitably flexible to describe transformations conceptually.

## 2.5    Graphs

Graphs have a three-folded role in this work. The first role of graphs is that every category is naturally a graph where objects are the vertices and morphisms are the edges. On the other hand, a graph is an abstract data model which we are formalizing in terms of category theory. Some concrete models following the graph model are property graphs and RDF graphs. The third role of graphs is that they serve as the most standard tool to model relationships in a database, for example, ER diagrams and various relational schemas are graphs. We want to emphasize that these graphs should not be confused.

**Definition 5 (Graph).** *A graph $G$ is a quad $G = (V, E, src, tgt)$ where $V$ is a set of vertices, $E$ is the set of edges, $src: E \to V$ is the source function and $tgt: E \to V$ is the target function. If $e \in E$ is an edge then its source vertex is $src(e) = v$ and its target vertex is $tgt(e) = w$.*

When we have graphs, it is natural to talk about paths. The following notation for paths is used in [24].

**Definition 6 (Path).** *Let $G = (V, E, src, tgt)$ be a graph. A path $p$ of length $n$ in the graph $G$ is a sequence of connected edges in $G$. The set of all paths of length $n$ is denoted by $\mathrm{Path}_G^{(n)}$. The set of all path of $G$ is $\mathrm{Path}_G = \cup_{n \in \mathbb{N}} \mathrm{Path}_G^{(n)}$.*

# 3  Functorial Instances and Databases

## 3.1  Functorial Representation of Relational Data

We can draw a correspondence that we use categories to encode database constraints and functors to create instances. Because database instances have to follow the constraints, the structure-preserving (and thus constraint-preserving) mapping, a functor, is a natural choice to model instances and transfer constraints to them.

David Spivak [24] represented a simple database definition language using categories and functors. Now we shortly recall this construction. Following his ideas, we extend relational construction to graph and hierarchical data models. When data models have their functorial representations, we can define data transformations as a solution to the lifting problem (Definition 4).

**Definition 7 (Categorical Path Equivalence Relation [24]).** *Let $G = (V, E, src, tgt)$ be a graph. A categorical path equivalence relation, denoted by $\cong$, is an equivalence relation on the set $\mathrm{Path}_G$ of all the paths of $G$ and it has the properties listed in Definition 3.2.4 in [24].*

We omit the full list of properties since the list is relatively long and for this work, the most important is to know that the relation $\cong$ is an equivalence relation on the set $\mathrm{Path}_G$.

**Definition 8 (Categorical Schema).** *A categorical schema is $C = (G, \cong)$ where $G$ is a graph and $\cong$ is a categorical path equivalence relation on $\mathrm{Path}_G$.*

**Definition 9 (Schema Category).** *Let $C = (G, \cong)$ be a categorical schema. The schema category $\mathsf{C}$ is the category whose objects are the vertices of the graph*

*G and the morphisms are the equivalence classes of the paths of G defined by $\cong$.*
*The composition is defined as path composition with respect to the equivalence*
*relation.*

The schema category consists of objects which are table descriptions, for
example, similar to that we have in the ER diagram. The morphisms are induced
by the foreign key constraints between the tables. Intuitively, a schema category
is the category induced by the corresponding ER diagram.

**Definition 10 (Instance Functor).** *Let* $\mathsf{C} = (G, \cong)$ *be a schema category.*
*An instance functor* $I \colon \mathsf{C} \to \mathsf{Set}$ *maps the schema category to the category of*
*sets and it satisfies the property that if* $p \cong q$, *then* $I(p) = I(q)$.

See Fig. 3(a) as an example of a relational instance functor. In Fig. 3(a) arrows
are based on the constraints between the attributes. Since functional dependencies can be composed, the compositions of the dependencies are defined. A set
of attributes trivially depends on itself which creates identity arrows.

For instance, we can ask a question related to Fig. 3(a): What is the channel
that the moderator with ModName `alicee` owns? The answer can be found when
we compose the arrow Moderator.FollowerID $\to$ Follower.ID with the arrow Fol-
lower.OwnChannel $\to$ Channel.ID. This gives us an arrow Moderator.FollowerID
$\to$ Channel.ID. The answer is the channel with id `C4` which can be read in Fig. 3(a).

The intuition behind a relational instance functor is that it sends each object
$c \in \mathsf{C}$ (corresponding table description or a column in the schema) to a set $I(c) \in$
$\mathsf{Set}$. The set $I(c)$ is the concrete instance of a table or a column. For example
in Fig. 3(a), $I(\text{ChannelMods}) = \{(C1, M1), (C2, M2), (C3, M1), (C3, M2)\}$. If a
morphism $f \colon c \to d \in \mathsf{C}$ corresponds a foreign key dependency between the
table descriptions $c$ and $d$ in the schema, then $I(f) \colon I(c) \to I(d) \in \mathsf{Set}$ is the set
valued function that sends the tuples of the table $I(c)$ to the tuples of the table
$I(d)$ along the functional dependency defined by the foreign key constraint.

## 3.2    Functorial Representation of the Graph and Hierarchical Data

Bumby et al. [2] gives a category theoretical formulation for graphs. Recall that we
previously defined a graph $G$ to be a quad $(V, E, src, tgt)$. Property graphs have
been studied from an algebraic and category theoretical perspective already in [23].

**Definition 11 (Graph as Functor).** *Let* $\mathsf{G}$ *be the two element category which*
*consists of the identity morphisms and two non-trivial morphisms as the diagram*

$$0 \underset{t}{\overset{s}{\rightrightarrows}} 1$$

*describes. Now a graph* $G$ *is a functor* $G \colon \mathsf{G} \to \mathsf{Set}$ *where* $G(0) = E$ *is the set of*
*edges,* $G(1) = V$ *is the set of vertices,* $G(s) \colon G(0) \to G(1) = src \colon E \to V$ *is the*
*source function and* $G(t) \colon G(0) \to G(1) = tgt \colon E \to V$ *is the target function.*
*Besides,* $G$ *maps identity morphisms of* $\mathsf{G}$ *to identity functions in* $\mathsf{Set}$.

We do not assume that the graph would have a schema. In this sense, the construction differs from the one that we gave to the relational data. In practice, we might have a graph schema available, for example, in the cases when we are transforming relational data into graph data.

When a graph schema is available, we can encode it in the category theoretical definition. If we have a strict schema for the graph, we can generalize Spivak's approach for the relational data and assign the schema information to the objects 0 and 1 in Definition 11.

The classical graph example is a social network. Let us take a property graph -oriented approach and set that the object 1 is associated with a graph schema ($person$ : {key, name, age}). The label $person$ is the label of the node and key, name and age are keys for the properties stored in nodes. For edges we can define similar structure by setting $0 = [knows : \{key, since\}]$. See Fig. 3(b) for the full construction.

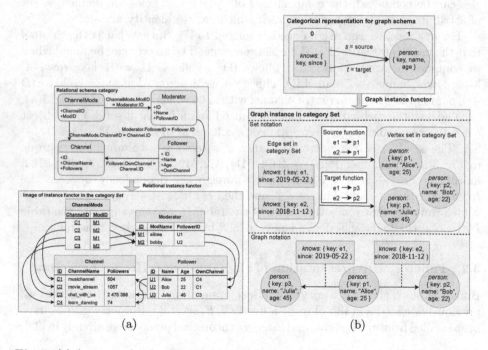

(a)                                                    (b)

**Fig. 3.** (a) An example of a relational instance functor. (b) The graph instance functor consists of the functor from the category that is a categorical representation for the graph schema to the category set. The graph is represented using the set notation and the conventional property graph notation.

As far as we know, hierarchical data, such as XML and JSON, do not have a category theoretical description that would have been studied previously. We use terms hierarchical data and tree data interchangeable. For any tree, we identify the characteristical feature that each node in the tree has exactly one parent node except the root. We can conceptually expand the tree construction so that the root is the unique node that has itself as a parent.

**Definition 12 (Tree as functor).** *Let* T *be the one element category whose object is 0 and the only non-trivial morphism is $p\colon 0 \to 0$. Diagrammatically the category is simply*

$$
\begin{array}{c}
p \\
\circlearrowright \\
0
\end{array}
$$

*Now a tree is a functor $T\colon \mathsf{T} \to \mathsf{Set}$ which sends the single element 0 to the set of nodes of the tree. The single non-trivial morphism $p\colon 0 \to 0$ is sent to the function that gives the parent node for each node in $T(0)$. If the node is the root $r$, then we define $T(p)(r) = r$.*

# 4 Data Transformations Between Functorial Instances

## 4.1 Intuition Behind Transformations Represented in Terms of Category Theory

Before formally discussing the transformations, we show a motivating example of how the theory in the previous sections manages to unify a big part of the transformation theory.

This example is continuation to Fig. 3(b) where we had the classical social network data stored in a relational database. In our opinion, the most obvious way to store a social network is to use simple vertex- and edge-tables. The relationships are defined by foreign key constraints. The *knows* table, which serves as the edge-table, has at least two foreign keys, *k.personID1* and *k.personID2*. These are connected to the person-table's primary key *p.personID*. Diagrammatically this can be expressed as

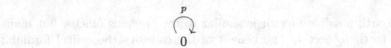

We note that this schema already defines a schema category (Definition 9).

Recall the category theoretical representation for the graph in Definition 11. We can transform the relational instance into a graph in multiple ways. The first way to map the relational schema category to the graph schema category is

$$
\text{on objects}
\begin{cases}
p \mapsto 1 \\
k \mapsto 0
\end{cases}
\text{and on morphisms}
\begin{cases}
(p.personID = k.personID1) \mapsto s \\
(p.personID = k.personID2) \mapsto t.
\end{cases}
$$

The objects 0 and 1 and morphisms $s$ and $t$ refer to the same objects and morphisms as in Definition 11. The second transformation is that we swap how the morphisms are mapped i.e. swap the roles of $s$ and $t$. Compared to the first transformation this inverses the direction of the edges in the resulting graph.

Besides these two mappings, we can find two more. The third possible functor collapses the relational schema i.e. it maps everything to the object 0 and its identity morphism:

$$\text{on objects} \begin{cases} p \mapsto 0 \\ k \mapsto 0 \end{cases} \text{and on morphisms} \begin{cases} (p.personID = k.personID1) \mapsto id_0 \\ (p.personID = k.personID2) \mapsto id_0. \end{cases}$$

The fourth possible functor is similar to the previous functor but maps everything to the object 1. The benefit of the category theoretical formulation for transformations is that we can mathematically characterize, that the transformation which sends the knows-table to vertices and person-table to edges, is not valid because such transformation is not a functor.

The transformations 3. and 4. have problems although they are well-defined functors. Thus functoriality is not a sufficient condition to characterize meaningful transformations. It does not make sense to map everything to edges (the result of the transformation 3.) because a valid edge needs to have a source and a target vertex. Also, a graph that contains only vertices without edges (the result of the transformation 4.) is not meaningful because edges are necessary for the most important graph operations. Thus we require that the functor should be *full* (Definition 2) to be relevant in practice. As we see, the transformations 3. and 4. as functors are not full but transformations 1. and 2. are.

## 4.2   Data Transformation as Lifting Problem

Data and schema transformations are usually modeled as mappings from a source database to a target database. We base our data and schema transformation on Kan lifts [21]. Lifting problems have been considered in database theory also previously in [25]. As Definition 4 shows, the lift consists of two components: a functor and a natural transformation. Informally, the functor part is a schema mapping which describes a set of rules which define how the data items are mapped at a schema level. The functor is required to be *full* (Definition 2) because functors which are not full are not practically meaningful as the discussion in the previous section shows. Along the functor, we have a natural transformation which is data mapping. The pair satisfies the universal property which creates certain classification for transformations. The nature of this classification is still an open question.

The category theoretical approach to data and schema transformations reveals a crucial problem in transformation research. The problem is the separation of data and schema. In a world where relational databases are still the dominant databases, the division of data and schema is obvious. But the problem is apparent with the schemaless or schema-free models such as graphs and documents. If graph and document data transformations are approached from the relational perspective, we are likely to face problems. With category theory, we can model as much structure as the data has. Modeling transformations as pairs of mappings describes transformations more rigorously than a single total function between data sets.

Let $I_1\colon \mathsf{C}_1 \to \mathsf{Set}$ and $I_2\colon \mathsf{C}_2 \to \mathsf{Set}$ be two data instances as functors where the functors can represent either relational, graph or hierarchical instance functors as described in Definitions 10, 11, and 12. The question is how do we generally find a transformation between the data instances $I_1$ and $I_2$. The problem can be expressed as a diagram

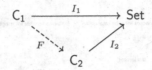

where the functor $F\colon \mathsf{C}_1 \to \mathsf{C}_2$ is the schema transformation mapping between the categorical representations of the schema categories $\mathsf{C}_1$ and $\mathsf{C}_2$. The second part of the transformation consists of a natural transformation $\varepsilon\colon I_2 \circ F \Rightarrow I_1$ which obeys certain laws. If we assume that we have the two diagrams

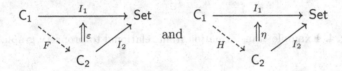

where the second diagram has a functor $H\colon \mathsf{C}_1 \to \mathsf{C}_2$ and $\eta\colon I_2 \circ H \Rightarrow I_1$ a natural transformation. We then require that there exists a *unique* natural transformation $\gamma\colon H \Rightarrow F$ such that $\eta = \varepsilon \circ (I_2 \circ \gamma)$.

**Definition 13 (Data and Schema Transformation).** *Let* $I_1\colon \mathsf{C}_1 \to \mathsf{Set}$ *and* $I_2\colon \mathsf{C}_2 \to \mathsf{Set}$ *be two data instances. A transformation from* $I_1$ *to* $I_2$ *is a Kan lift* $(\mathrm{Rift}_{I_2} I_1\colon \mathsf{C}_1 \to \mathsf{C}_2,\ \varepsilon\colon I_2 \circ \mathrm{Rift}_{I_2} I_1 \Rightarrow I_1)$ *so that the functor* $\mathrm{Rift}_{I_2} I_1$ *is a full functor.*

We recall our example relational database instance in Fig. 3(a). In order to transform the relational instance to a property graph we need to construct a functor from the relational schema category to the graph schema category and define the natural transformation. Figure 4 describes the full transformation and the coloring codes the corresponding elements in each category. Informally, the natural transformation in the example could be understood so that for each object in the relational schema category, we have a mapping that tells how the corresponding relational data object in the category Set is mapped to the graph data object in the category Set.

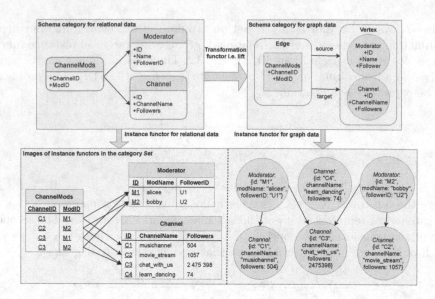

**Fig. 4.** Example transformation from relational to property graph.

# 5   Conclusions and Future Work

When the variety and amount of data grows, the need for polystores and multi-model databases is urgent. The efficient utilization of the systems requires a precise theory of how the systems operate and how they are modeled. So far, there has been extensive research on practical and implementational aspects. Without a proper theoretical framework, the field is left scattered. We are answering this challenge by formalizing the three most common data models and the data and schema transformations between them. We continued previous research and contributed by formalizing graph and hierarchical models functorially. We then focused on data and schema transformations between the functorial instances. Kan lifts require more studying as a basis for transformations but it seems a promising direction.

Query transformations form another half of the transformation systems. A query can be transformed correctly if the data is transformed correctly. This ties both transformations together which makes the modeling challenge still harder. Future work would include formalizing and unifying query transformations. In the case of SQL, the topic has already been studied in [25].

We identify that there is a need to model temporal data better. The problem of temporality is rarely addressed in polystore, multi-model database, and transformation research. Usually, the implicit assumption, especially in transformation frameworks, is that the systems are dealing with static data. Of course, that is hardly ever true and data changes and expands constantly. We believe that with category theory we can naturally include a time component to data.

**Acknowledgement.** This paper is partially supported by Finnish Academy Project 310321 and Oracle ERO gift funding.

# References

1. Abramsky, S., Coecke, B.: Categorical quantum mechanics (2008)
2. Bumby, R.T., Latch, D.M.: Categorical constructions in graph theory. Int. J. Math. Math. Sci. **9**, 791947 (1986). https://doi.org/10.1155/S0161171286000017
3. Codd, E.F.: A relational model of data for large shared data banks. Commun. ACM **13**(6), 377–387 (1970). https://doi.org/10.1145/362384.362685, https://doi.org/10.1145/362384.362685
4. Coecke, B., Paquette, É.: Categories for the Practising Physicist, pp. 173–286. Springer, Berlin Heidelberg (2011). https://doi.org/10.1007/978-3-642-12821-9_3
5. Coecke, B., Sadrzadeh, M., Clark, S.: Mathematical foundations for a compositional distributional model of meaning. CoRR abs/1003.4394 (2010). http://arxiv.org/abs/1003.4394
6. Cruttwell, G.S.H., Gavranovic, B., Ghani, N., Wilson, P.W., Zanasi, F.: Categorical foundations of gradient-based learning. CoRR abs/2103.01931 (2021). https://arxiv.org/abs/2103.01931
7. Daimler, E., Wisnesky, R.: Informal data transformation considered harmful. arXiv:2001.00338, January 2020. http://arxiv.org/abs/2001.00338, arXiv: 2001.00338
8. Das, S., Srinivasan, J., Perry, M., Chong, E., Banerjee, J.: A tale of two graphs: property graphs as RDF in oracle (2014). https://doi.org/10.5441/002/EDBT.2014.82, https://openproceedings.org/EDBT/2014/edbticdt2014industrial_submission_28.pdf
9. De Virgilio, R., Maccioni, A., Torlone, R.: Converting relational to graph databases. In: First International Workshop on Graph Data Management Experiences and Systems, pp. 1–6. ACM, June 2013. https://doi.org/10.1145/2484425.2484426
10. Dziedzic, A., Elmore, A.J., Stonebraker, M.: Data transformation and migration in polystores. In: 2016 IEEE High Performance Extreme Computing Conference, HPEC 2016, Waltham, MA, USA, 13–15 September 2016, pp. 1–6. IEEE (2016). https://doi.org/10.1109/HPEC.2016.7761594
11. Fong, B., Spivak, D., Tuyéras, R.: Backprop as functor: a compositional perspective on supervised learning. In: 2019 34th Annual ACM/IEEE Symposium on Logic in Computer Science (LICS), pp. 1–13 (2019). https://doi.org/10.1109/LICS.2019.8785665
12. Gadepally, V., et al.: The bigdawg polystore system and architecture. In: 2016 IEEE High Performance Extreme Computing Conference (HPEC), pp. 1–6 (2016). https://doi.org/10.1109/HPEC.2016.7761636
13. van Heerdt, G., Kappé, T., Rot, J., Sammartino, M., Silva, A.: A categorical framework for learning generalised tree automata. CoRR abs/2001.05786 (2020). https://arxiv.org/abs/2001.05786
14. Holubová, I., Klettke, M., Störl, U.: Evolution management of multi-model data. In: Gadepally, V., Mattson, T., Stonebraker, M., Wang, F., Luo, G., Laing, Y., Dubovitskaya, A. (eds.) DMAH/Poly -2019. LNCS, vol. 11721, pp. 139–153. Springer, Cham (2019). https://doi.org/10.1007/978-3-030-33752-0_10

15. Jananthan, H., Zhou, Z., Gadepally, V., Hutchison, D., Kim, S., Kepner, J.: Poly-store mathematics of relational algebra. In: 2017 IEEE International Conference on Big Data (Big Data), pp. 3180–3189. IEEE Computer Society, Los Alamitos, December 2017. https://doi.org/10.1109/BigData.2017.8258298

16. Kadish, B., Diskin, Z.: Algebraic graph-oriented = category theory based. manifesto of categorizing database theory (1994)

17. Lane, S.: Categories for the Working Mathematician. In: Graduate Texts in Mathematics, Springer, New York (1998), https://doi.org/10.1007/978-1-4612-9839-7

18. Leclercq, E., Savonnet, M.: A tensor based data model for polystore: an application to social networks data. In: Proceedings of the 22nd International Database Engineering & Applications Symposium, IDEAS 2018, pp. 110–118. Association for Computing Machinery, New York (2018). https://doi.org/10.1145/3216122.3216152

19. Liu, Z., Lu, J., Gawlick, D., Helskyaho, H., Pogossiants, G., Wu, Z.: Multi-model database management systems - a look forward. In: Poly/DMAH@VLDB (2018)

20. Lu, J., Holubová, I., Cautis, B.: Multi-model databases and tightly integrated polystores: current practices, comparisons, and open challenges. In: Cuzzocrea, A., et al. (eds.) Proceedings of the 27th ACM International Conference on Information and Knowledge Management, CIKM 2018, Torino, Italy, 22–26 October 2018, pp. 2301–2302. ACM (2018). https://doi.org/10.1145/3269206.3274269

21. nLab authors: Kan lift, May 2021. http://ncatlab.org/nlab/show/Kan%20lift

22. Riehl, E.: Category Theory in Context. Aurora: Dover Modern Math Originals, Dover Publications, Mineola (2017). www.math.jhu.edu/~eriehl/context.pdf

23. Shinavier, J., Wisnesky, R.: Algebraic property graphs (2020)

24. Spivak, D.I.: Functorial data migration. CoRR abs/1009.1166 (2010). http://arxiv.org/abs/1009.1166

25. Spivak, D.I.: Database queries and constraints via lifting problems. Math. Struct. Comput. Sci. **24** (2013)

26. Spivak, D.I.: Category Theory for the Sciences. MIT Press, Cambridge (2014)

27. Sun, W., Fokoue, A., Srinivas, K., Kementsietsidis, A., Hu, G., Xie, G.: Sqlgraph: an efficient relational-based property graph store. In: Proceedings of the 2015 ACM SIGMOD International Conference on Management of Data, pp. 1887–1901. ACM, May 2015. https://doi.org/10.1145/2723372.2723732

28. Wells, C.: Category theory for computing science. Theory Appl. Categ. **22**, 515 (2012)

# Towards Generic Fine-Grained Transaction Isolation in Polystores

Nuno Faria[✉][ID], José Pereira[ID], Ana Nunes Alonso[ID], and Ricardo Vilaça[ID]

INESC TEC and University of Minho, Braga, Portugal
{nuno.f.faria,jose.o.pereira,ana.n.alonso,ricardo.p.vilaca}@inesctec.pt

**Abstract.** Transactional isolation is a challenge for polystores, as along with the limited capabilities of each datastore, we have to contend with their sheer diversity. However, transactional isolation is increasingly desirable as a variety of datastores are being sought after for roles that go beyond data lakes. Transactional guarantees are also relevant for reliability at scale. In this paper, we propose that transactional isolation in polystores can be achieved by leveraging the query engine, i.e., basing some of the responsibilities of a traditional transactional storage manager (TSM) on the query language itself. This has the key advantage of greatly simplifying design and implementation, as it doesn't need to be re-invented for each datastore, and should increase performance, by taking advantage of dynamic query optimization where available. We demonstrate the feasibility of the proposal with a simple proof-of-concept and experiment.

**Keywords:** Transactions · Snapshot isolation · Polystores

## 1 Introduction

Polystores aim at combining the diversity of data models, query languages, interfaces, and architectures of multiple datastores [17, 22]. This enables executing queries expressed in, or even combining, the preferred data model, the best query abstractions, and ideal query engines for each use case. The focus has thus been on big data and analytical workloads.

However, diverse data models and query capabilities are not the sole reason for the current datastore diversity. Increasingly, the ability to handle updates in a variety of challenging scenarios has been the driving force behind novel datastore proposals. For instance, Apache Cassandra is well known for its ability to handle very high update throughput [23]. Redis provides a variety of data structures, including Conflict-free Replicated Data Types (CRDTs) for geographical scalability [10].

It is thus interesting to accommodate this diversity in update processing capabilities of datastores, which raises the issue of update consistency and atomicity in each of them and across multiple of them. Transactional updates are also desirable even in mostly static data lakes to correct and remove data (e.g., due

© Springer Nature Switzerland AG 2021
E. K. Rezig et al. (Eds.): Poly 2021/DMAH 2021, LNCS 12921, pp. 29–42, 2021.
https://doi.org/10.1007/978-3-030-93663-1_3

to the GDPR and other "right to be forgotten" regulations) and ultimately for reliability, as data corruption on loading has shown to be a frequent issue [7].

Traditionally, transactional isolation and recovery are the responsibility of the transactional storage manager (TSM) layer [21]. Depending on the strategy used, these are achieved by the combined effect of the lock manager, the buffer pool (i.e., for latching and holding different versions), and the log manager. These features are implemented separately and lie beneath the query engine, which then operates within the abstraction of an isolated and recoverable data space. More recently, transactional isolation has also been provided for NoSQL datastores as a custom middleware layer that wraps the native store [19].

Unfortunately, transactional isolation in polystores is harder than in traditional database systems or homogeneous big datastores, and often identified as a key research challenge [28,30]. The first issue is that target datastores have wildly different isolation and consistency criteria, and not just different implementations of similar criteria. Namely, some systems, such as MongoDB [26] or Neo4j [5], provide multi-operation isolation and recovery. Other systems, such as HBase, do not offer multi-operation isolation but provide multi-versioning and a re-do log, that can be used for transactional isolation at the middleware level [19]. Still, some systems (e.g., Cassandra [23]) exhibit no isolation at all and offer only eventual consistency [31], which is central to their value proposition as distributed and scalable. The second issue is how to enforce a single transactional context for an operation reading from or updating multiple datastores. Even datastores that have transactional support such as MongoDB or Neo4j do not support XA [1] transaction interfaces for two-phase commit. Therefore, individually wrapping or modifying each datastore with a transactional storage management layer is both unfeasible and undesirable.

In this paper, we assume Snapshot Isolation [9] as the target transactional isolation criterion and the availability of a multi-version optimistic concurrency control mechanism. We divide transactional processing into two main concerns: the first involves capturing write operations and, when commit is requested, validating that there are no write-write conflicts with concurrent transactions; the second is the ability to, at any point during the execution of a given transaction, reconstruct the current snapshot by reconciling values written by previously committed transactions, items updated by the current transaction, and avoiding values written by concurrent transactions. We address only the latter and focus on the computation needed to deliver the snapshot in a polyglot query engine.

Our first requirement is to provide transactional isolation and recovery, while at the same time allowing unfettered access to native stores. This precludes, for instance, cluttering the data with version information. The second requirement stems from the observation that the best approach for computing isolated snapshots varies for different datastores and that an efficient implementation must take advantage of each one's strengths.

The main insights in this paper are that reconstructing a transactional snapshot across a diversity of datastores (1) is itself a polyglot data processing problem and (2) that we can take advantage of an optimizing query engine to make it simpler, portable, and efficient. We are, as the saying goes, "eating our own dog-food."

The rest of this paper is organized as follows: Sect. 2 describes the background and assumptions for our proposal; Sect. 3 details the design of a proof-of-concept system for transactional snapshot reconstruction; Sect. 4 evaluates the proposed approach with an experiment; and finally, Sect. 5 discusses the main conclusions, remaining challenges, and future research directions.

# 2 Background and Assumptions

## 2.1 Query Processing

We assume as the baseline a cloud multi-datastore query engine such as Cloud-MdsQL [22] offering a SQL-like language that can embed statements in native query languages of diverse datastores as table expressions, i.e., *native table expressions*. It follows the mediator/wrapper architecture from multi-database systems: A logically centralized mediator – the Common Query Engine (CQE) – handles client connections, parses and optimizes queries, and then hands subsets of the resulting plan for each target datastore to each wrapper, that extracts native query fragments or converts relational operators in the plan and handles execution and data transfer.

In practice, this means that ad-hoc views of data from multiple datastores can be defined and used in relational queries. A relational data model, extended with non-atomic list and dictionary types, is used as the target for such views and the domain for queries in the CloudMdsQL common query language. The major advantage of this approach is that it is able to fully exploit the power of each datastore with native queries without having to fully map data to a common data model, while at the same time globally optimizing the composite query, e.g., by pushing down selection predicates, using bind join, performing join ordering, or planning intermediate data shipping.

## 2.2 Versions and Snapshot Isolation

We assume Snapshot Isolation [9] as the target criterion. In contrast to traditional ANSI isolation levels based on 2-phase locking, using a multi-version concurrency control mechanism has clear advantages for read-only transactions and parallel/distributed systems, and is now widely preferred.

This means that there can be multiple versions of each data item stored at the same time and that a version is visible to a transaction if and only if it was committed before the transaction started. For simplicity, we consider only full Snapshot Isolation, with multi-statement consistency, and not the weaker single-statement Read Consistency levels that are also available in various systems.

Assuming that the minimum visibility (commit) timestamp for an item is $cts$ and that the maximum (starting) visibility timestamp for a transaction is $sts$, we can consider these possible states for each usable version of an item:

**Visible-to-All (or Storage):** Committed versions labeled with a *cts* that is less than or equal to the starting timestamps *sts* of all currently executing transactions, thus, visible-to-all transactions unless overwritten.

**Visible-to-Some (or Cache):** Committed versions labeled with a *cts* that is greater than the starting timestamp *sts* of some currently executing transactions, thus, invisible to such transactions even if not overridden. Keeping these versions separate from those visible-to-all avoids non-repeatable reads.

**Visible-to-One (or Temporary):** Uncommitted versions associated with a single transaction. These versions ensure that a transaction reads its own writes and at the same time avoid causing dirty reads in concurrent transactions.

When a version is written, it starts in the visible-to-one state, proceeds to visible-to-some when committed, and eventually becomes visible-to-all as other concurrent transactions finish. Some systems might in fact keep around some obsolete versions, visible-to-none, after a newer visible-to-all version exists.

When reading, a transaction first considers its own visible-to-one versions, then those visible-to-some – considering the timestamp – and finally those visible-to-all. This process, which obtains correct versions for all data items requested by some transaction, is the *snapshot reconstruction* and is the focus of this paper.

This distinction of versions in terms of visibility is not how most multi-version systems are described but is key to our insight in Sect. 3. Instead, systems are usually described in terms of strategies used to physically store different versions. As an example, PostgreSQL keeps them all in the main heap/file, explicitly tagged with *t_xmin* and *t_xmax* that can be compared to current visibility boundaries, termed the *snapshot*. This avoids copying old data when new versions are added, at the expense of keeping obsolete versions until vacuumed [27,29]. Oracle labels versions with the *system change number* (SCN) [8,12] and these reside: in the main heap/file, while visible-to-one and locked, latest visible-to-some, or if visible-to-all; other visible-to-some versions are kept separately in *rollback segments*. This optimizes for short-lived transactions, where a new version quickly becomes visible-to-all. A different example is provided by Google's Spanner, which keeps visible-to-one versions directly in the client in unlogged structures and takes advantage of versioning in BigTable to manage committed versions, visible-to-some or visible-to-all [14].

## 2.3  Simplifying Assumptions

Besides snapshot reconstruction, Snapshot Isolation requires precluding concurrent updates to the same item. As an example, Oracle and PostgreSQL rely on aborting transactions in lock queues on commit to ensure that the first committer wins. In distributed systems, such as Omid [19], this is achieved with a centralized validation server. A recovery mechanism is also required and usually relies on logging to ensure atomicity and durability. In this paper, we omit both of these important issues and focus exclusively on the read path for snapshot reconstruction.

We make the additional simplifying assumption of not considering the ability of a transaction to read its own writes, i.e., we ignore visible-to-one (or temporary) versions during snapshot reconstruction. Moreover, we assume that all writes are done atomically at commit time, as this simplifies representation and the manipulation of timestamps. Our proposal could be extended to accommodate such possibilities, although the current simpler form would already be useful and is actually how some systems work [14].

# 3  Proof-of-Concept

## 3.1  Version Representation

The first pillar of our proposal is the use of regular tables or collections to hold versions of data items in different visibility categories according to Sect. 2.2, in contrast to using custom data structures encapsulated within a transactional storage manager layer. In detail, we separate visible-to-all (or storage) from visible-to-some (or cache) versions. The approach could be extended by considering a third table or collection for visible-to-one (or temporary) versions, which we are not addressing in this proof-of-concept.

Our key insight, which makes our proposal suitable for a polystore and compatible with a wide spectrum of datastores, is the following: *It is not necessary to keep individual version numbers for visible-to-all (or storage) versions.* The reason for this is that, by definition, all these versions are visible to all transactions unless overwritten. Therefore, their final visibility depends only on whether reconstruction picks up a more recent version while traversing cached (visible-to-some) versions. In other words, it is as if we consider that all storage (visible-to-all) versions are implicitly labeled with $ts - 1$, where $ts$ is the oldest version in cache (visible-to-some).

The first corollary is that a transactional update and query system can be layered on top of an existing datastore without changing its content, in particular, without polluting data with additional version meta-data or multiple versions for each item, which would break compatibility with existing non-transactional applications. Additionally, this also decreases the space overhead imposed on the system, comprised by recently modified rows. With a sufficiently large storage, this overhead can be considered effectively zero. The second corollary is that the datastore does not need to be able to filter versions, which is hard or even impossible to do in pure key-value stores. In fact, previous transaction isolation systems that can be layered on existing datastores, such as Spanner [14] or Omid [19], assume that the datastore can hold and filter versions or, in the latter, store additional version meta-data with each item.

In detail, our general approach is that for each storage table ($S$) in any of the supported datastores, we create an additional table for the corresponding visible-to-some versions ($S\_Cache$). The cache accommodates data with the original schema plus three extra fields: $from$ and $to$, which specify a record's validity, and $deleted$, which identifies deleted records. The primary key for this table is

| a) S | | b) S_Cache | | | | | c) S_Snapshot | |
|---|---|---|---|---|---|---|---|---|
| k | v | k | v | from | to | deleted | k | v |
| k1 v1 | | k1 | v01 | 1 | 4 | false | k1 | v10 |
| k2 v2 | | k1 | v10 | 5 | 20 | false | k2 | v2 |
| k3 v3 | | k1 | v100 | 21 | ∞ | false | k4 | v4 |
| k4 v4 | | k3 | ⊥ | 4 | ∞ | true | | |

**Fig. 1.** Example of the cache of storage $S$ ($S\_Cache$) and resulting snapshot for transaction $T$. $T$'s starting timestamp $= 15$, meaning it will read $(k1, v10)$ and $(k3, \bot)$ from the cache and the remaining records from the storage. $k3$ will not be present in the snapshot since it is flagged as deleted. (Color figure online)

composite, with the original key in the base storage table and $from$. As this table is not used by non-transactional applications, and only indirectly by transactional applications, the additional data do not create a compatibility issue.

Figure 1 provides an example. Figure 1(a) shows some base storage table $S$ with key $k$ and value $v$. Depending on the application and the underlying datastore, both $k$ and $v$ can be composite values. The base table contains items with keys $k1$ to $k4$ with corresponding base values $v1$ to $v4$. Figure 1(b) shows the version cache table, added by our proposal. In detail, $S\_Cache$ shows that the value for $k1$ has been updated three times: $v01$ is valid from timestamp 1 to 4; $v10$ from 5 to 20; and $v100$ from 21. We can also see that $k3$ has been removed by version 4.

## 3.2 Snapshot Reconstruction

The second pillar of our proposal is that we describe snapshot reconstruction for each transaction as a query to the common query engine. This is made possible by representing versions of items with different visibility as regular tables or collections.

Figure 2 outlines the logical query used to reconstruct each table in a transaction's snapshot. It finds out which keys in the cache (visible-to-some) are relevant considering the current transaction's starting timestamp $sts$. These keys are used to filter out the corresponding rows from the storage. The result is merged with the readable values from the cache. A complex query involving multiple tables requires computing this plan for each table.

Figure 1(c) shows the example of the reconstructed snapshot for a transaction reading from starting timestamp $sts = 15$. Records selected in each table are highlighted in green, and tombstones hiding items in red. In detail, $k1$ has been recently updated and the appropriate value corresponding to the starting timestamp of 15 is selected from $S\_Cache$, avoiding an even more recent value with timestamp 21. $k3$ is present in $S\_Cache$ as a tombstone and thus is removed from the snapshot. Finally, $k4$ and $k2$ are obtained from the base storage table.

In short, by using a query for reconstructing the snapshot, we are able to provide isolation while, at the same time, provide a simpler alternative to

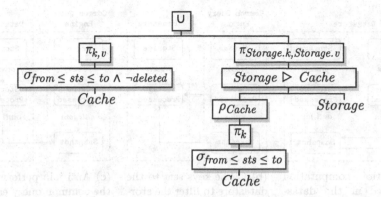

**Fig. 2.** Logical plan for snapshot reconstruction. *Storage* and *Cache* are the tables from Fig. 1; $\sigma, \pi, \rho, \triangleright, \cup$ are the relational selection, projection, renaming, left anti join, and union operators, respectively.

specialized transactional layers or modifications to multiple datastores. It is, however, interesting to determine to what extent the resulting performance is acceptable.

### 3.3  Execution Alternatives and Optimization

The attainable performance is related to the possibility of finding an optimal physical plan for the proposed reconstruction query. Defining snapshot reconstruction as a query at the common query engine level opens up the possibility of alternative physical plans, leading to decisions by the database administrator and the automatic optimizer.

The key decision is the placement of the cache table relative to the original storage. Ideally, they would be placed right next to each other, i.e., the same datastore, providing optimal data locality and enabling the entire reconstruction plan to be pushed down to the datastore. However, since the underlying query engine might not support joining the different structures, this solution is not always viable. Therefore, the version cache can be placed in a different datastore, that should be selected to provide optimal performance for the required operations. In systems such as CloudMdsQl, auxiliary tables can be stored in the common query engine itself, instead of an external datastore.

The next decision is how to distribute the logical query plan across the common query engine and external datastores. Depending on where each cache table is placed relative to the corresponding storage table and the capabilities of the query engine in the external datastore, there are three main options for what can be delegated to the datastore, depicted in Fig. 3: alternative (a) shows the ideal case of pushing the entire computation to the datastore, which should also allow for additional processing that needs to be performed over the entire snapshot to be made there; (b) sends the cache keys to the datastore to filter the storage but performs the union operation and the remaining processing in the

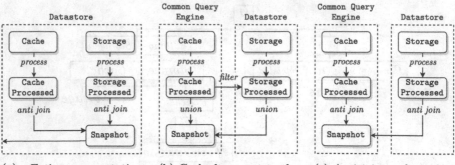

(a) Entire computation performed in the datastore.

(b) Cache keys sent to the datastore to filter the storage.

(c) Anti join performed in the common query engine.

**Fig. 3.** Different alternatives for cache placement and snapshot computation. The "process" step here depicted can be a wide range of operators (filter, order, join, aggregate, ...) intended to be performed over the snapshot but are pushed down in order to favor index usage, reduce record materialization, and reduce data transfer.

common query engine; (c) performs only basic storage processing in the datastore (if possible), leaving the merging process and remaining processing to the common query engine.

Finally, when considering snapshot reconstruction sub-plan as part of a larger query, an optimizer should be able to globally reorder and select physical operators. For instance, when executing a join operation, the query engine might opt for first joining the caches for different tables and obtain an empty result, thus avoiding the need to filter the storage. To quickly assess if these alternatives have a substantial impact on execution time, which justifies using an optimizer, and if the resulting overhead is tolerable, we evaluate in Sect. 4 different plan implementations with different queries and datastores.

### 3.4 Concurrent Updates

We are focusing only on transactional snapshot reconstruction during query execution and avoiding the discussion of how update operations are handled. However, the reconstruction process needs to tolerate that operations needed for updates – producing new versions – may occur concurrently.

When a transaction is committed, new versions of data items labeled with corresponding versions need to be inserted into the cache. This can be done one item at a time without impact in reconstruction as long as no currently executing transactions have a starting timestamp equal or greater than the currently committing transaction. This is true by definition, as the starting timestamp assigned to a transaction should be the commit timestamp of the latest committed transaction. Recovery would need a re-do log to ensure that all items from committed transactions are eventually inserted in the cache.

We now consider the task which materializes cache records into the storage, i.e., *flush*, and removes them, i.e., *garbage collection*. Let us assume that a record in the cache $C$, $r_c$, has the same key as some record $r_s$ in the storage $S$, meaning $r_c$ overwrites $r_s$ in the snapshots of transactions with begin time greater or equal to $r_c.from$. We can only flush $r_c$ if no current or future transaction can ever read $r_s$, i.e., the smallest begin timestamp of all currently executing transactions ($\epsilon$), is greater or equal to $r_c.from$. This $\epsilon$ can be easily computed with a log that stores the identifier, timestamp, and status of every transaction. When multiple versions of the same key can be flushed, the most recent one is chosen. After that, the flushed records can be safely removed from the cache.

An interesting property of this process is that it can crash at any time without compromising consistency, not requiring multi-record atomicity guarantees or needing to halt transaction execution. An incomplete flush means both flushed and non-flushed records are still present in the cache, and thus will still be considered for reads for current and future transactions. An incomplete garbage collection still has the guarantee that every removed cache record is persisted in the storage, while the remaining ones will overwrite the storage with the exact same value.

## 4    Experiment

We use a polystore inspired by CloudMdsQL [6], with MongoDB and Cassandra as datastores. Briefly, queries are written with a low code visual builder or the corresponding SQL-like language, with embedded native queries for different datastores. The common query engine is based on PostgreSQL, using the FDW interface for datastore wrappers. This system includes custom wrappers for Cassandra and MongoDB that optimize filter push-down, by combining them with the native query languages. While MongoDB's aggregation pipeline is expressive enough to build the entire snapshot natively, the same is not possible in Cassandra, and as such it relies exclusively on the common query engine to join the cache with the storage.

Therefore, we have multiple steps where the query is transformed and possibly optimized: (1) in the initial translation to PostgreSQL SQL; (2) within PostgreSQL itself; (3) in the wrapper; and finally (4) in the datastore itself. We use step 1 to determine placement and step 3 to push-down selections and projections. We have, however, limited control of step 2 in how we re-write the query in step 1 or how we provide statistics back in step 3. We deployed the system on two Google Cloud instances (8 N1 vCPUs, 8 GB RAM, 500 GB SDD), located on us-east1 and us-east4 (RTT of 11 ms), one hosting the query engine and the other the MongoDB and Cassandra datastores. The cache sizes are set to 1% of their respective storage sizes.

Our experiment consists in running various simple queries – *select all* (returns all rows), *filter* (returns one row), small join (joins one row), large join (joins all rows), and *aggregation* (performs a sum) – on TPC-C's *order_line* and *item* tables, stored in both MongoDB and Cassandra. By manipulating placement of tables and the common query engine, we obtain several physical

**Table 1.** Performance of different physical plans with MongoDB and Cassandra. The bordered cells mark the best plan for each query in each datastore.

| Query type | MongoDB Baseline (ms) | NG | NL | FJ | LJ | NI | NA | OD | Cassandra Baseline (ms) | FJ | LJ | NI | OD |
|---|---|---|---|---|---|---|---|---|---|---|---|---|---|
| Select all | 11682 | 17 | 151 | 5 | 7 | 6 | 8 | 5 | 15702 | 2 | 6 | 1 | 1 |
| Filter | 13 | 9 | 10 | 14 | 11 | 12 | 46 | 12 | 15 | 1 | 1 | 1 | 0 |
| Small join | 13 | 5 | 8 | 100 | 94 | 98 | 95 | 94 | 28 | 4 | 9 | 10 | 8 |
| Large join | 15266 | 15 | 156 | 6 | 10 | 7 | 5 | 6 | 19740 | 2 | 5 | 1 | 2 |
| Aggregation | 299 | 171 | 5.7K | 1.4K | 1.4K | 1.4K | 93 | 1.9k | 8842 | 7 | 14 | 7 | 10 |

**NG** - MongoDB Native GROUP | **NL** - MongoDB Native LOOKUP | **FJ** - SQL FULL JOIN | **LJ** - SQL LEFT JOIN | **NI** - SQL WHERE NOT IN | **NA** - SQL WHERE NOT ANY | **OD** - SQL ORDER BY + DISTINCT

plans. Considering the alternatives of Fig. 3, when using MongoDB, alternative (a) is implemented with a native GROUP (*NG*, equivalent to PostgreSQL's ORDER+DISTINCT [2]) and a native LOOKUP (*NL*, equivalent to PostgreSQL's LEFT JOIN [3]). With MongoDB and Cassandra, alternative (c) makes use of FULL JOIN (*FJ*), LEFT JOIN (*LJ*), NOT IN (*NI*), and ORDER+DISTINCT (*OD*). Note that each implementation generates different execution trees. Finally, we also use NOT ANY (*NA*) with MongoDB to implement alternative (b).

Table 1 displays the read overhead comparatively to the transaction-less alternative. The first conclusion is that different physical plans have a profound impact on query execution time, with one reaching up to 58× the baseline! Most strikingly, *it is clear that different plans are optimal in different scenarios*, which is a compelling argument for the use of an optimizer.

Finally, these results show less than 10% of read overhead for most cases with both datastores, which compares favorably to the measured cost of corresponding transactional mechanisms in a traditional SQL database system [20]. The exception is the aggregation query with MongoDB. While the NOT ANY approach can execute the partial aggregation natively in it, greatly reducing data transfer, the engine filters the storage with the cache keys using, for this particular case, a suboptimal index scan implemented with the keys' bounds. Since each of the thousands of keys are completely different, the scan will consider thousands of bounds. For this case, a better alternative would be a *hash anti join*, which should bring the overhead closer to the other queries.

## 5    Discussion

In this paper, we address a challenge – transaction isolation in polystores – that has seen very little previous attention, even if identified as a key research challenge [28, 30]. Transactional support is a challenge even in multi-model datastores, naturally more integrated than polystores, where support for multi-model transactions seems to be non-existent [24].

The main competing approach for transactional isolation in polystores is Polypheny-DB [32]. In contrast to our proposal, which aims at running read-only transactions with little interference and at fine-grained conflict resolution for update transactions, Polypheny-DB assumes two-phase locking with coarse granularity, which limits concurrent updates and makes them conflict with read-only transactions.

We are also aware of a different proposal that has been prototyped in Cloud-MdsQL [22], as part of the same research project. Like our current proposal, it aimed at Snapshot Isolation and fine-grained conflict resolution but it relied on the implementation, from scratch, of a custom wrapper or even core changes, to each datastore. It also assumed the version cache is always co-located, which often resulted in changing the native schema.

Similar motivation can be found in DeltaLake [7], aimed at incremental loading or correction of data in a data lake with coarse-granularity. In contrast to our proposal, it is not aimed at polystores but only at data in Parquet files directly managed by Spark. Therefore, snapshot reconstruction in DeltaLake boils down to reading the right subset of file fragments, making updates and removals very costly as a new version of the affected files needs to be written. It is also not clear how it would be extended to polystores.

Our approach is to define transactional isolation in terms of additional tables, managed themselves within the polystore, and generic queries that can be mapped to a common query engine layer and multiple datastores. This takes advantage of query optimization to achieve the optimal execution plan for each particular polystore configuration. In fact, a preliminary experiment shows that the overhead of transactional isolation is comparable to what has been measured in traditional SQL systems [20].

An interesting outcome of this experiment regards the feasibility of the proposed approach: To what extent keeping updated versions in a separate table can be reconciled with full use of the interface of each datastore? Namely, can a native query for some datastore always be modified to account for such versions? In our experiment, this is very easy to do with a key-value store such as Cassandra, where obsolete versions returned from the datastore can easily be replaced by the correct versions from the cache. Our experience with MongoDB is different: We cannot easily patch the result from a native query, which can be an arbitrarily complex "aggregation pipeline." On the other hand, this makes MongoDB expressive enough that the query can be modified to the reconstruction by itself. We postulate that this might be generally true: Whenever the native query engine is complex enough to make it hard to patch the result, it should be expressive enough to be itself used for reconstruction.

The main threat to the validity of our experiment is that we omit the write path. We expect to approach this by defining how updates on a view should be translated to changes in the cache table, which can be implemented, for example, using INSTEAD OF triggers or rules [4]. This possibility is limited by known bounds on updatable views as the reverse mapping may not always exist [13] and the challenges of translating an update $u$ to a view $V$ into a set of updates

$U$ to the underlying data $D$, namely [15,16]. Additionally, we have to consider multiple data models and, in the CloudMdsQL, the effect of ad-hoc views, for which we can resort to bi-directional transformations, with weaker guarantees on update properties [11,25]. Finally, we have to coordinate the recovery of heterogeneous multi-statement transactions with the various guarantees of individual datastores.

We can thus identify several lessons learned and outstanding challenges for transactional polystores:

*Optimization and DBA are Needed.* We have shown that structuring snapshot reconstruction as a data processing problem allows optimization (different plans are optimal in different conditions) and provides an opportunity for a DBA to intervene.

*Useful for Different Datastores.* Datastores with a more complex QE make it harder to store changes and reconstruct the snapshot outside (e.g. MongoDB) than simple key-value stores, but on the other hand, they make it easier to use their own QE for reconstruction, which makes the approach feasible across a large spectrum of datastores.

*Datastore Interfaces Matter.* It is highly relevant that the data-store language is amenable to processing and manipulation, without having to rewrite the parser. For instance, MongoDB's aggregation pipeline is much easier to handle than the SQL-like language in Cassandra. It is thus a challenge to achieve this and still be user-friendly for writing native queries.

*Various Isolation Criteria are Possible.* Polystores are inherently distributed and likely make strict snapshot isolation problematic. Moreover, it is likely that the "one size does not fit all" motto is also true in terms of isolation level. A possible alternative is a relaxed criterion such as TOPSI [18].

*Update Processing is an Open Problem.* Updates issued at the common QE level are issued on views. This means that they have to be translated back to the original data model for the underlying datastore.

*Interaction with Native Readers and Writers is an Open Problem.* Our proposal provides transactional isolation when all readers and writers access datastores through the common query engine. A consistent view of a prefix of updates to native readers should also be possible by judiciously scheduling checkpointing operations. It is unclear, however, if it is possible to do the reverse: Allowing native clients to update datastores without disturbing isolation.

**Acknowledgments.** Special thanks to the anonymous reviewers for their helpful feedback. Partially funded by project AIDA – Adaptive, Intelligent and Distributed Assurance Platform (POCI-01-0247-FEDER-045907) co-financed by the European Regional Development Fund (ERDF) through the Operational Program for Competitiveness and Internationalisation (COMPETE 2020) and by the Portuguese Foundation for Science and Technology (FCT) under CMU Portugal.

# References

1. Distributed transaction processing: The XA specification (1991). https://pubs.opengroup.org/onlinepubs/009680699/toc.pdf
2. MongoDB 4.4 manual - aggregation pileline stages: $group (2020). https://docs.mongodb.com/manual/reference/operator/aggregation/group/
3. MongoDB 4.4 manual - aggregation pileline stages: $lookup (2020). https://docs.mongodb.com/manual/reference/operator/aggregation/lookup/
4. PostgreSQL documentation - 40.4. rules on insert, update, and delete (2020). https://www.postgresql.org/docs/13/rules-update.html
5. Transaction management - the Neo4j java developer reference v4.3 (2020). https://pubs.opengroup.org/onlinepubs/009680699/toc.pdf
6. Nunes Alonso, A., et al.: Building a polyglot data access layer for a low-code application development platform (experience report). In: Remke, A., Schiavoni, V. (eds.) DAIS 2020. LNCS, vol. 12135, pp. 95–103. Springer, Cham (2020). https://doi.org/10.1007/978-3-030-50323-9_6
7. Armbrust, M., et al.: Delta lake: high-performance acid table storage over cloud object stores. Proc. VLDB Endow. **13**(12), 3411–3424 (2020). https://doi.org/10.14778/3415478.3415560
8. Bamford, R.J., Jacobs, K.R.: Method and apparatus for providing isolation levels in a database system, 9 February 1999. US Patent 5,870,758
9. Berenson, H., Bernstein, P., Gray, J., Melton, J., O'Neil, E., O'Neil, P.: A critique of ANSI SQL isolation levels. ACM SIGMOD Rec. **24**(2), 1–10 (1995)
10. Biyikoglu, C.: Under the hood: Redis CRDTs (conflict-free replicated data types) (2018)
11. Bohannon, A., Pierce, B.C., Vaughan, J.A.: Relational lenses: a language for updatable views. In: Proceedings of the Twenty-Fifth ACM SIGMOD-SIGACT-SIGART Symposium on Principles of Database Systems, pp. 338–347 (2006)
12. Burleson, D.K.: Oracle Internals: Tips, Tricks, and Techniques for DBAs. CRC Press, Boca Raton (2017)
13. Codd, E.F.: Recent investigations into relational data base systems. Technical report RJ1385, IBM, April 1974
14. Corbett, J.C., et al.: Spanner: Google's globally distributed database. ACM Trans. Comput. Syst. (TOCS) **31**(3), 1–22 (2013)
15. Dayal, U., Bernstein, P.A.: On the updatability of relational views. In: VLDB, vol. 78, pp. 368–377. Citeseer (1978)
16. Dayal, U., Bernstein, P.A.: On the correct translation of update operations on relational views. ACM Trans. Database Syst. (TODS) **7**(3), 381–416 (1982)
17. Duggan, J., et al.: The BigDAWG polystore system. SIGMOD Rec. **44**(2), 11–16 (2015). https://doi.org/10.1145/2814710.2814713
18. Faria, N., Pereira, J.: Totally-ordered prefix parallel snapshot isolation. In: Proceedings of the 8th Workshop on Principles and Practice of Consistency for Distributed Data, PaPoC 2021. Association for Computing Machinery, New York (2021). https://doi.org/10.1145/3447865.3457966
19. Gómez Ferro, D., Junqueira, F., Kelly, I., Reed, B., Yabandeh, M.: Omid: lock-free transactional support for distributed data stores. In: 2014 IEEE 30th International Conference on Data Engineering, pp. 676–687 (2014). https://doi.org/10.1109/ICDE.2014.6816691

20. Harizopoulos, S., Abadi, D.J., Madden, S., Stonebraker, M.: OLTP through the looking glass, and what we found there. In: Proceedings of the 2008 ACM SIGMOD International Conference on Management of Data, SIGMOD 2008, pp. 981–992. Association for Computing Machinery, New York (2008). https://doi.org/10.1145/1376616.1376713
21. Hellerstein, J.M., Stonebraker, M., Hamilton, J.: Architecture of a database system. Found. Trends Databases **1**(2), 141–259 (2007). https://doi.org/10.1561/1900000002
22. Kolev, B., Valduriez, P., Bondiombouy, C., Jiménez-Peris, R., Pau, R., Pereira, J.: CloudMdsQL: querying heterogeneous cloud data stores with a common language. Distrib. Parallel Databases **34**(4), 463–503 (2015). https://doi.org/10.1007/s10619-015-7185-y
23. Lakshman, A., Malik, P.: Cassandra: a decentralized structured storage system. ACM SIGOPS Oper. Syst. Rev. **44**(2), 35–40 (2010)
24. Lu, J., Holubová, I.: Multi-model databases: a new journey to handle the variety of data. ACM Comput. Surv. (CSUR) **52**(3), 1–38 (2019)
25. Macedo, N., Pacheco, H., Cunha, A., Oliveira, J.N.: Composing least-change lenses. In: Electronic Communications of the EASST, vol. 57 (2013)
26. Schultz, W., Avitabile, T., Cabral, A.: Tunable consistency in MongoDB. Proc. VLDB Endow. **12**(12), 2071–2081 (2019). https://doi.org/10.14778/3352063.3352125
27. Stonebraker, M.: The design of the POSTGRES storage system. In: Proceedings of the 13th International Conference on Very Large Data Bases, VLDB 1987, pp. 289–300. Morgan Kaufmann Publishers Inc., San Francisco (1987)
28. Stonebraker, M.: The case for polystores. ACM SIGMOD Blog (2015). https://wp.sigmod.org/?p=1629
29. Suzuki, H.: The internals of PostgreSQL: Chapter 5 concurrency control (2021). https://www.interdb.jp/pg/pgsql05.html
30. Tan, R., Chirkova, R., Gadepally, V., Mattson, T.G.: Enabling query processing across heterogeneous data models: a survey. In: 2017 IEEE International Conference on Big Data (Big Data), pp. 3211–3220 (2017). https://doi.org/10.1109/BigData.2017.8258302
31. Vogels, W.: Eventually consistent. Commun. ACM **52**(1), 40–44 (2009)
32. Vogt, M., et al.: Polypheny-DB: towards bridging the gap between polystores and HTAP systems. In: Gadepally, V., et al. (eds.) DMAH/Poly-2020. LNCS, vol. 12633, pp. 25–36. Springer, Cham (2021). https://doi.org/10.1007/978-3-030-71055-2_2

# Data Governance in a Database Operating System (DBOS)

Deeptaanshu Kumar[1], Qian Li[3(✉)], Jason Li[2], Peter Kraft[3],
Athinagoras Skiadopoulos[3], Lalith Suresh[4], Michael Cafarella[2],
and Michael Stonebraker[2]

[1] Carnegie Mellon University, Pittsburgh, USA
[2] Massachusetts Institute of Technology, Cambridge, USA
[3] Stanford University, Stanford, USA
qianli@cs.stanford.edu
[4] VMware, Palo Alto, USA

**Abstract.** This paper documents the data governance facilities in
DBOS, a database-oriented operating system under construction at Stanford and MIT. Because all operating system state is stored in a high
performance main-memory relational DBMS, DBOS has architected a
novel data provenance system for all application data. This system uses
a high-volume column store for historical provenance information, and
provenance data can be queried in SQL. Hence, at its core, DBOS is a
polystore data system. Complementing this capability are facilities motivated by GDPR including support for personal data, purposes, and the
right to be forgotten.

## 1 Introduction

At Stanford and MIT, we are building a new operating system stack, based
on sophisticated data management: the Database Operating System (DBOS).
Herein we briefly motivate the need for a new stack and then turn to novel
data provenance capabilities that are facilitated by DBOS. We note that this
provenance system requires a collection of polystore capabilities.

Specifically, we are motivated by a collection of hardware and software trends
that have occurred since the current Unix/Linux architecture was devised some
50 years ago. First, the scale of operating system (OS) resources under management has increased by several orders of magnitude. From the uniprocessor
environments of the 1970's we have evolved to current data centers with thousands of processors. For example, the MIT/Lincoln Labs Supercloud [1] on which
DBOS has been build encompasses some 9000 cores. Similar expansion of storage has also occurred. Hence, operating system state (files, tasks, messages,
etc.) is several orders of magnitude larger than 50 years ago, and warrants a
new approach to state management. Second, Unix/Linux is now elderly software, having been extended/modified/maintained for many, many years. As such,
development velocity is slowing; for example, there is no multi-node support and
sophisticated multi-core management has been slow in appearing. As a result,

© Springer Nature Switzerland AG 2021
E. K. Rezig et al. (Eds.): Poly 2021/DMAH 2021, LNCS 12921, pp. 43–59, 2021.
https://doi.org/10.1007/978-3-030-93663-1_4

multi-node capabilities must be provided by a second piece of system software (e.g. Kubernetes). This results in a duplication of services, for example two schedulers, and more difficulty in efficient resource utilization. Third, modern data centers now have heterogeneous hardware under management, for example GPUs, TPUs, and FPGAs. However, there is no ability in Linux to manage multiple kinds of processors. Lastly, a data center OS would benefit a great deal from DBMS services. For example, DBMSs provide consistency guarantees on concurrent updates, crash recovery and a high-level language (SQL) for querying OS state.

As a result, we have rearchitected the Linux stack to store *all* OS state in a multi-node, main memory, transactional DBMS. This full function RDBMS will run on top of a microkernel which provides interrupt handling, raw device drivers and very little else. Essentially all OS services (file system, messages, scheduling, etc.) are implemented in SQL on top of this DBMS. Normal user tasks run at the top level in protected fashion, as shown in Fig. 1.

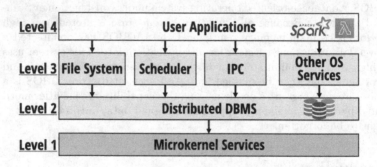

**Fig. 1.** Proposed DBOS stack.

This architecture has a number of compelling advantages relative to the traditional architecture. First, there is a single piece of software that is managing a multi-node hardware environment. This removes the duplication of function found in current multi-node environments. Second, many OS facilities (e.g. ls, chdir) can be implemented in SQL in a lot less code than in C++. Hence, we expect the footprint of our stack to be smaller than the current one. Third, DBMS services (concurrency control, crash recovery, high availability) are available to all OS functions, resulting in greater functionality (a transactional file system, for example). Lastly, DBMS services are implemented exactly once and then used by everybody, resulting in minimal code duplication. At the present time, we have an initial version of DBOS running as noted in [28], and performance is encouraging. File system services, messages, and task scheduling are competitive in our stack relative to the traditional one. In [28], we also documented our plan for constructing a complete end-to-end DBOS in additional implementation phases.

In this paper we discuss our approach to data governance. System administrators want a complete record of who did what to which objects. This record is useful when answering questions such as:

- Could user X have leaked information to user Y?
- Data element X has been found to be erroneous. Find all data elements that could have been corrupted by this error.
- Find the history of users who have written to file F.
- Find all applications run by user X.
- Find all files copied by user X.

Most large enterprises implement one or more governance systems. A popular choice is Splunk [2], which requires a user to define "events" of interest, which Splunk will then capture from application systems. Often organizations, for example the MIT Supercloud, implement more than one such system, each dealing with different applications. This results in a piecemeal approach to data governance in which the complete picture is spread over several semantically distinct systems. In addition, deploying any new software requires manual intervention to capture new events from the added systems. Most large organizations struggle to meet the ever growing requirements requested by management in this area. Such requirements are unlikely to abate, given the recent legislative and regulatory interest in this area.

Since all OS state is in a DBMS, DBOS enables automatic provenance capture, which will allow easier coverage of events without manual intervention. In Sect. 2, we detail our current DBOS support for data provenance. In Sect. 3 we turn to demonstrating that there is very little overhead to running DBOS provenance, and that interesting provenance queries run with good performance. Then, Sect. 4 turns to the polystore implications of our provenance system and the future directions we are exploring in this area. Section 5 discusses one aspect of the polystore nature of storage, especially in data lakes, which is the use of data catalogs. Section 6 describes several design challenges and our plan to address them. Finally, Sect. 7 discusses GDPR capabilities, and Sect. 8 presents related work.

## 2  DBOS Data Provenance

### 2.1  Provenance Architecture

All DBOS operating system state is stored in a main memory DBMS, in our case VoltDB [3]. This includes multiple tables implementing a file system, a scheduling table and a interprocess communication (IPC) table. There are likely to be additional tables storing OS state as the project evolves. For example, the Message table contains the following fields.

```
Message (sender_id, receiver_id, message_id,
         date_time, message_contents, other_fields)
```

The sender activates a stored procedure in VoltDB, which inserts a row in this table with the various fields filled in. The Message table is partitioned across the various nodes in Supercloud. The partition key is receiver_id, so the row is added to the Message partition at the node of the receiver. As noted in [28] this is a single-row single-table operation which is very fast. An efficient implementation of messages would then use a database trigger to alert the receiver, who could use SQL to retrieve the message contents and delete the row in the table. Unfortunately, VoltDB lacks database triggers, so our implementation requires the receiver to poll the database for the message contents. Even with this limitation, DBOS messages are surprisingly performant, as noted in [28].

In [28] we also detailed implementations of a file system and a scheduler using VoltDB tables with a similar architecture.

To implement a complete provenance system, DBOS merely needs to capture all reads and writes to the message table and other tables with relevant OS state. There are several possible ways to do so. First, a conventional DBMS would log all changes to all tables for crash recovery purposes. However, VoltDB uses command logging, as it offers higher performance in their environment [17]. Hence the actual data update is not logged, just the SQL that performed the operation. In addition, a complete provenance system would also require us to capture reads as well as writes.

A second possible implementation is to use VoltDB "change capture". This facility spools all database updates to a file or other location. With no DBOS code, this will capture writes but not reads. If VoltDB supported database triggers, those could be a third possible implementation.

At the present time, we have a system running that uses VoltDB change capture to deal with all write events. To get to a complete system, we plan to migrate to a facility that performs data capture in the DBOS stored procedures that read and write database tables. That way we can capture all reads and writes to table of interest.

## 2.2 Provenance Specification

For every table in the DBOS VoltDB data base, the table owner must specify the level of provenance they desire. The options are:

- Capture the existence of each write operations
- Capture write operations including the actual data written
- Capture the existence of each read operations
- Capture read operations including the actual data read.

We have had substantial discussions about the granularity of provenance capture. On the one hand, we could capture coarse granularity, for example that user X wrote File Y at time T. Alternately, we could capture that user X wrote block L at time Y or even that user X wrote byte B at time Y. This will obviously dramatically change the size of the provenance database when DBOS is in "capture existence" mode. Our current thinking is to allow user specification of granularity on a file/table basis. Obviously, there may be additional modes for the provenance system as we gain more experience with it.

## 2.3 Provenance Database

Obviously, provenance capture entails a massive amount of data especially if the actual data read or written is captured. A high performance OLTP DBMS like VoltDB is ill-suited to the capture of a massive amount of historical data. As a result, we are spooling provenance data transactionally to Vertica, a multi-core, multi-node DBMS based on column store technology that can readily manage petabytes of provenance data. In a DBOS environment, we expect an instance of VoltDB and an instance of Vertica will run on most DBOS nodes.

According to our industrial partners, access control is handled by standard SQL capabilities. Hence, they are worried about legal, but suspicious events, which we call the Edward Snowden effect (ESE). As such, the main use of a provenance database is for after-the-fact monitoring, as we discuss in the next section. Of course, provenance is also useful for detecting error propagation.

## 2.4 Provenance Queries

In this section, we present ten representative provenance queries, which guide our implementation. This list comes primarily from tasks of interest at DBOS industrial partners.

**1. File/DB touch**—For a file F or a table T, who was the last person to write each block/record. Who was the first person to do so? Which block/record has the most updates in the last week? In the last year?

**2. Connectivity**—If X made a network connection with Y, then there is a bi-directional arc between X and Y. Construct the connection graph in the last week. Do the same for the last year. Construct the connection graph of people who talked in the last year but not in the last week. Do the same for systems, described below.

**3. Compromised systems/users**—A user interacted with a system if the scheduler ran a task on the system on his/her behalf. Who interacted with potentially compromised system S in the last month? What systems did a potentially compromised user interact with in the last month? Trace all connections (transitively) from a compromised system S in the last month.

**4. Downstream provenance**—Find all blocks/records that could have resulted from information in block/record X. In other words, find a block Y that was written by some user who previously read block X within 5 s. This is "one hop" provenance. Complete provenance requires the transitive closure of this operation.

**5. Upstream provenance**—Find any block/record X that could have been influenced by block/record Y. In other words, somebody read X and wrote Y - transitively.

**6. Debugging**—What is the state of a file/table at time T. Now "single step" forward for 3 h.

**7. Could X have leaked info to Y?**—We define possible leakage as X wrote a file block and Y read the same block within 1 min. In addition, X sent a message to Y, or X wrote a DBMS record and Y read it within 1 min. This is "one-hop" possible leakage. Complete possible leakage is the transitive closure of this operation.

**8. Ranking suspicious objects**—Administrators are often called upon to rank suspicious objects or behaviors: network packets from potential intrusions, files that are potentially infected, and user data reads that are potentially inappropriate. To rank an object, we can compute an object score using provenance-derived statistics. For example, scoring a particular file open might need to know how many individuals open the file on a typical day. The provenance system should allow administrators to specify and efficiently compute different "object ranking views" that use provenance data.

**9. Input auditing**—An organization wants to know that it has the legal rights to all of the data resources used to compute a particular output (possibly a sensitive ML model). For file X, the system should: (1) compute every ancestor file of X, and (2) consult a database of file rights to make sure it has legal right to all X's ancestors. That database might be partially derived from GDPR activity, but probably also reflects commercial transactions and other information.

**10. Pipeline Modeling**—A data pipeline is a long sequence of programs that yields a set of data products. If pipelines are first-class objects, then the provenance system can answer valuable questions valuable to administrators, such as, "Did pipeline X complete successfully on July 23?" and "What pipeline produced file Y?"

The query processing implications of these queries are discussed in Sect. 2.6.

## 2.5   Provenance Schema

There are two possible approaches to a Vertica provenance schema. First, for any update, we can capture (old_value, new_value) pairs from VoltDB using change capture or our own stored procedures. For inserts, there is no old value and for deletes, there is no new value. For any operation, we insert the appropriate record into Vertica. As such, Vertica manages an insert-only provenance database. The second option for updates is to capture only the new value, and perform a Vertica update (rather than an insert). Since Vertica does not overwrite data, the historical record is preserved with appropriate timestamps and we store two records, without duplicating data between them. We plan to explore the performance and ease of querying for both options.

## 2.6   Provenance Query Processing

Some of the above queries (1, 6, 8, and 10) can be expressed in normal SQL. On the other hand, several (2, 3, 4, 5, 7, and 9) require transitive closure, which is available in some SQL engines but not others. Specifically, Vertica does not have built-in support for transitive closure. There has been a lot of work in this area [4,9,29]. However, in Vertica it will likely be fastest to code a breadth first algorithm, removing duplicates between iterations. A depth first exploration would require many more user queries and would make parallelism difficult to exploit. On the other hand, breadth-first means running a transitive closure iteration as a parallel SQL query, adding the result to the answer being assembled, removing duplicates at each iteration.

In query 7, in our opinion, indirect leakage is quite rare. Hence, one could stop after one or two iterations, with very low probability of missing a leakage path. Since the iteration is in user code, we can watch the size of the answer being assembled and stop if it does not grow.

Furthermore, one can maintain the transitive closure for each of these queries dynamically, incrementally updating the result when events occur. Alternatively, one can compute the transitive closure only when there is a provenance query. The tradeoff, of course, is the ratio of VoltDB updates to provenance queries. When provenance queries are rare (the usual case), computing the transitive closure in advance is probably the wrong thing to do.

Lastly, in query 7 if (X, Y) is a possible leakage path, then there is no reason to find additional instances of this possibility. As such, this is a "first match" query in which additional instances are not useful.

Although we could run Vertica at level 4 in the diagram of Fig. 1 (i.e. in user space) performance would suffer. Our planned implementation uses the VoltDB store procedures for read and write. If Vertica is run in user space, then an extra two messages will be required. Hence, we are planning to run both DBMSs in the kernel at level 2.

The trend in data warehouse systems is to separate compute from storage, pioneered by systems such as BigQuery [27] and Snowflake [30]. In this way, a storage layer with perhaps limited compute is separate from a compute layer. Of course, the reason for this architecture is to allow compute resources to be scaled up and down elastically as query needs change. Vertica is moving toward this architecture, and in time, most warehouse vendors will offer elasticity on a query-by-query basis.

With this separation, there is the option of pushing portions of a provenance query into the storage layer. In a recent paper [32], some of us analyzed the desirability of pushing down filters and joins into the storage layer. When data blocks are re-referenced frequently, it will be desirable to perform most-to-all of query processing in the compute layer. Alternately, when re-reference is low, then it is best to push down query pieces into the storage layer, when possible. Since provenance queries are expected to be infrequent, it will generally be advantageous to push down as much computation as possible.

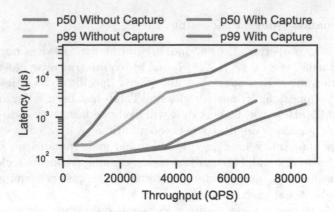

**Fig. 2.** Throughput versus median and tail latency for a social network workload with and without provenance capture for writes.

## 3 Performance

To demonstrate the practicality of provenance capture, we instrumented a simple DBOS workload to capture all write operations including the actual data written, then measured workload performance with and without capture. We implemented this instrumentation using VoltDB's change data capture feature, exporting all information to a remote Vertica server. Our benchmark uses the simple Twitter clone Retwis [26], adapted to store all data in VoltDB instead of in Redis. This workload stores all data in VoltDB tables (e.g., a "posts" table) so provenance capture requires logging updates to these table. We execute a workload of 100% writes to a single VoltDB partition, repeatedly making posts for randomly selected users.

We show all results for this benchmark in Fig. 2. We measure throughput versus median and tail latency with an increasing amount of offered load. We find that overhead associated with provenance capture slightly reduces maximum achievable throughput. It has little effect on latency at lower loads, but increases latency somewhat at higher loads. A DBA would have to decide whether detailed provenance was worth the overhead, given the particulars of his load.

We next evaluate query performance on this captured data. We adapt two of the queries from Sect. 2.4 to Retwis and measure their latency in both Vertica and VoltDB, showing results in Fig. 3.

The first query is "Who was the last person to write a post?":

```
select USERID from RETWISPOSTS order by TIMESTAMP desc limit 1;
```

We show the performance of this query in Fig. 3a. With 100M rows, Vertica can execute this query in 17 ms, while VoltDB slows down and eventually times out when given too much data.

The second query is "Who posted the most since time X?":

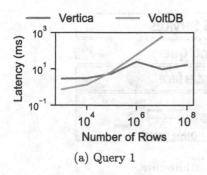
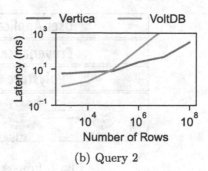

(a) Query 1    (b) Query 2

**Fig. 3.** Performance of provenance queries on social network data using Vertica and VoltDB.

```
select agg.USERID, agg.cnt
  from (select USERID, count(*) as cnt from RETWISPOSTS
    where TIMESTAMP >= 100 group by USERID) as agg
  order by agg.cnt desc limit 1;
```

Figure 3b demonstrates the performance of this query. As before, Vertica can execute this more complex query in 313 ms given 100M rows, while VoltDB slows down and eventually times out with too much data.

These experiments demonstrate that a dedicated OLAP system like Vertica can easily handle provenance queries on large amounts of data. They also demonstrate the need for a polystore in provenance management, as a dedicated OLTP system like VoltDB is not capable of executing large-scale provenance queries.

## 4  Polystore Implications

As noted previously, DBOS is a fairly simple polystore that spools provenance data from VoltDB to Vertica. However, it is obviously a good idea to support a file system on top of Vertica. For gigantic files, this will offer a compressed column store implementation which will outperform the VoltDB row store. Also, there is no reason to disallow users from storing DBMS data in Vertica, if they so choose. As such, we will have two different DBMSs generating provenance information.

More generally, there will potentially be other DBMSs in which user data is stored and/or files supported. On a case-by-case basis, we will explore supporting such other DBMSs. Also, over time we expect to have to support provenance information in multiple data warehouse-oriented column stores. This situation could arise if applications insist on spooling their provenance data to a preferred DBMS. This leads to the general polystore architecture of Fig. 4.

With multiple provenance stores, standard SQL queries will access only one of the repositories. However, figuring out which one will require a data catalog, discussed in the next section. Also, the scope of our transitive closure queries will be all systems. We distinguish two cases of interest. In the first case provenance information is separable and there is no cross-talk between the systems. In this

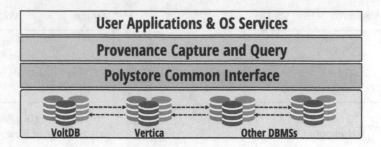

**Fig. 4.** Proposed polystore architecture.

case there is no possibility of a user reading a file or a database that spools to one repository and then writing a file or a database that spools elsewhere. Hence, one can run the transitive closure queries on each repository individually and then merge the answers. On the other hand, there will be situations where provenance information is not separable. This will lead to a more complex query processing strategy, whereby intermediate results must be traded between provenance stores.

However, it is a reasonable assumption that a provenance system need only support warehouse-oriented DBMSs and only for a subset of possible queries. As such polystore complexity is limited.

## 5   Support for Data Catalogs

The previous section noted the problem of finding metadata across multiple storage systems. Obviously, the metadata within a single DBMS is correct; however, enterprises are typically running several-to-many DBMSs. Also, metadata for files is often not captured anywhere. A common architecture is to move all such data to a data lake (or lakehouse, if you wish) and then build a catalog for lake objects.

There are a number of recent data catalog systems that do exactly this. These are standalone systems that serve as authoritative sources of metadata for all the datasets in an organization. Commercial systems include Alation, Collibra, and data.world. Open source systems include ckan, Amundsen, and Magda.

Data catalogs allow metadata queries by humans and external systems. For example, a compliance system might compare the access permissions of an observed database with the data privacy requirements stated in the organization's data catalog. Catalogs can also be instrumental in enabling better organizational data search.

In addition, data catalogs also play an important role in data access control and information security initiatives. For example, companies frequently implement course-grained or fine-grained access control based on data classifications stored within these catalogs.

In our conversations with commercial users of such systems, we have observed two common problems. First, the catalogs are incomplete. Although most of these systems include crawlers that will traverse existing data assets and help populate the catalog, there is still some human curation effort needed to ensure datasets have correct schemas, personal data settings, and so on. Moreover, many users build semi-private datasets that are inaccessible to crawlers and are never added to the catalog. Second, the catalogs fail to attract wide audiences inside the organizations that build them. This might be due to the poor quality of the catalogs, or because the catalogs simply do not deliver enough compelling value to the typical data users.

We wish to make two points in this section. First, if an enterprise decided to run DBOS everywhere, then a rudimentary data catalog is automatically constructed. This DBOS catalog is by definition complete and accurate, avoiding the criticisms discussed above. Also, if DBOS provenance is used, then the lineage of every object is automatically provided. This is a powerful form of metadata, which will help users uncover the semantic definition of a data set, even when it is missing or incomplete.

# 6 Design Challenges

We now describe a few ongoing design challenges for any useful provenance system, and how we address them in DBOS.

## 6.1 Provenance Data Capture

Data capture is a serious challenge for provenance systems. Past efforts have addressed this challenge in two main ways, both unsatisfying:

1. Users must rewrite their code with a new toolchain, which generally yields high-quality data at the cost of high human effort. With this approach, the coverage of data provenance often suffers.
2. Automatic instrumentation of unmodified code, which generally yields low-quality data at a low human cost. With this approach, the usefulness of data provenance often suffers.

The design of DBOS alters this playing field dramatically. Since provenance is integrated with the OS itself, all important operations are captured and logged. We expect this design to make a big difference.

However, DBOS provenance still has shortcomings. For example, suppose OS-visible operations do not reflect operations that downstream users are interested in. Consider a privacy policy-compliance process that scans every file in DBOS and generates a per-user report file describing possible violations. The DBOS provenance system will show that each output report file is dependent on every file in the system. In most cases, such provenance information is either misleading or useless. Capturing such provenance data is not helpful to the application being run, and another (presumably higher level) system is required.

Another problem arises when data crosses DBOS-visible boundaries. In particular, the provenance of any dataset that escapes via traditional I/O channels (e.g., a screen, a log file, or over a network socket) can no longer be tracked with confidence. Disabling traditional display and network access would make DBOS unusable for many applications.

We can mitigate this problem by sandboxing stored procedures and either noting in the provenance record when bytes left the DBOS system, or disabling such operations altogether for sensitive data. There are several solutions of interest in this space. For example, cloud providers already use techniques like runtime sandboxing [24] and restricting process privileges via mechanisms like SEC-COMP [15]. In addition, sandboxing techniques in dynamic information flow control (IFC) systems like Trapeze [5] are also applicable in our setting.

These issues are serious. While DBOS' current provenance design partially addresses them, they are still questions for ongoing research. One approach is discussed in the next subsection.

## 6.2  Application Integration

Organizations operate with multiple data abstractions. Obviously, organizational activity can be captured as files, records, processes, and function invocations. But organizations also have pipelines, approval processes, business patterns, and other "objects" that intersect with, but are not identical to, computational objects.

For example, "did marketing approve the latest commercial?" is a business question, but it can also be framed as a provenance question when combined with a file identified as "the latest commercial", a user group identified as "marketing", and a particular process execution identified as "approve".

DBOS can enable integration of provenance with these external non-provenance concepts in two ways.

**Concept-As-View**—The user can define views that model external concepts. For example, the table of "commercials" might be written as a view over the set of DBOS files that are in the commercials directory and which have a member of the marketing team as an owner. An important property of such a system is the use of user-defined functions as part of the view definition. This allows arbitrary domain-specific questions to be asked of the DBOS and its provenance objects.

**Federated Query Optimization**—A user query that involves non-provenance objects might involve query processing over multiple schemas, for example a relational database of DBOS files and a graph database of provenance information. We plan to study optimization across multiple systems so that user queries can be executed in reasonable amounts of time.

## 7  Support for Capabilities Motivated by GDPR

### 7.1  Personal Data

GDPR legislates special support for personal data. One of us is a lawyer specializing in privacy issues such as this one. Although it would be very helpful to have an algorithm decide what fields are personal data and what ones are not, such a feature seems out of reach, since personal data is somewhat subjective. Instead, a human must specify what is personal data. In a DBOS environment, this requires tagging every column of every table in a DBOS instance with a notation whether it is personal data or not. Furthermore, it is equally difficult to automatically mark derived data (materialized views, query results). Hence, it is assumed that all derived data will be appropriately marked, and we will not try to build a system to automatically mark derived data.

Such a marking system can be added trivially to the system catalogs (metadata).

## 7.2  Purposes

GDPR legislates that every person with personal data stored in a service have the right to decide for what purposes his/her data can be used. Example purposes might be medical research or advertising. Hence, the service provider decides on a collection, K, of (otherwise uninterpreted) strings, called purposes. Every item of personal data is tagged with the purposes the owner of that data item allows for that data element.

Although in theory, there can be tens or hundreds of purposes, we expect the normal case will be a half a dozen or less. Otherwise, it will be too confusing for users to say yes/no to each of tens of purposes. In a previous paper [13], we advocated using extra bits in each record to store this yes/no information. However, when the number of purposes is small, we think an alternate implementation will be more efficient.

For every column of personal data and for each purpose, we plan to store in DBOS an exception list of record identifiers of persons who have opted out of allowing their data to be used for that purpose. We expect the normal case is that people will not opt out, so these lists will not be onerous to store. Every query which is sent to a service must include one of the authorized purposes.

The query executor just needs to add the following processing step whenever it picks up a piece of personal data:

– Look up the person ID in the appropriate exception list
– If found, do not return the requested data element.

We anticipate the exception lists for a table will be small and will be cached in main memory when the table is active. A bit-oriented implementation will require one bit per record. This scheme requires one record identifier per person that opts out. As long as the opt out rate is low (less than 1%), this scheme will be more efficient. We can also use delta encoding for record identifiers to cut down on the amount of space they consume.

## 7.3  The Right to be Forgotten

Any person, P, with personal data in a service can request to be forgotten. In this case all personal data (defined above) should be deleted by the service.

It is assumed that P presents their identifier, I, or the service can look it up. The identifier is assumed to be the key of one or more tables.

If there is a "path" from the key to an item of personal data, then this item must be deleted (nulled). A path is defined as a collection of column names, $N_1, \ldots, N_k$, such that $(I, N_1), (N_1, N_2), \ldots, (N_{k-1}, N_k)$ are the composite keys of intermediate tables and $N_k$ is the key of a table, T, with personal data. Any personal data in the appropriate row of T should be nulled.

We expect to look for efficient ways to perform this operation. In addition, we GDPR legislated that a service has 30 days to perform this operation. Hence, it is possible to batch such requests and perform them in bulk. We expect to see if this technique is more efficient than forgetting people one at a time.

## 8    Related Work

There has been a substantial amount of provenance research, including work on data models, query processing, and practical systems.

**Provenance Models**—There has been a vast amount of theoretical and model-related provenance research. Cheney, Chiticariu, and Tan provide a useful overview [7]. Provenance queries are generally divided among three models:

- *Why provenance* queries that identify all the source values contributed to the computation of a particular output,
- *How provenance* queries that describe the computation that combined the source values, and
- *Where provenance* queries that describe where a particular piece of output information was copied from.

For most of our DBOS target queries, *why provenance* and *where provenance* are likely the most relevant model.

**Query Processing**—Query processing is a major thrust of provenance work. Green, *et al.* [8] showed that query processing for why-provenance queries can be viewed as an example of a broader class of query processing methods that can also be used in probabilistic and incomplete databases. Recent work [22] takes a user's example *why provenance* query and rewrites it to match user guidance about which entities should be included or not; this method might be a good fit to typical DBOS scenarios. Chiticariu, *et al.* [12] introduced a system that permits manual annotations of relational data, along with a mechanism for users to describe how annotations should be propagated.

**Data Collection**—For many non-relational systems, there is an additional challenge associated with non-relational software: how to actually capture the provenance. The noWorkflow [20] system automatically collects information about Python programs at code-definition time as well as runtime. Vamsa [21] uses static analysis of Python programs to derive provenance for machine learning models. Chapman, *et al.* [6] aim to capture provenance for data preprocessing code; they introduce a set of operators that closely resemble common prepreprocessing patterns, then annotate Python code with their standard operators. Scientific workflow systems [10,14,18,31] ask users to manually annotate code for provenance collection. Dagger asks users to annotate data at certain interfaces between code blocks [25]. Other systems [11,19] collect provenance via automatic automatic instrumentation of a process' interaction with the computational environment; this is perhaps the most similar approach in previous work to what DBOS does today.

All of these systems struggle to obtain provenance data that is relevant and complete without huge human effort. Unlike relational databases with their fixed set of operators, general-purpose programs have neither a fixed set of operations, nor an obvious best place for instrumenting those operations. In work to date, either the programmer must manually annotate existing code to capture provenance information, at great human effort; or the system must try to automatically instrument unmodified code, and thereby potentially capture confusing "operations" at an inappropriate level of granularity.

By moving many operations into a relational model, DBOS has some data capture advantages over previous work. Many OS operations—such as file create, or network transmissions, or process launches—can be observed as a standard relational INSERT. In many cases, the semantics of these operations are broadly understood and can support a range of likely downstream queries.

However, there is nothing that requires a DBOS-visible operation to make sense to a future provenance query-writer; consider that a user launching a single program from a shell will appear to be a new entry in a process table, as will just one of the many independent processes that together allow a modern web browser to operate. As a result, even though DBOS operates via the relational model, some aspects of DBOS data capture closely resemble the challenges usually associated with general-purpose program provenance.

**Practical Systems**—There are many issues that arise when building practical provenance systems, especially when the volume of provenance data grows very large. Zheng and Ives examine how to build a provenance system that is efficient and tamper-proof enough for long term archival use [33]. The Smoke system [23] is an in-memory database explicitly designed for efficient provenance capture and querying, employing specialized optimizations when provenance queries are known in advance, which is likely in many use cases. As provenance is especially useful in data science use cases, the NBSafety [16] system is tailored for preserving provenance in notebook-style settings where cell dependencies are easy to lose track of.

## 9    Conclusions

In this paper we have presented a provenance system built into the DBOS operating system. This automatically captures a lot of provenance events without manual intervention by a user. We have show that the run-time overhead of the system is modest and query performance on the provenance database is reasonable. The polystore implications of our approach were also discussed. Our plan going forward is to build a complete end-to-end DBOS implementation.

# References

1. Mit supercloud (2021). https://supercloud.mit.edu/
2. Splunk (2021). https://www.splunk.com/
3. VoltDB (2021). https://www.voltdb.com/
4. Agrawal, R., Jagadish, H.: Direct algorithms for computing the transitive closure of database relations. In: VLDB, vol. 87, pp. 1–4 (1987)
5. Alpernas, K., et al.: Secure serverless computing using dynamic information flow control. In: Proceedings of the ACM Programming Languages (OOPSLA), October 2018. https://doi.org/10.1145/3276488,https://doi.org/10.1145/3276488
6. Chapman, A., Missier, P., Simonelli, G., Torlone, R.: Capturing and querying fine-grained provenance of preprocessing pipelines in data science. Proc. VLDB Endow. **14**(4), 507–520 (2020). https://doi.org/10.14778/3436905.3436911
7. Cheney, J., Chiticariu, L., Tan, W.C.: Provenance in databases: why, how, and where. Found. Trends Databases **1**(4), 379–474 (2009). https://doi.org/10.1561/1900000006
8. Chiticariu, L., Tan, W.C., Vijayvargiya, G.: Dbnotes: a post-it system for relational databases based on provenance. In: Conference: Proceedings of the ACM SIGMOD International Conference on Management of Data, Baltimore, Maryland, USA, June 14-16, 2005, pp. 942–944, January 2005. https://doi.org/10.1145/1066157.1066296
9. Dar, S., Ramakrishnan, R.: A performance study of transitive closure algorithms. ACM SIGMOD Record. **23**(2), 454–465 (1994)
10. Frew, J., Bose, R.: Earth system science workbench: a data management infrastructure for earth science products, pp. 180–189, January 2001. https://doi.org/10.1109/SSDM.2001.938550
11. Frew, J., Metzger, D., Slaughter, P.: Automatic capture and reconstruction of computational provenance. Concurr. Comput. Pract. Exp. **20**, 485–496 (2008). https://doi.org/10.1002/cpe.1247
12. Green, T.J., Karvounarakis, G., Tannen, V.: Provenance semirings. In: Proceedings of the Twenty-Sixth ACM SIGMOD-SIGACT-SIGART Symposium on Principles of Database Systems, PODS 2007, pp. 31–40. Association for Computing Machinery, New York (2007). https://doi.org/10.1145/1265530.1265535,https://doi.org/10.1145/1265530.1265535
13. Gadepally, V., Mattson, T., Stonebraker, M., Wang, F., Luo, G., Laing, Y., Dubovitskaya, A. (eds.): DMAH/Poly -2019. LNCS, vol. 11721. Springer, Cham (2019). https://doi.org/10.1007/978-3-030-33752-0
14. Lin, C., et al.: A reference architecture for scientific workflow management systems and the view SOA solution. IEEE Trans. Serv. Comput. **2**, 79–92 (2009). https://doi.org/10.1109/TSC.2009.4
15. Linux: Linux seccomp. https://man7.org/linux/man-pages/man2/seccomp.2.html
16. Macke, S., Gong, H., Lee, D.J.L., Head, A., Xin, D., Parameswaran, A.: Fine-grained lineage for safer notebook interactions (2021)
17. Malviya, N., Weisberg, A., Madden, S., Stonebraker, M.: Rethinking main memory OLTP recovery. In: 2014 IEEE 30th International Conference on Data Engineering, pp. 604–615. IEEE (2014)

18. McPhillips, T., Song, T., Kolisnik, T., Aulenbach, S., Freire, J.: al et: Yeswork-flow: a user-oriented, language-independent tool for recovering workflow informa-tion from scripts. Int. J. Digit. Cur. **10**(1), 298–313 (2015)
19. Muniswamy-Reddy, K.K., Holland, D.A., Braun, U., Seltzer, M.: Provenance-aware storage systems. In: Proceedings of the Annual Conference on USENIX 2006 Annual Technical Conference, ATEC 2006, p. 4. USENIX Association (2006)
20. Murta, L., Braganholo, V., Chirigati, F., Koop, D., Freire, J.: noworkflow: cap-turing and analyzing provenance of scripts. In: Ludäscher, B., Plale, B. (eds.) Provenance and Annotation of Data and Processes, pp. 71–83. Springer, Cham (2015)
21. Namaki, M.H., et al.: Vamsa: Automated Provenance Tracking in Data Science Scripts, pp. 1542–1551. Association for Computing Machinery, New York (2020). https://doi.org/10.1145/3394486.3403205
22. Namaki, M.H., Song, Q., Wu, Y., Yang, S.: Answering why-questions by exem-plars in attributed graphs. In: Proceedings of the 2019 International Conference on Management of Data, SIGMOD 2019, pp. 1481–1498. Association for Computing Machinery, New York (2019). https://doi.org/10.1145/3299869.3319890,https://doi.org/10.1145/3299869.3319890
23. Psallidas, F., Wu, E.: Smoke: fine-grained lineage at interactive speed. Proc. VLDB Endow. **11**(6), 719–732 (2018). https://doi.org/10.14778/3199517.3199522
24. PyPy: Pypy's sandboxing features. https://doc.pypy.org/en/release-2.0-beta2/sandbox.html
25. Rezig, E.K., et al.: Dagger: a data (not code) debugger. In: 10th Conference on Innovative Data Systems Research, CIDR 2020, Amsterdam, The Netherlands, 12–15 January 2020, Online Proceedings. www.cidrdb.org (2020). http://cidrdb.org/cidr2020/papers/p35-rezig-cidr20.pdf
26. Salvatore Sanfilippo: Retwis: a twitter toy-clone (2014). https://github.com/antirez/retwis
27. Sato, K.: An inside look at google bigquery. White paper (2012). https://cloud.google.com/files/BigQueryTechnicalWP.pdf
28. Skiadopoulos, A., et al.: DBOS: a DBMS-oriented Operating System. Submitted for publication (2021)
29. Valduriez, P., Khoshfian, S.: Parallel evaluation of the transitive closure of a database relation. Int. J. Parallel Program. **17**(1), 19–42 (1988)
30. Vuppalapati, M., Miron, J., Agarwal, R., Truong, D., Motivala, A., Cruanes, T.: Building an elastic query engine on disaggregated storage. In: 17th USENIX Sym-posium on Networked Systems Design and Implementation (NSDI 2020), pp. 449–462. USENIX Association, Santa Clara, February 2020. https://www.usenix.org/conference/nsdi20/presentation/vuppalapati
31. Wolstencroft, K., et al.: The Taverna workflow suite: designing and executing workflows of Web Services on the desktop, web or in the cloud. Nucl. Acids Res. **41**(W1), W557–W561 (2013). https://doi.org/10.1093/nar/gkt328,https://doi.org/10.1093/nar/gkt328
32. Yang, Y., et al.: Flexpushdowndb: Hybrid pushdown and caching in a cloud DBMS. In: VLDB, vol. 14 (2021)
33. Zheng, N., Ives, Z.G.: Compact, tamper-resistant archival of fine-grained prove-nance. Proc. VLDB Endow. **14**(4), 485–497 (2020). https://doi.org/10.14778/3436905.3436909

# ACID-V: Towards a New Class of DBMSs for Data Sharing

Muhammad El-Hindi$^{(\boxtimes)}$, Zheguang Zhao$^{(\boxtimes)}$, and Carsten Binnig$^{(\boxtimes)}$

Technical University Darmstadt, Darmstadt, Germany
{muhammad.el-hindi,zheguang.zhao,carsten.binnig}@cs.tu-darmstadt.de

**Abstract.** Recently, a new class of systems for shared and collaborative data management has gained more and more traction. Different from classical DBMSs, systems for shared data need to provide additional guarantees to ensure the integrity of data and transaction execution. In this paper, we propose to extend the ACID properties used by classical DBMSs with a new Verifiability component to enable users to specify the required guarantees of verifiability in a declarative manner.

## 1  Introduction

*Motivation.* Recently, a new class of systems for shared and collaborative data management has gained more and more traction. Examples of such systems include Veritas [2], BlockchainDB [1], FalconDB [5], Fides [4] and Spitz [8]. Compared to classical DBMSs that are designed for being used by a single party, these systems enable multiple parties to manage a shared database (DB) in a collaborative manner. For example, think of a shared database for medical patient records. Here, hospitals and doctors would be able to directly share and modify patient data to keep track of diagnoses and treatments a patient received. Clearly, shared DBs provide many opportunities not only in the medical domain such as for large-scale epidemic studies [6], but also for many other fields where access to a shared DB enables more effective collaboration or new use cases (e.g., financial domain [7] or supply chains [3]).

However, different from classical DBMSs, systems for shared data need to provide additional guarantees to ensure the integrity of data and transaction execution (called *verifiability* guarantees in the following). The main reason for this is that when manipulating a shared database in a collaborative manner there is often some mutual distrust between the different parties that jointly access the shared database since they often have different interests (e.g., think of an insurance company and a hospital that use a shared database for medical records). Hence, the goal of the verifiability guarantees is to govern the shared database; i.e., to guarantee that the shared database is only modified based on a predefined and agreed upon set of transactions that every party adheres to and that none of the parties can tamper with the data in a different manner.

If we now look at how existing systems for shared data (such as those mentioned at the beginning) provide verifiability, we can observe that these systems

E. K. Rezig et al. (Eds.): Poly 2021/DMAH 2021, LNCS 12921, pp. 60–64, 2021.
https://doi.org/10.1007/978-3-030-93663-1_5

typically take a very implementation-centric approach and often do not integrate well with the ACID guarantees of classical DBMSs. Moreover, the concrete guarantees that such systems provide are very different from system to system and often hard-baked into their execution model. FalconDB, for instance, is based on blockchains to implement verifiability and uses an incentive-based scheme where nodes are encouraged to verify the execution of queries asynchronously to hide the high verification cost. As a result, however, potentially unverified queries from malicious servers stay undetected. In contrast to that, updates are always verified synchronously for the entire network.

*Vision.* In this paper, we propose to take a more principled and more database-centric approach to provide verifiability for shared data systems. The main idea is to extend the ACID properties used by classical DBMSs with a new *Verifiability* component which results in the *ACID-V* properties. To be more precise, similar to the other components in ACID such as the well-known isolation property, we propose to specify the guarantees of verifiability in a declarative manner using different verification levels (i.e., strict or more loose). Moreover, we believe that the integration of verification with the ACID properties not only is a natural fit and gives applications well-defined guarantees but it enables a new class of shared DBMSs that decide based on the verification level what optimizations and concrete execution strategies are best suited to meet the desired guarantees.

## 2   From ACID to ACID-V

### 2.1   Adding the V to ACID

In classical databases, transactions are governed by the ACID properties. As mentioned before, the concrete properties that should be satisfied can be defined declaratively and are implemented by databases in various ways. For example, for the I (solation) in ACID, a user can declare the specific isolation level (e.g., read committed, serializable) that a transaction should run under. This isolation level is then guaranteed by a database through its concurrency control scheme (e.g., optimistic vs. pessimistic). Similarly, we propose to add a new Verifiability property that user can specify declaratively and that database systems can implement in different ways. Further, looking at Verifiability from a conceptional perspective enables users to reason about the guarantees a system provides independent from implementation details.

To add the V to ACID, we extend the classical transaction state model of ACID-compliant DBMSs by a *verified* state. For simplicity, Fig. 1 visualizes the extended state model for ACID-V for the case in which all nodes in a shared DBMS act honestly. We will briefly discuss some aspects of malicious behavior later in Sect. 2.3. As we can see, in our state model a transaction can only reach the *verified* state after it reached the *committed* state.

Modeling *verified* as a state that follows the *committed* state has several advantages. First, since verification is typically an expensive step the model leaves some freedom when the transition from *committed* to *verified* happens (i.e., directly after the commit or if it can be deferred). Moreover, it enables

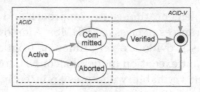

**Fig. 1.** Simplified state model for ACID-V. The classical transaction state model is extended with a *Verified* state.

the user to declare which state is allowed to be read by other transactions (e.g., if committed but unverified can be read or if all state must be verified before becoming visible). Second, the *verified* state is an optional state as shown in Fig. 1, i.e., not all *committed* transactions need to be verified, which allows partial verification to reduce the overhead.

## 2.2   Verification Levels

While a formal definition of ACID-V and a more complete discussion of possible verification levels are out of scope for this paper, in the following we show how a first set of different verification levels can be defined based on the state model we introduced before. Based on this we will discuss what implications different levels can have on the integrity of data/execution and a system's performance.

*Strict Verification (SV).* This verification level requires that all transactions need to be verified. Moreover, all transactions are allowed to read only verified state. A similar guarantee can be provided by the online verification schemes of existing systems such as Veritas and BlockchainDB which guarantee that the result of a transaction (or database operation) is verified before becoming visible to other transactions. For the actual execution of transactions, this level implies that transactions should transition as fast as possible from the *committed* state to *verified* since otherwise (i.e., if there are too many committed but unverified transactions) this can lead to low performance or in worst case starvation. However, clearly strict verification thus has a high overhead and might lead to inferior performance when compared to more relaxed levels that we discuss below.

*Unstrict Verification/Full (UV-f).* Compared to the previous level, this is a more relaxed verification level since it allows transactions to read from committed but not yet verified state. That is, even if the verification of a transaction is still pending, other transactions can access its committed state. However, all transactions are still being verified (hence it is called *full*) and unsuccessful verification in case of malicious behavior needs to be handled as we discuss below in Sect. 2.3. In contrast to the *SV* level, though, this makes room for different optimizations. Most importantly, transactions are not blocked by potentially expensive verification protocols since verification can be executed in batches and in a deferred manner. This is similar to deferred verification schemes that are available in existing systems (e.g., [8] or [1]). But still, verification should not lag behind too much. This can be controlled by setting an additional parameter that specifies how many committed but unverified transactions are allowed.

*Unstrict Verification/Partial (UV-p).* This verification level relaxes the guarantees of the previous level (UV-f) even further. In UV-f, transactions are allowed to access committed, but unverified state. However, unlike UV-f in *partial unstrict verification* (UV-p) we do not enforce that all transactions need to be verified. Consequently, this verification level assumes that *verified* is an optional state of a transaction. In this level, a user can thus explicitly request to verify only a subset of transactions. Hence, UV-p could be used to limit the verification overhead to some (e.g., important) transactions or to provide probabilistic guarantees by verifying only a sample of all transactions.

### 2.3 Handling Malicious Behavior

As mentioned before, in ACID-V it is important to take the effects of potentially malicious behavior of individual peers into account (i.e., in case they do not execute transactions in a correct manner). That is, if the verification fails for a particular transaction (e.g., due to incorrect execution by a malicious peer) all dependent subsequent transactions need to be rolled back in order to guarantee a correctly verified state of the database as specified in the verification level. For strict verification levels, this is less of a problem since no other transaction can read committed but unverified state from other transactions and hence only the effects of the transactions where the verification failed need to be reverted. However, for unstrict verification handling malicious behavior is more difficult since transactions can read from committed and not yet verified transactions and thus erroneous state can propagate across multiple dependent transactions.

## 3 Future Directions

In this paper we presented our vision for ACID-V compliant DBMSs to enable data sharing. As a core contribution, with ACID-V we propose to specify the guarantees of verifiability in a declarative manner and let the DBMS decide on what optimizations and concrete execution strategies are best suited to meet the guarantees of a particular verification level. In the future, we think that this model of ACID-V compliant DBMSs can trigger many follow-up work. First, the verification levels proposed in this paper are just an initial direction and we think that this requires a more profound discussion of what levels data sharing applications actually require. Second, similar to isolation levels that have triggered different implementation strategies (optimistic vs. pessimistic), we think ACID-V will also enable a wide variety of different implementation strategies (e.g., beyond using blockchains) to implement the desired guarantees of verification.

**Acknowledgments.** This work partly grew out of discussions within and support of the National Research Center ATHENE, the BMWi project SafeFBDC (01MK21002K), and the BMBF project TrustDBle (16KIS1267).

# References

1. El-Hindi, M., et al.: Blockchaindb - a shared database on blockchains. Proc. VLDB Endow. **12**(11), 1597–1609 (2019)
2. Gehrke, J., et al.: Veritas: shared verifiable databases and tables in the cloud. In: CIDR. www.cidrdb.org (2019)
3. Kamilaris, A., et al.: The rise of blockchain technology in agriculture and food supply chains. Trends Food Sci. Technol. **91**, 640–652 (2019)
4. Maiyya, S., et al.: Fides: managing data on untrusted infrastructure. In: ICDCS, pp. 344–354. IEEE (2020)
5. Peng, Y., et al.: Falcondb: blockchain-based collaborative database. In: ACM SIGMOD, pp. 637–652. ACM (2020)
6. Smith, E.R., Flaherman, V.J.: Why you should share your data during a pandemic. BMJ Glob. Health **6**(3) (2021)
7. Tapscott, D., Tapscott, A.: Blockchain Revolution: How the Technology Behind Bitcoin Is Changing Money, Business, and the World. Penguin, Westminster (2016)
8. Zhang, M., et al.: Spitz: A verifiable database system. PVLDB **13**(12), 3449–3460 (2020)

# Polystore Systems and DBMSs: Love Marriage or Marriage of Convenience?

Marco Vogt[✉], David Lengweiler, Isabel Geissmann, Nils Hansen,
Marc Hennemann, Cédric Mendelin, Sebastian Philipp, and Heiko Schuldt

Databases and Information Systems Research Group, Department of Mathematics
and Computer Science, University of Basel, Basel, Switzerland
{marco.vogt,david.lengweiler,isabel.geissmann,nils.hansen,marc.hennemann,
cedric.mendelin,sebastian.philipp,heiko.schuldt}@unibas.ch

**Abstract.** Polystore systems allow to combine different heterogeneous data stores in one system and also offer different query languages for accessing data. While this addresses a large number of requirements especially when providing access to heterogeneous data in mixed workloads, most polystore systems are somewhat limited in terms of their functionality. In this paper, we make the case to 'upgrade' polystore systems towards full-fledged databases systems, leading to the notion of *PolyDBMSs*. We summarize the features of such PolyDBMSs and exemplify the implementation on the basis of our PolyDBMS Polypheny-DB.

**Keywords:** Polystore systems · Database management systems

## 1  Introduction

In the last years, *polystore systems* have become popular as an attempt to bridge the heterogeneity of data models and to combine the best-of-breed in a single system – by seamlessly integrating the concepts of multistore databases and polyglot persistence [3]. A multistore database system combines heterogeneous data stores and manages data across these stores by offering a single query interface and a single query language. Polyglot persistence offers different query languages for accessing data. Most existing polystore systems focus on selected aspects but do not provide the full-fledged feature set of a database system.

According to a summary given in [2], Ted Codd identified the following functionality a full-fledged database system has to provide: (i) *Storage* of data (ii) *Retrieval* and *update* of data (iii) *Access* support from remote locations (iv) User accessible *metadata catalog or data dictionary* (v) Support for *transactions and concurrency* (vi) Facilities for *recovering* the database in case of damage (vii) Enforcing *constraints*, and (viii) Support for *authorization* of access and update of data. When deploying polystore systems in real world applications, it has turned out that the full DBMS functionality is required, not (only) the support for heterogeneous data stores and different query languages.

In this paper, we make the case for upgrading polystore systems to full-fledged databases – for which we introduce the term *PolyDBMSs* – and we discuss the

© Springer Nature Switzerland AG 2021
E. K. Rezig et al. (Eds.): Poly 2021/DMAH 2021, LNCS 12921, pp. 65–69, 2021.
https://doi.org/10.1007/978-3-030-93663-1_6

challenges for the different database functionality. We exemplify this on the basis of Polypheny-DB [4,5], the polystore database system we have introduced in our previous work. Polypheny-DB has been published under an open source license[1] and participates in 2021 to the Google Summer of Code (GSoC) program.

The contribution of the paper is twofold: first, we identify the challenges polystore systems have to meet to provide the features of a full-fledged DBMS. Second, we exemplify based on Polypheny-DB how these feature can be provided.

## 2   From Polystore Systems to "PolyDBMSs"

In this section, which is organized along Codd's DBMS features as summarized in [2], we discuss the challenges for polystore systems in general, leading to a novel kind of *PolyDBMS*, and how they are addressed in Polypheny-DB.

### 2.1   Storage of Data

*PolyDBMSs* need to support different data storage engines optimized for various types of data and workloads. These data stores are internally based on different data models (relational, documents, wide-columns, key-values, graphs, etc.) and are queried using different query languages and methods. This is an inevitable feature all PolyDBMSs have to provide intrinsically.

*Polypheny-DB* currently supports relational, document, and wide-column stores and different data sources. The connection to data stores and data sources is handled by *adapters*. *Data Stores* are used as physical storage and execution engines and are fully maintained by and under exclusive control of Polypheny-DB. In order to be able to guarantee correctness, the stores are only accessed through Polypheny-DB. *Data Sources* allow mapping data on (remote) database systems into the schema of Polypheny-DB. There are also adapters for querying file systems or CSV files. Data source adapters are less complex than data store adapters and usually only support a subset of the functionality. Polypheny-DB allows that data sources are queried by other systems in parallel. Hence, Polypheny-DB does not provide support for constraints or data replication/partitioning on entities originating from data sources, only for the ones from data stores. The optimization offered by a storage system can be leveraged when pushing down a complete query (or at least parts of it) whenever possible. In order to optimize the data transfers, query results are read on demand.

### 2.2   Retrieval and Update of Data

*PolyDBMSs* intrinsically need to support the retrieval of data using multiple query languages and methods. Furthermore, PolyDBMSs should also offer data modification queries – which usually goes beyond the feature set of polystores.

---

[1] https://github.com/polypheny/Polypheny-DB.

*Polypheny-DB* supports DML and DDL operations. The most mature query language supported by Polypheny-DB is its own SQL dialect *PolySQL*. It features a common set of operations including JOIN, GROUP BY and HAVING clauses, set operations, inner queries and WITH clauses. Additionally, it provides a large set of query and aggregation functions [2] and it comes with functions specifically for media and blob data. Furthermore, Polypheny-DB supports a distance function for *k*-NN similarity search. Polypheny-DB also supports the *MongoDB Query Language*. Moreover, support for the Contextual Query Language is currently being added. With the *Explore-by-Example* interface and the *Dynamic Query Builder*, Polypheny-DB also supports two innovative query methods [4].

## 2.3   Access Support from Remote Locations

*PolyDBMSs* should offer the query functionality identified in Sect. 2.2 also from remote locations by offering appropriate APIs and query interfaces.

The JDBC interface of *Polypheny-DB* supports the retrieval of meta data and the control of transactions. It also provides prepared statements and batch inserts and updates. The REST-based query interface allows accessing and modifying data using GET, POST, PATCH, and DELETE requests. Results are returned as JSON.

## 2.4   User Accessible Metadata Catalog or Data Dictionary

In addition to the usual metadata maintained by a DBMS, *PolyDBMSs* also need to keep metadata on data distribution across different data stores.

*Polypheny-DB* comes with a data dictionary that has a browser-based user interface (Polypheny-UI). It allows to view and alter the schema and it can be used to browse and modify the data, manage data stores and data sources, and execute queries using the supported query methods and languages. In addition to accessing schema information using Polypheny-UI, it is also possible to retrieve the schema using the JDBC meta functions provided by our JDBC driver.

## 2.5   Support for Transactions and Concurrency

*PolyDBMSs* need to offer transaction support at their interface. This is particularly relevant when data accessed within an application is internally spread across several data stores.

*Polypheny-DB* supports concurrent queries, guaranteeing atomicity and isolation using transactions for data stored on its underlying data stores. For data stored on data sources, support for transactions can be limited and depends on the capabilities of the data source. The isolation of concurrent transactions is ensured on the polystore level. Due to data partitioning and replication, only the polystore has the necessary information for ensuring the isolated execution of transactions. Locking on the underlying data stores is deactivated for performance reasons whenever possible. Polypheny-DB uses *strong strict two-phase*

---

[2] https://polypheny.org/documentation/PolySQL/Operators/.

*locking (SS2PL)* [1] for the isolation of concurrent transactions. The SS2PL implementation in Polypheny-DB comes with the necessary deadlock detection.

### 2.6  Facilities for Recovering the Database in Case of Damage

*PolyDBMSs* need to support two types of failure cases: (i) failures of the Poly-DBMS as a whole and (ii) failures of single data stores/data sources.

*Polypheny-DB* distinguishes between data recovery in the underlying data stores, and schema recovery, which includes data placement (i.e., the physical schema mapping). For *data recovery*, Polypheny-DB assumes that the selected underlying data stores work correctly and thus delegates recovery there. For the data stores integrated in Polypheny-DB (e.g., file store), a proper recovery mechanism is implemented in the adapter. *Schema recovery* is under the responsibility of Polypheny-DB. It leverages the whole catalog containing the schema information which is persistently stored using a transactional storage system featuring a write-ahead log. On start-up, all persistent placements of an entity are restored. For entities without a persistent placement, only the schema is restored.

### 2.7  Enforcing Constraints

*PolyDBMSs* need to enforce constraints that span two or more data sources, not just constraints within a single store that are natively enforced there.

*Polypheny-DB* enforces primary key, foreign key, and uniqueness constraints. The enforcement is done on the polystore level by extending the query plan. The major challenge with implementing constraint enforcement on the polystore level is that constraints need to be enforced even if data is stored on data stores that do not natively support constraints. Furthermore, data can be partitioned across multiple data stores which makes the full delegation of constraint enforcement to the underlying data stores unfeasible. Hence, constraint enforcement may only (partly) be delegated to underlying stores whenever applicable.

### 2.8  Support for Authorization of Access and Update of Data

In a *PolyDBMSs*, each single store is supposed to provide necessary mechanisms for authorizing accesses. In addition, this support also needs to be provided globally at the PolyDBMS level.

*Polypheny-DB* supports basic authentication, but there is not yet a complete mechanism for a role or user-based authorization of specific actions.

## 3  Conclusion

Polystore systems combine several distributed and potentially heterogeneous data stores underneath one or several interfaces. Usually, even though the data stores might be full-fledged database systems, polystore systems lack one or several features of a complete DBMS. In this paper, we make the case to 'upgrade' polystore systems to full-fledged DBMSs, leading to the notion of *PolyDBMSs*. We have surveyed the requirements at the PolyDBMS level and we have briefly presented how these challenges have been implemented in Polypheny-DB, which combines the advantages of a polystore system with the ones of a DBMS.

**Acknowledgments.** This work has been partly funded by the Swiss National Science Foundation, project Polypheny-DB (contract no. 200021_172763).

# References

1. Bernstein, P., Hadzilacos, V., Goodman, N.: Concurrency Control and Recovery in Database Systems. Addison-Wesley Longman, Boston (1987)
2. Connolly, T., Begg, C.: Database Systems: A Practical Approach to Design, Implementation, and Management. Pearson, Boston (2014)
3. Tan, R., Chirkova, R., Gadepally, V., Mattson, T.G.: Enabling query processing across heterogeneous data models: a survey. In: Proceedings of the 2017 IEEE International Conference on Big Data (BigData 2017), pp. 3211–3220. IEEE, Boston (2017). https://doi.org/10.1109/BigData.2017.8258302
4. Vogt, M., et al.: Polypheny-DB: towards bridging the gap between polystores and HTAP systems. In: Gadepally, V., et al. (eds.) DMAH/Poly-2020. LNCS, vol. 12633, pp. 25–36. Springer, Cham (2021). https://doi.org/10.1007/978-3-030-71055-2_2
5. Vogt, M., Stiemer, A., Schuldt, H.: Polypheny-DB: towards a distributed and self-adaptive polystore. In: 2018 IEEE International Conference on Big Data, pp. 3364–3373. IEEE (2018). https://doi.org/10.1109/BigData.2018.8622353

# WIP: PODS: Privacy Compliant Scalable Decentralized Data Services

Jonas Spenger[1,2](✉), Paris Carbone[1,2], and Philipp Haller[2]

[1] RISE Research Institutes of Sweden, Stockholm, Sweden
{jonas.spenger,paris.carbone}@ri.se
[2] Digital Futures and EECS, KTH Royal Institute of Technology, Stockholm, Sweden
{jspenger,parisc,phaller}@kth.se

**Abstract.** Modern data services need to meet application developers' demands in terms of scalability and resilience, and also support privacy regulations such as the EU's GDPR. We outline the main systems challenges of supporting data privacy regulations in the context of large-scale data services, and advocate for causal snapshot consistency to ensure application-level and privacy-level consistency. We present PODS, an extension to the dataflow model that allows external services to access snapshotted operator state directly, with built-in support for addressing the outlined privacy challenges, and summarize open questions and research directions.

**Keywords:** Decentralized data services · Dataflow model · Privacy compliance · GDPR

## 1 Introduction

Implementing and maintaining distributed data services is becoming an increasingly complex task across two frontiers. At one end, there is strong demand for data decentralization across multiple data stores, scalability and improved resilience to failures [4,17,23]. At the other end, there is demand for user data protection and support for users to exercise their data protection rights [5,9]. Building large and complex data services over a single ACID (atomicity, consistency, isolation, and durability) database is no longer a realistic implementation approach for meeting today's demands [18]. Existing scalable solutions to building such services instead settle on weaker consistency models such as eventual consistency, which has become the norm for building large-scale data services.

In this work, we identify the core challenges that privacy regulations such as GDPR [9] and CCPA [5] add to the already existing set of requirements for building scalable data services, at the intersection of privacy-policy driven demands and systems driven demands. In particular, we argue that stronger types of consistency are required, and feasible to achieve given the necessary paradigm shift in modelling data services.

To that end, we propose PODS, a dataflow model that provides built-in support for consistent continuous processing of user data, as well as access to

E. K. Rezig et al. (Eds.): Poly 2021/DMAH 2021, LNCS 12921, pp. 70–82, 2021.
https://doi.org/10.1007/978-3-030-93663-1_7

causally snapshot consistent state such as materialized views used by external services. Our model is currently under implementation on top of the Akka actor framework [12] and features causal consistency for cross-state reads via the use of distributed consistent snapshotting [6], and the serializable execution of privacy requests. The solution supports ideas from recent positions on data-privacy protection systems [16,19,22] while expanding on the capabilities of modern dataflow systems [2,7], proposing stronger types of guarantees and ways of stateful processing relevant to data privacy.

In summary, we claim the following contributions: (1) We outline the main systems challenges for supporting data privacy regulations in the context of large-scale data services. (2) We argue that eventual consistency is insufficient for supporting privacy regulations and advocate the adoption of causal snapshot consistency, as implemented on dataflow systems. (3) We propose PODS, a system model capable of addressing all outlined challenges. (4) We summarize open questions and propose several research directions for resilient, scalable and privacy-protecting services on dataflow systems.

## 2 Problem Scope and Challenges

### 2.1 Privacy Regulation Preliminaries

Data privacy regulations such as the EU's General Data Protection Regulation (GDPR) [9] and the California Consumer Privacy Act (CCPA) [5] have shaped the landscape for data privacy conformance and the proper handling and protection of user data. The GDPR mainly concerns with how *controllers* (the data service providers) process and collect the data of *data subjects* (the users), and what rights the data subject has over its *personal data* (any data relating to an identifiable natural person). The data subject may issue *privacy requests* (our notation) to the controller, these are requests to exercise the rights of the data subject. Evidently, enforcing compliance becomes more complex as data service architectures become decentralized. To illustrate this issue we focus on three fundamental data subject rights (*i.e.*, privacy requests) from the GDPR [9]:

**1. Right of Access (Art. 15).** The right of access grants the data subject access to information from the data service (controller) within one month's time on what personal data of the data subject is being processed, how it is being processed, the period for which the data will be stored, the purposes of the processing, the recipients of the processed data, and more.

**2. Right to Erasure (Art. 17).** The right to erasure grants the data subject the right to erase all personal data concerning the data subject within one month from the time of the request. This would include data that has been processed, and data for which there is no longer a legal ground for processing.

**3. Right to Objection (Art. 21).** The right to objection grants the data subject the right to object to certain types of processing if there are no legitimate grounds for the processing. Such a request should be processed within one month.

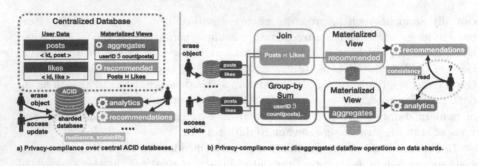

**Fig. 1.** Centralized and decentralized privacy compliant service composition.

## 2.2   Problem Intuition

**Consistent Privacy Requests.** From a data management systems perspective, granting the rights to perform privacy requests such as access, erasure and objection, can be considered as additional *operations* that need to be performed. To illustrate this, consider the example in Fig. 1a of a social network that records the posts and likes of users, and computes aggregates and recommendations based on these, which are used for an analytics and recommendations service, respectively. In the example the data subject issues an *erasure/access/objection* request to the central database management system (DBMS) with support for ACID (atomicity, consistency, isolation, durability) transactions. This request is committed transactionally with an immediate effect. In this setting, ACID transactions ensure trivially that the client and external services access a consistent view of completed operations and privacy requests.

In reality, however, most data services today are not built around a central DBMS with ACID guarantees. Instead, they employ decentralized storage and processing across geographically distributed data centers. The lack of support for ACID transactions in this setting makes it challenging to support the consistent execution of privacy requests (in contrast to regular user operations, privacy requests are expected to be executed with stronger guarantees). To that end, a dataflow-driven design has been proposed (exemplified in Fig. 1b) for data privacy compliance by construction [16]. In this design, data services can be built organically from data shards, dataflow operators, and materialized views. Data shards are data sources owned by the users of the system. External services are composed using dataflow operators that subscribe to shards or other intermediate dataflow dependencies defined by other services, and end in materialized views. Data access by an external service is limited to reading from materialized views (*e.g.*, the recommended view in Fig. 1b) that are composed on the fly through consumption of data events originating from the user shards. This is a promising architecture that aligns well with current trends in cloud computing. However, the current state of the art in distributed dataflow computing lacks two properties that we consider necessary for serving privacy requests, namely: causal consistency and serializability of privacy requests.

**Dataflow Causal Consistency.** Supporting materialized views in the distributed dataflow model is currently limited to eventual consistency [16] which is insufficient for serving privacy requests. To illustrate the problem consider the external observer in Fig. 1b that accesses state from the recommendations service. Assume that an erasure request has been completed such that a user's post is no longer visible. Subsequently, the same observer reads state from the analytics service where the aggregate post count still includes the user's post (*i.e.*, the erasure request has not yet reached the aggregates view). Given that the erasure request was already observed in a prior access that precedes the second read, this exposes a causality violation. In practice, numerous causality violations can naturally occur in externally accessed dataflow graph state. For example, eventually consistent materialized views may roll-back due to failure recovery; and reading from different materialized views may be inconsistent as one view may contain the effects of a privacy request whereas the other view may not contain these effects. Instead, an external observer (user or external system) should only read causally consistent snapshotted state of completed operations. More specifically, if an observer performs two subsequent read requests, $r_1$ and $r_2$ with causal relationship $r_1 \prec r_2$ that observe two states $s_1$ and $s_2$, then there should be a causal relationship between the states $s_1 \preceq s_2$, such that the observed operations and privacy requests that yield the state $s_1$: $o_1, \ldots, o_n$, are a prefix of those that yield $s_2$: $o_1, \ldots, o_m$, with $n \leq m$.

**Serializability of Privacy Requests.** Whereas causal consistency addresses the order of which operations are observed externally, the internal execution order of dataflow operations, including privacy requests, is still subject to arbitrary stream alignment. For example, propagating events may be reordered if they are separated into two different streams, and later joined into a single stream, because the joined ordering can be an arbitrary interleaving of the two streams. Such a reordering of privacy requests could result into partially applied operations and therefore offer an inconsistent view of the system. To ensure the correct execution of privacy requests we also require them to be serializable. This means that for every privacy request $p$, all operations preceding it need to take effect before $p$, whereas all subsequent operations need to observe the effect of $p$. More formally, consider the sequence of operations $o_1, \ldots, o_{k-1}, p_k, o_{k+1} \ldots o_n$, and $p_k$ is a privacy request, then the effect should be equivalent to an execution that executes and completes $o_1, \ldots, o_{k-1}$ before the privacy request $p_k$ starts its execution, and $o_{k-1}, \ldots, o_n$ start execution after $p_k$ completes.

**Executing Privacy Requests.** The serializability and causal-consistency describe the order in which the requests are to be executed. Yet, there is a need to materialize privacy requests on top of distributed dataflow operators. For example, an access request should produce the requested data and return it to the requester. For an erasure/objection request, the correct execution may be more complicated as the request modifies state. The dataflow operator needs to correctly update its own state, and also emit sufficient information to dependent dataflow operators such that they can perform the request accordingly.

## 2.3  Supporting Privacy on Dataflows: Challenges Overview

We have identified the need for dataflow systems to provide built-in support for privacy requests. A look into modern/popular dataflow streaming [1,7] as well as serverless programming [4,17,23] solutions used to build data services reveals fundamental design challenges for supporting privacy regulations. These include a lack of causally consistent externally queryable state support, and support for serializable transactions. To that end, we derive a set of challenges towards the creation of scalable distributed programming systems, able to support privacy requests (access, erasure, objection) consistently. Intuitively, there is a need to combine the programming flexibility of actor models with the support for ad-hoc external queries and transactional ACID guarantees of DBMSs and the end-to-end reliability and scalability of modern dataflow stream processing systems. Based on these intuitions we outline the following challenges. While a number of previous systems address one or more of the challenges, to the best of our knowledge no existing system addresses all challenges simultaneously.

C1 **Dataflow composition for high-performance data streaming:** providing the compositional construction of dataflow graphs and enabling high-performance data streaming.
C2 **Automated resilience to failures:** dealing with partial process and network failures that might occur throughout the execution of data services while maintaining exactly-once processing semantics.
C3 **Automated scaling of data services:** automatically and elastically scaling the system to meet increasing and decreasing load.
C4 **Snapshot consistent externally queryable state:** providing external services access to causally snapshot consistent state of dataflow operators.
C5 **Support for privacy requests and data ownership:** supporting serializable privacy requests, ensuring that users have control of and access to their raw and derived data.
C6 **Transparent handling of privacy requests:** The privacy requests should be handled transparently by the system. In effect, the application developer should not need to implement any logic for handling privacy requests.

## 3  Proposed Extensions to Dataflow Architecture

At a high level, PODS resembles most existing dataflow system models [2,7,13], supporting arbitrary stateful event logic, compositional subscription to event streams and pipelined task execution. Its main distinctions lie at the execution logic employed within its dataflow tasks, called pod tasks. A pod features two distinct components, one handling regular event input logic and another handling state operations. This grants PODS the flexibility to transparently employ all special yet necessary local actions that can collectively ensure global system properties such as serializability of privacy requests and dataflow causal consistency. In this section, we discuss its core design choices.

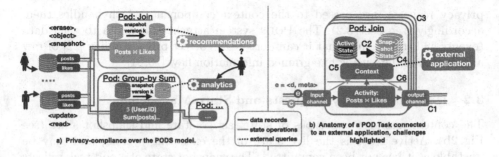

**Fig. 2.** Privacy compliant service composition with the PODS model.

## 3.1 Overview of the PODS Model

PODS is a dataflow model that processes user event streams and privacy requests. We adopt the notion of user shards [16] for all per-user data ingestion and introduce pod tasks for all stateful processing including the composition of materialized views. Figure 2a shows an example of a privacy-compliant service in PODS, while Fig. 2b depicts the anatomy of a pod task. We further detail the design of user shards and pods, which constitute the overall behavior of the model.

**User Shards.** All user data is ingested in "user shards" (adopted from [16]) that may be materialized on different data stores. A user shard creates a set of per-user data updates, e.g., new posts or likes as well as state requests including `erase`, `object` and system-invoked `snapshot` operations (Fig. 2a). All user shard streams are expected to be persistently logged and replicated. This makes them replayable and available in order to support rollback recovery.

**Pod Tasks.** Pods execute the application and privacy request handling logic. In detail, pods: 1) subscribe to input streams and generate output streams; and 2) execute operations on the input stream events, and have two side effects: a) pod state is updated and b) new output events are generated. In contrast to existing dataflow models, PODS makes a clear separation between state and logic, one stateless control-flow component handles the application logic, and another stateful contextual component handles operations on state. Beyond this, pod tasks allow external services to query their snapshotted state.

We highlight the anatomy of a pod task in Fig. 2b. This detailed view shows that a pod task consists of two components, a stateless *activity* component, and a stateful *context* component. Pod tasks are connected to other pods and user shards via a set of input and output channels. Events received by a pod on one of its input streams are processed sequentially, one at a time. Thus, the processing of a single event including its effects on the local state can be considered an atomic operation. Each input/output stream maintains a FIFO order of events; however, there is no deterministic ordering across streams. Application-level events are passed to the activity, the activity may access state via the *context* component, and emit messages on the output channels. Other events, such as control events and privacy requests, are passed to the context component, which handles them accordingly (see Sect. 3.2). The PODS system attaches metadata to each data (events and state), such that it can derive the correct privacy policy [22] of raw and processed data using fine-grained information flow [15,21].

## 3.2 Handling Privacy Requests and State Management

The context manages two types of state, active state and snapshot state (see Fig. 2b). Active state is the live state of the executing system, and may be unstable as it has not been committed. The snapshot state of a pod task reflects its latest globally coordinated state snapshot of the dataflow graph and it can be used to support materialized views. Control operations, such as privacy request operations, are handled transparently by the context component (the control events are passed to the context component, not the activity), for which the context component may emit control events to other pods.

Both snapshot operations and privacy requests can make use of a similar broadcast and alignment dissemination scheme to enforce ordering. Similarly to classic marker-based snapshotting protocols (e.g., Chandy-Lamport [8]), markers can be inserted in dataflow inputs and further broadcasted to all outputs in order to separate those operations that precede and those that succeed a snapshot. To enforce the complete effect of certain operations an additional alignment phase is necessary [6]. The alignment makes every dataflow task prioritize pending changes across its inputs until all markers are received. This enforces all operations prior to a marker to complete before triggering a snapshot. Privacy requests can follow an identical broadcast and alignment scheme within a pod. This can enforce serializability for privacy requests.

External services can interact with the PODS system by querying the state of user shards and live pod tasks directly through an asynchronous RPC query (illustrated by the dotted lines in Fig. 2b). Updates on active pod state are not directly visible to external queries. This is because read operations would not expose the right level of isolation for external service access. Therefore, queries submitted by an external service receive the latest snapshotted version of that state from the pod context. Since snapshots within the pods dataflow are atomically committed across all pod tasks, subsequent external access requests would access the same or a newer version of the corresponding global state of the system. Via the use of a globally coordinated snapshotting method [6] it is guaranteed that an operation is either included in all pod snapshots, or pending to be committed in the next global snapshot.

Privacy requests that arrive at the pod are executed by the context component after the alignment phase. An access request can be executed on the local state, whereas erasure and objection requests are more difficult as they modify state. We can execute an erasure/objection request by using differential updates or by recomputing the state [16]. If these options are not available (*e.g.,* non-relational operators, user-defined functions), we can perform the operation directly on the state. The semantics and efficient/correct execution remains an open question which we intend to explore further (see Sect. 4).

Implementing a system with the presented properties efficiently is challenging. Whereas causal snapshot consistency has been shown to be supported in high-performance systems [6]; enforcing serializability of privacy user requests comes with an overhead from dissemination and synchronization of alignment markers. Further, certain privacy requests may cause large updates, which take a long time to complete. The total system overhead from privacy compliance, however, may be amortized through the batched execution of privacy requests, given that GDPR allows up to one month to process a privacy request.

### 3.3  Privacy Request Example

Let us revisit the example from Sect. 2 and exemplify how the PODS system can successfully deal with a privacy request (see Fig. 2a). Consider the `erasure` request submitted by the client. This request first arrives at a user shard. The shard can handle this request by erasing all data that belongs to the requesting client. We can find the corresponding data because of the information about the data origin contained in the metadata. This privacy request is then broadcast along all outgoing channels of the shard to the two other pod tasks (together with auxiliary information), the Join pod and the Group-by pod. The request arrives at the Join pod, and is passed to the context component which applies it to the active state and snapshot state. Similarly, the request is applied to the Group-by pod. If another pod subscribes to both the Join pod and the Group-by pod, the two streams are joined, and the privacy request will act as an alignment marker to ensure the serializability of the privacy request. This way, the request is propagated and applied consistently to the whole system.

### 3.4  Addressing the Outlined Privacy Dataflow Challenges

The specific features of the PODS model enable us to address the outlined challenges of privacy-compliant dataflows from Sect. 2.3, the challenges are highlighted in the Fig. 2b.

**C1 Dataflow Composition for High-Performance Data Streaming.** The PODS model enables constructing dataflow graphs composed of pod tasks interconnected via channels (see C1 in Fig. 2b). This design for high-performance data streaming is inspired to a large extent by state-of-the-art data streaming systems such as Apache Flink [6, 7].

**C2 Automated Resilience to Failures.** Since PODS adopts the stateful stream processing paradigm and user shard streams are replayable, exactly-once stream processing methods such as distributed consistent snapshotting [6] and rollback recovery are applicable to ensure failure-recovery to a consistent active state.

**C3 Automated Scaling of Data Services.** The PODS model enables scaling elastically according to load. A pod can either scale the number of messages that it can handle through executing messages concurrently on activities that are replicated across physical nodes, or scale its state by partitioning the state into shards across nodes (*e.g.,* using consistent hashing). This should be feasible and requires little to no synchronization for activities that access disjoint state or conflict-free state (*e.g.,* keyed state [6]). Joint state has a synchronization overhead and may not be scalable, the developer could be notified of this through static checking and encouraged to use other types of state. The decision on when (policy) and how (mechanism) to elastically reconfigure [10] can be handled by the context component.

C4 **Snapshot Consistent Externally Queryable State.** Updates on pod states are not directly visible to external queries. Instead, external queries are handled differently by the context components. All external read requests are granted access to the latest snapshotted state of a pod which is acquired via a global causally consistent checkpoint mechanism (see Sect. 3.2). This ensures that state is atomically committed across all pod tasks, and only completed operations are observable to external services.

C5 **Support for Privacy Requests and Data Ownership.** Supporting `access`, `erasure`, and `objection` requests requires us to be able to locate and update all data, raw or processed, belonging to or derived from a data subject. We can locate all data from a data subject by traversing the static dependencies of the dataflow system, and through the data ownership information in the metadata. Once the data has been located we can apply the requested operation on it. Privacy requests in PODS dataflows are directly related to the user state and not the application logic, thus, they are handled differently than regular application operations. Privacy requests broadcast to all outgoing channels (similar to snapshot markers), and aligned on pod tasks with multiple input streams (see Sect. 3.2). This way we can ensure a serializable ordering of the operations.

C6 **Transparent Handling of Privacy Requests.** The application developer does not need to implement any logic for handling privacy requests, this is instead handled by the stateful context component within the pod task (see C6 in Fig. 2b). In effect, the application developer only needs to write the activity component's application logic, agnostic to any privacy/control logic.

## 4    Open Questions and Research Directions

The design for the PODS model presented in the previous section leaves a few questions unanswered, for which we outline research directions in the following.

**A More Flexible Programming Model.** Supporting a wider range of scalable data services requires evolving dataflow graphs dynamically by adding and removing user shards and pod tasks at runtime. Generalizing pod tasks to actor-like entities could enable iterative computations which require cyclic data dependencies. However, cyclic data dependencies could conflict with assumptions that are critical for ensuring consistency, and the semantics of dynamic changes to the dataflow graph are still unclear. This research direction devises ways to efficiently ensure both consistency guarantees and privacy compliance in the presence of cyclic data dependencies and dynamic deployments.

**Efficient Information Flow Tracking.** With the PODS model we propose to enable servicing privacy requests by employing fine-grained information-flow tracking [15,21]. This poses an efficiency challenge for aggregate data. For example, computing aggregate data over all users of a system would have to track its origin to all users of the system. Efficient processing of such aggregate data would require a form of *declassification* [14] as it has been studied in the field of information-flow security. This research direction explores adaptations of declassification to enable efficient information flow tracking.

**Execution of Privacy Requests.** The execution of privacy requests has unclear semantics, for example, it is unclear how to handle a request on data associated to multiple users; and the efficient execution of privacy requests remains challenging [19]. There are various trade-offs between approaches depending on the workload. Further, many issues do not appear until implementing the full specification. This research direction looks at the efficient handling of fine-grained privacy requests for relational and user-defined functions, both for general workloads, and applied to specific case studies.

**Consistent Integration with External Services.** Data computed by a dataflow graph in the PODS model can be exported to external services which read from materialized views with snapshot consistency. Pull-based, snapshot-consistent reads have been presented in Sect. 3. However, it remains an open challenge (a) to support push-based updates and (b) to propagate privacy requests to external services with atomic consistency. Push-based updates pose a challenge due to the (strong) consistency on which external services should be able to rely. This research direction explores interfaces and protocols that enable atomically-consistent operations across dataflow graphs and external services, in order to provide end-to-end exactly-once data processing.

## 5   Related Work

**Data Privacy Compliance.** The PODS model was inspired by a position paper on "GDPR compliance by construction" by Schwarzkopf et al. [16]. In this work they propose a design that consists of user shards, a dataflow that computes on inputs from the user shards, and materialized views that are generated by the dataflow. Privacy requests are performed on the user shards, and these updates cause the dependent dataflow operators and materialized views to eventually update implicitly through the "partially-stateful dataflow model" [11]. In our model, we expose the pod state to external services, in replacement of materialized views, in order to provide causally consistent snapshot state of the system across views (such reads also access the metadata). The privacy requests are executed serializably using alignment markers; and we aim to support user-defined functions with the fine-grained information flow tracking, and declassification for aggregate data. Further, we adopt ideas from Data Capsules [22] to hold data together with metadata that specifies the policy of the data. The data capsule system consists of a data capsule manager that maintains the data capsule graph and tracks all data capsules, and verifies that analysis programs that access the data do not violate any policy. In the PODS system we enforce all data and events to be coupled with metadata (although our metadata is more limited), and have no central manager as this information is decentralized. The MONPOLY system [3] uses logs to detect policy violation by formalising GDPR requirements into metric first-order temporal logic formulas. The GDPR for Akka Persistence supports encrypting data such that it later can be shredded by erasing the encryption key, this feature can be used to implement the right to be forgotten even when encrypted personal data may leak to logs.

**Data Services.** Apache Flink [7] is a stream-processing framework for dataflow programs. Flink is known for the use of aligned snapshotting to achieve causal snapshot consistency [6]. PODS also builds on the same general dataflow model [2,7,13], and expands it further with the native alignment of privacy requests and view maintenance of all pod states. This new capability allows PODS to expose causally consistent shapshotted states for external reads featuring strong serializability of privacy requests. Flink Stateful Functions [20] runs on a runtime built on Apache Flink. Stateful functions are virtual, i.e. they don't consume any resources if idle, and the state and compute are separated. They provide built-in resilience in form of fault-tolerance and exactly-once semantics, and also support cyclical message patterns. Similarly, other serverless systems separate compute and state [4,17,23]. Durable Functions [4] provides server-less, elastic, failure-resilient, and consistent execution of workflows. It consists of orchestrations, i.e. reliable workflows, entities, i.e. actor-like addressable units, and critical sections, i.e. for synchronization. Cloudburst [17] is a function-as-a-service platform for stateful functions, for which state is held in a lattice-based distributed key-value store, and functions are executed in virtual machines with a local cache. Kappa [23] is a serverless computing framework that offers check-pointing for long-running tasks (and uses checkpointing for fault-tolerance). The outlined challenges are partially solved by these mentioned works, however, to the best of our knowledge, none of these projects provides built-in support for privacy compliance or for externally queryable snapshotted state.

## 6   Conclusion

We have presented PODS, a practical model for building scalable data services with privacy compliance as a core concern. Services in PODS can be built organically and execute reliably on decentralized infrastructures. To avoid inconsistencies between application-level operations and privacy requests, PODS employs transactional dataflow snapshots which capture a consistent view of the pod tasks' state, the snapshotting occurs asynchronously. PODS adopts best practices from distributed actor programming and serverless frameworks, which makes it flexible for supporting elastically scalable, replicated and fault tolerant services that respect their users' privacy by construction. The architecture of the PODS model allows the privacy request logic to be handled transparently, in effect the application developer is agnostic of any privacy logic.

**Acknowledgements.** We would like to thank the anonymous reviewers for their helpful comments. This work was partially funded by the Swedish Foundation for Strategic Research (SSF grant no. BD15-0006) and by Digital Futures.

# References

1. Akidau, T., et al.: Millwheel: fault-tolerant stream processing at internet scale. Proc. VLDB Endow. **6**(11), 1033–1044 (2013). https://doi.org/10.14778/2536222. 2536229, http://www.vldb.org/pvldb/vol6/p1033-akidau.pdf
2. Akidau, T., et al.: The dataflow model: a practical approach to balancing correctness, latency, and cost in massive-scale, unbounded, out-of-order data processing. Proc. VLDB Endow. **8**(12), 1792–1803 (2015). https://doi.org/10.14778/2824032. 2824076, http://www.vldb.org/pvldb/vol8/p1792-Akidau.pdf
3. Arfelt, E., Basin, D., Debois, S.: Monitoring the GDPR. In: Sako, K., Schneider, S., Ryan, P.Y.A. (eds.) ESORICS 2019. LNCS, vol. 11735, pp. 681–699. Springer, Cham (2019). https://doi.org/10.1007/978-3-030-29959-0_33
4. Burckhardt, S., Gillum, C., Justo, D., Kallas, K., McMahon, C., Meiklejohn, C.S.: Serverless workflows with durable functions and netherite. CoRR abs/2103.00033 (2021). https://arxiv.org/abs/2103.00033
5. California Legislature: California consumer privacy act of 2018 (CCPA) (2018). https://leginfo.legislature.ca.gov/faces/codes_displayText.xhtml?division=3.& part=4.&lawCode=CIV&title=1.81.5
6. Carbone, P., Ewen, S., Fóra, G., Haridi, S., Richter, S., Tzoumas, K.: State management in apache flink®: consistent stateful distributed stream processing. Proc. VLDB Endow. **10**(12), 1718–1729 (2017). https://doi.org/10.14778/3137765. 3137777, http://www.vldb.org/pvldb/vol10/p1718-carbone.pdf
7. Carbone, P., Katsifodimos, A., Ewen, S., Markl, V., Haridi, S., Tzoumas, K.: Apache Flink™: stream and batch processing in a single engine. IEEE Data Eng. Bull. **38**(4), 28–38 (2015). http://sites.computer.org/debull/A15dec/p28.pdf
8. Chandy, K.M., Lamport, L.: Distributed snapshots: determining global states of distributed systems. ACM Trans. Comput. Syst. **3**(1), 63–75 (1985). https://doi. org/10.1145/214451.214456
9. Council of the European Union: Regulation (EU) 2016/679 of the European parliament and of the council of 27 April 2016 on the protection of natural persons with regard to the processing of personal data and on the free movement of such data, and repealing directive 95/46/ec (general data protection regulation) (2016). https://eur-lex.europa.eu/legal-content/EN/TXT/?uri=OJ:L:2016:119:TOC
10. Fragkoulis, M., Carbone, P., Kalavri, V., Katsifodimos, A.: A survey on the evolution of stream processing systems. CoRR abs/2008.00842 (2020). https://arxiv. org/abs/2008.00842
11. Gjengset, J., et al.: Noria: dynamic, partially-stateful data-flow for high-performance web applications. In: Arpaci-Dusseau, A.C., Voelker, G. (eds.) 13th USENIX Symposium on Operating Systems Design and Implementation, OSDI 2018, Carlsbad, CA, USA, 8–10 October 2018, pp. 213–231. USENIX Association (2018). https://www.usenix.org/conference/osdi18/presentation/gjengset
12. Lightbend Inc: Akka. https://akka.io/. Accessed 21 May 2021

13. Murray, D.G., McSherry, F., Isaacs, R., Isard, M., Barham, P., Abadi, M.: Naiad: a timely dataflow system. In: Kaminsky, M., Dahlin, M. (eds.) ACM SIGOPS 24th Symposium on Operating Systems Principles, SOSP '13, Farmington, PA, USA, 3–6 November 2013, pp. 439–455. ACM (2013). https://doi.org/10.1145/2517349. 2522738

14. Sabelfeld, A., Sands, D.: Dimensions and principles of declassification. In: 18th IEEE Computer Security Foundations Workshop, (CSFW-18 2005), 20–22 June 2005, Aix-en-Provence, France, pp. 255–269. IEEE Computer Society (2005). https://doi.org/10.1109/CSFW.2005.15

15. Salvaneschi, G., Köhler, M., Sokolowski, D., Haller, P., Erdweg, S., Mezini, M.: Language-integrated privacy-aware distributed queries. In: Proceedings ACM Programming Language 3(OOPSLA), pp. 167:1–167:30 (2019). https://doi.org/10. 1145/3360593

16. Schwarzkopf, M., Kohler, E., Frans Kaashoek, M., Morris, R.: Position: GDPR compliance by construction. In: Gadepally, V., et al. (eds.) DMAH/Poly -2019. LNCS, vol. 11721, pp. 39–53. Springer, Cham (2019). https://doi.org/10.1007/ 978-3-030-33752-0_3

17. Sreekanti, V., et al.: Cloudburst: stateful functions-as-a-service. Proc. VLDB Endow. **13**(11), 2438–2452 (2020). http://www.vldb.org/pvldb/vol13/p2438-sreekanti.pdf

18. Stonebraker, M., Çetintemel, U.: "One size fits all": an idea whose time has come and gone. In: Aberer, K., Franklin, M.J., Nishio, S. (eds.) Proceedings of the 21st International Conference on Data Engineering, ICDE 2005, 5–8 April 2005, Tokyo, Japan, pp. 2–11. IEEE Computer Society (2005). https://doi.org/10.1109/ICDE. 2005.1

19. Stonebraker, M., Mattson, T.G., Kraska, T., Gadepally, V.: Poly'19 workshop summary: GDPR. SIGMOD Rec. **49**(3), 55–58 (2020). https://doi.org/10.1145/ 3444831.3444842

20. The Apache Software Foundation: Apache Flink stateful functions (2021). https:// flink.apache.org/stateful-functions.html. Accessed 14 June 2021

21. Volpano, D.M., Irvine, C.E., Smith, G.: A sound type system for secure flow analysis. J. Comput. Secur. **4**(2/3), 167–188 (1996). https://doi.org/10.3233/JCS-1996-42-304

22. Wang, L., et al.: Data capsule: a new paradigm for automatic compliance with data privacy regulations. In: Gadepally, V., et al. (eds.) DMAH/Poly -2019. LNCS, vol. 11721, pp. 3–23. Springer, Cham (2019). https://doi.org/10.1007/978-3-030-33752-0_1

23. Zhang, W., Fang, V., Panda, A., Shenker, S.: Kappa: a programming framework for serverless computing. In: Fonseca, R., Delimitrou, C., Ooi, B.C. (eds.) SoCC 2020: ACM Symposium on Cloud Computing, Virtual Event, USA, 19–21 October 2020, pp. 328–343. ACM (2020). https://doi.org/10.1145/3419111.3421277

**DMAH 2021**

# Privacy-Preserving Distributed Support Vector Machines

Simone Bottoni[1]([✉]), Stefano Braghin[2], Theodora Brisimi[2],
and Alberto Trombetta[1]

[1] University of Insubria, Varese, Italy
{sbottoni,alberto.trombetta}@uninsubria.it
[2] IBM Research Europe, Dublin, Ireland
stefanob@ie.ibm.com, theodora.brisimi@ibm.com

**Abstract.** Federated machine learning is a promising paradigm allowing organizations to collaborate toward the training of a joint model without the need to explicitly share sensitive or business-critical datasets. Previous works demonstrated that such paradigm is not sufficient to preserve confidentiality of the training data, even to honest participants. In this work, we extend a well-known framework for training sparse Support Vector Machines in a distributed setting, while preserving data confidentiality by means of a novel non-interactive secure multiparty computation engine, that preserves data confidentiality. We formally demonstrate the security properties of the engine and provide, by means of extensive empirical evaluation, the performance of the extended framework both in terms of accuracy and execution time.

**Keywords:** Distributed support vector machines · Privacy-preserving machine learning · Secure federated learning

## 1 Introduction

In an era of "big data", computationally efficient and privacy-aware solutions for large-scale machine learning problems become crucial. This becomes very relevant in the healthcare domain where large amounts of data are stored in different locations and owned by different entities. Past research has been focused on centralized algorithms, which assume the existence of a central data repository (database) that stores and processes the data from all participants. Such an architecture, however, can be impractical when data are not centrally located, it does not scale well to very large datasets, and introduces single-point of failure risks which could compromise the integrity and privacy of the data. Given the large amount of data that is widely spread across hospitals/individuals, a decentralized and computationally scalable methodology is very much in need.

*Motivating Scenario.* Hospitals want to create reliable and accurate models on the data that they own but for regulatory and compliant constraints they cannot

© Springer Nature Switzerland AG 2021
E. K. Rezig et al. (Eds.): Poly 2021/DMAH 2021, LNCS 12921, pp. 85–102, 2021.
https://doi.org/10.1007/978-3-030-93663-1_8

share data with other institutes. Within national boundaries, it might be possible to leverage governmental aggregators, but it is not always feasible to share data across borders, or even between organizations. Legislations like General Data Protection Regulation (GDPR)[1], California Consumer Privacy Act (CCPA)[2] and Safe Shield[3] provide definitions and levels of sensitivity in personal data and instruct all the entities involved in the data process pipeline how such categories of data should be managed. These data handling instructions further specify under which conditions data can be exchanged, with the general assumption that clear text data should not be openly shared with other entities. This constraint conflicts with the basic requirement of sharing data to train a joint model. Hence, a mechanism to securely compute models in a federated fashion is required.

Federated learning allows the hospitals to train a machine learning model without sharing their data. However, this mechanism is vulnerable to attacks, for example, in the inference problem [15] where an attacker can leak sensitive information about the participants' private data from the machine learning algorithm parameters [19].

To preserve privacy, federated learning can use various methods. Specifically, Secure Multi-party Computation (SMC), Differential Privacy, Homomorphic Encryption [25], or a combination of them, as in [23,26]. Each of these methods has its advantages and disadvantages. SMC provides a complete Zero-Knowledge property, where each party involved knows nothing except its input and output, but this is difficult to achieve efficiently [8]. Differential Privacy prevents a third party from being able to associate data with an individual and protects their privacy, at the cost of losing a certain amount of the model's accuracy [17]. Finally, the Homomorphic Encryption guarantees privacy protection through parameter exchange under the encryption mechanism. The model's accuracy is preserved but this technique adds a non-negligible communication cost [27].

In this work we present a method based on the Homomorphic Encryption technique, and in particular, using the Paillier Homomorphic Encryption scheme [21], which is a method widely used in the previously described scenario. We choose to use a Homomorphic Encryption approach given the fact that it can preserve the privacy of data from any external adversary, it does not have any model precision loss and, finally, it is possible to apply this security method over an existing federated learning model. This is obtained without modification to the original algorithm, beside the encryption and decryption of the coefficients [27]. A similar approach to our work was considered in [12]. The authors propose a secure weighted aggregation scheme based on the Paillier Homomorphic Encryption where they try to protect the privacy of the clients' data from information leakage. The architecture of their protocol includes multiple clients that solve a machine learning problem with the coordination of a central unit that has the purpose to aggregate the values received from the clients. In their protocol, they evaluate the data disparity, i.e., the different amounts of data that

---

[1] https://eur-lex.europa.eu/legal-content/EN/TXT/?uri=OJ:L:2016:119:TOC.

[2] https://oag.ca.gov/privacy/ccpa.

[3] https://eur-lex.europa.eu/eli/dec_impl/2016/1250/oj.

the federated learning participants own. For the security of that protocol, the authors take into account both the privacy problems in data disparity evaluation and the privacy-preserving aggregation security issue. They also consider the possibility that both the central server and/or the clients send fraudulent messages to the others clients.

In [16] the authors present the xMK-CKKS, a multi-key homomorphic encryption protocol for a privacy-preserving federated learning method that is an improvement of the state-of-art MK-CKKS protocol [4]. They apply this scheme to FedAvg [18], a federated learning method based on iterative model averaging. The authors apply their solution to a smart healthcare scenario with 10 IoT devices and a central unit that computes the model aggregates. They compare their solution with a federated learning method based on the Paillier encryption scheme assuming that this last solution is not secure because all the devices share the same secret key and public key. They show that their solution loses less than 0.5% accuracy compared to the federated learning scheme and reduces the communication cost, the computational cost, and the energy consumption compared to the Paillier solution.

More recent work was presented in [10], where the author proposes a multi-party privacy-preserving federated machine learning framework, called PFMLP. This framework is based on partially homomorphic encryption, in particular, they used an improved Paillier algorithm, that adds a random integer in the encryption, which can speed up the training by 25–28%. They consider a Federated Network that includes a server that aggregates the encrypted model gradients and sends back the results to the clients. The security of their solution is based on the fact that the server does not have any key, so it can not see any plaintext avoiding the inference problem.

All previous works take into account a central unit with the purpose to aggregate the model coefficients shared from the clients. Our work does not involve the use of a single central unit, in fact, all the clients act both as a node and an aggregator. Our protocol also avoids the security problem related to the fact that all the devices share the same secret key and public key, generating different compatible keys in a particular way.

In this paper, we present Secure Homomorphic Sum protocol (SHSP), a novel SMC protocol that can be applied to any federated learning method. Encrypted messages are exchanged between agents containing the parameters of a model that they all jointly want to learn. To illustrate it in practice, we apply the proposed encryption scheme on top of a federated learning method, where agents jointly solve the sparse Support Vector Machine (sSVM) in a distributed privacy-preserving manner without exchanging their raw data. As a case study to illustrate our algorithm, we apply it in a healthcare scenario, where we study the heart disease problem.

The paper is organized as follows. Section 2 presents an overview of the distributed sSVM algorithm based on a framework called cluster Primal Dual Splitting (cPDS). In Sect. 3 we explain the protocol and its variation that adapts cPDS to be secure. In Sect. 4 we present the datasets, how we executed the tests, and the setting that we used. In Sect. 5 we show the results that we have obtained and we finally discuss them in Sect. 6. We conclude in Sect. 7 depicting some future work.

## 2   Federated Primal Dual Split Method

We will be extending the work presented in [2], that describes a federated learning of predictive models from federated data. Specifically they apply the cPDS framework to the sSVM.

Let us briefly summarize the work presented in [2]. Suppose a set $\mathcal{P}$ of agents that want to collaborate to train a sSVM global model to separate two classes. Each participant $p \in \mathcal{P}$ owns a subset $\mathcal{D}_p \subseteq \mathcal{D}$ of the entire dataset and maintains a copy $(\boldsymbol{\beta}_j, \beta_{j0})$ of the classifier parameters to be estimated. In each iteration of the method the parameters $(\boldsymbol{\beta}_j, \beta_{j0})$ are updated, using data locally stored in the agent and the coefficients that the agent receives from its neighbors. In every iteration each agent updates $\mathbf{x}_j = (\boldsymbol{\beta}_j, \beta_{j0}) \in \mathbb{R}^{d+1}$, $\mathbf{y}_j \in \mathbb{R}^{n_j}$, $\mathbf{q}_j \in \mathbb{R}^{n_j}$ and $\boldsymbol{\lambda}_j \in \mathbb{R}^{d+1}$.

We illustrate in Algorithm 1 the cPDS updates that each agent $j$ is performing. The effectiveness of this approach has been demonstrated against state-of-the-art of local and distributed methods in [2].

## 3   Method

From a high-level point of view, the protocol presented in Sect. 2 can be viewed as a sequence of iterations in which, at every stage, a set of nodes sends its own locally computed weights to an aggregator that sums them, and afterward uses the aggregated value as input for the next stage. Note that this is an abstraction of the actual protocol. In cPDS each node is at the same time aggregator and worker, as each nodes receives weights from its neighbours and sends the weights it computed on its own data to the neighbours as well.

In what follows, we describe how an aggregator may sum the coefficients sent by the nodes in an oblivious way, obtaining the aggregated value of their sum without knowing their actual values. The proposed approach is based on a simple deployment of the Paillier encryption scheme, known to be additively homomorphic [21]. This, in turn, allows us to define a secure version of the protocol presented in Sect. 2 in which the weights collected by an aggregator are not directly accessible neither to the aggregator nor to the other nodes (except – of course – the weights a node has sent itself). In this way, it is not possible for a party acting in the protocol to infer the weights computed by other parties and, in turn, no party is able to perform an inference attack on the data that parties exchange during the protocol's stages. In this work, we do not address attacks different from inference attacks or – as an example – collusion attacks [24]. Other attack scenarios can be addressed by combining works previously presented, such as [17] and [15], to the framework presented in remainder this section. This is

---

**Algorithm 1:** cPDS method

---

1 **Function** main():
2     $x_j^0, y_j^0, q_j^{-1}, q_j^0, \lambda_j^{-1}, \lambda_j^0 = initialize()$
3     **for** $k \leftarrow 0$ **to** $max\_iter$ **do**
4        $x_j^{k+1} = compute\_local(\lambda_j^k)$
5        $\lambda_j^{k+1} = \lambda\_update(x_j^{k+1})$          // requires information exchange
6     **end**
7
8 **Function** initialize():
9     $x_j^0 \in \mathbb{R}^{d+1}$
10     $y_j^0 \in \mathbb{R}^{n_j}$
11     $q_j^{-1} = 0$
12     $q_j^0 = \Gamma_j(A_j^\intercal x_j^0 - y_j^0)$
13     $\lambda_j^{-1} = 0$
14     $\lambda_j^0 = x_j^0 - \sum_{i \in N_j \cup \{j\}} w_{ji} x_i^0$
15     **return** $x_j^0, y_j^0, q_j^{-1}, q_j^0, \lambda_j^{-1}, \lambda_j^0$
16
17 **Function** compute_local($\lambda_j^k$):
18     $x_j^{k+1} =$
       $\underset{x_j}{\operatorname{argmin}}\{\langle 2q_j^k - q_j^{k-1}, \Gamma_j A_j x_j\rangle + g_j(x_j) + \langle 2\lambda_j^k - \lambda_j^{k-1}, x_j\rangle + 0.5\|x_j - x_j^k\|_{\Theta_j}^2\}$
19     $y_j^{k+1} = \underset{y_j}{\operatorname{argmin}}\{f_j(y_j) + \langle q_j^k, -\Gamma_j y_j\rangle + 0.5\|y_j - A_j x_j^{k+1}\|_{\Gamma_j^\intercal \Gamma_j}^2\}$
20     $q_j^{k+1} = q_j^k + \Gamma_j(A_j x_j^{k+1} - y_j^{k+1})$
21     **return** $x_j^{k+1}$
22
23 **Function** $\lambda\_update$():
24     $\lambda_j^{k+1} = \lambda_j^k + x_j^{k+1} - \sum_{i \in N_j \cup \{j\}} w_{ji} x_i^{k+1}$
25     **return** $\lambda_j^{k+1}$

---

possible because the framework here presented preserves confidentiality of the weights computed locally by each node, but does not make any assumption on how the weights have been computed.

We begin by presenting the Paillier-based secure sum protocol. Consider a set $\mathcal{P}$ of nodes, or *participants*, $\{p_1, \ldots, p_m\}$ and a dataset $\mathcal{D}$. Each participant $p \in \mathcal{P}$ owns a subset $\mathcal{D}_p \subseteq \mathcal{D}$ of the entire dataset.

According to the federated machine learning protocol described in [2], each participant of the federated machine learning task acts as an aggregator for the weights computed by its neighbors. Such neighbors are predefined according to the network topology connecting the various agents. Departing from traditional approaches, we remark that our protocol does not require multiple interaction steps among the nodes and an aggregator. There are two possible scenarios about network topology, as shown in Fig. 1a and Fig. 1b. The first scenario implies that all nodes that participate in the computation have at least two neighbors. On the

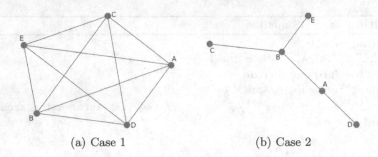

(a) Case 1                          (b) Case 2

**Fig. 1.** Simplified depiction of possible topological scenarios

other side, in the second scenario is it possible to find some nodes that have only one neighbor. In this case, it is necessary to modify the protocol to compute the sum. In the following, we present the protocol, its variation, and how we provide security to the machine learning model.

### 3.1  Keys Generation and Encryption

We assume the presence of a trusted *keys generator* that computes the cryptographic material (keys and random values) and distributes it to the appropriate parties participating in the protocol execution. We can safely assume that after the key generation and distribution phase the key generator may go offline.

The keys generator computes, for each node, a *master private key* msk and a set of *secret encryption keys* $\{pk_1, \ldots, pk_m\}$, where $m$ is the number of node's neighbors. The detailed procedure for the generation of the keys, based on the Paillier keys generation scheme, is summarized in Algorithm 2.

We note that the parameters for key generation are the same as in the Paillier scheme, and follow the same rules. Such parameters are used to generate a *master private key* msk that is used by a node to decrypt the aggregated value that it obtains after the sum of all the values that it has received from its neighbors (the associated public key is not used in our protocol, and so it is not generated). We detail how the nodes use these keys and which values (and how many times) are exchanged among the nodes in the next section.

Referring to the Algorithm 2 we note that the set of *secret encryption keys* $\{pk_1, \ldots, pk_m\}$ are generated following the Paillier public key rules, but in addition, a random value $r_i$ is added, different for each key of the set. Such keys will be used by the node's neighbors to encrypt the values before exchanging them. The decryption of one encrypted value can only happen after having summed up all the other ones, using the associated *master private key* msk. If a node tries to decrypt an encrypted value before having summed it with the other values, it obtains an obfuscated value with the secret $r_i$. We detail the security of the message in Sect. 3.4.

Note that the association between node's neighbors and keys $\{\mathsf{pk}_1, \ldots, \mathsf{pk}_m\}$ could be further randomized to reduce collusion risks.

---

**Algorithm 2:** Secure Homomorphic Sum protocol

---

1  **Function** parameters_generation():
2      Choose $p$, $q$ random primes such that $\gcd(pq, (p-1)(q-1)) = 1$
3      Compute $n = pq$ and $\lambda = \mathrm{lcm}(p-1, q-1)$
4      Select random integer $g$ where $g \in \mathbb{Z}_{n^2}^*$
5      Check the existence of $\mu = (L(g^\lambda \bmod n^2))^{-1} \bmod n$, where $L(x) = \frac{x-1}{n}$
6      **return** $n, g, L, \mu$
7
8  **Function** master_private_key($L, \mu$):
9      $msk = (\lambda, \mu)$
10     **return** $msk$
11
12 **Function** secret_encryption_keys($n, g$):
13     Select $m-1$ random numbers, $\{r_1, \ldots, r_{m-1}\}$ from $Z_n$
14     Set $r_m = -\sum r_i$
15     Let $p_i = (n, g, r_i)$ be the secret key associated to agent $i$
16     **return** $\mathcal{P} = \{p_1, \ldots, p_m\}$
17
18 **Function** encryption($p_i, m_i$):
19     Check $m_i < n$
20     Select $r < n$ such that $r \in \mathbb{Z}_n^*$
21     Ensure that $\gcd(r, n) = 1$
22     $c_i = g^{m_i} * g^{r_i} * r^n \bmod n^2$
23     **return** $c_i$
24
25 **Function** decryption($msk, c$):
26     $m = L(c^\lambda \bmod n^2)\mu \bmod n$
27     **return** $m$

---

### 3.2  Protocol

The protocol assumes that a node $p$ has $m \geq 2$ neighbors. All the nodes work both as a simple node and as an aggregator. In the following, we present how the protocol works taking into account only one node as an aggregator; these operations must be applied to all nodes in parallel, considering each node as an aggregator.

The trusted *keys generator* sends to the aggregator node a *master private key* and a secret encryption key $p_m$ taken from the set of keys $\mathcal{P}$; then it sends to each neighbor of the aggregator a different key always taken from the set of *keys* $\mathcal{P}$. The secret encryption keys are distributed to the nodes so that all the nodes that participate in the computation group have only one key present in the set and all the keys must be allocated.

At each iteration of the algorithm presented in Sect. 2, each participant $i$ computes its algorithm parameters based on its data. Then everyone encrypts its coefficients with the secret encryption key $p_i$, and sends the encrypted value to the node designated as the aggregator. When the aggregator has received all the encrypted data from all its neighbors, it encrypts its algorithm's coefficients with its secret encryption key $p_m$ and aggregates the values by summing all encrypted values that it has received, obtaining a value $E = \sum e_i$. Because of Paillier Encryption schema construction, this results in $E = g^{(v_1+r_1)+(v_2+r_2)+...+(v_m+r_m)}$. Knowing that $\sum r_i = 0$ this is equivalent to $E = g^{v_1+v_2+...+v_m}$, the aggregator can decrypt the aggregated value $E$ with its *master private key* msk to obtain the plaintext.

Because of the presence of $r_i$ in the keys, without first adding all the values, it is not possible to recover with enough confidence the values from the decryption of individual ciphertexts.

### 3.3   A Variation of the Protocol

The protocol presented in the previous section implies that a node $p$ has $m \geq 2$ neighbors. In fact, if we were deploying the previously described protocol in a scenario like the one in Fig. 1b, where there are some nodes as $C$, $D$ and $E$ with exactly one neighbor, when these will be aggregators they could leverage their secret encryption keys to extract the values of the coefficients of the nodes $A$ and $B$. For example, if we consider $C$ as the aggregator, it could encrypt its algorithm's coefficients with its secret encryption key, sum with the encrypted values that it has received from $B$ and then it can decrypt with its *master private key*. This way, $C$ obtains a plaintext that is an aggregated value composed by its value and the value of $B$. To obtain the $B$'s plaintext the aggregator must only subtract its coefficients. Thus, it would be able to infer some information about the nature of the data that the neighbor node possesses.

This variation adapts the protocol to work correctly with the presence of nodes with only one neighbor in the graph's topology.

The solution that we propose to solve this problem uses dummy links. The keys generator, which knows the graph topology, when seeing a node that has only one neighbor, instead of generating only two secret encryption keys p1, p2, generates a third key p3. This last key is sent to a random node that is a neighbor of the only neighbor node that has the aggregator. In this way, the node that is the only neighbor of the aggregator sends to the aggregator two different values, its value and the other one that has received from one of its neighbors. Applying this solution, the protocol can be considered as the standard one defined in the previous paragraph. The security of this protocol's variation is the same that the standard protocol has, because, using the third values encrypted with the third key, the aggregator can't recover with enough confidence the right values and it can't infer any information about the data.

## 3.4  Security Considerations

We now present the proof that our protocol is secure in an honest-but-curious scenario. In this scenario, we consider a passive adversary that listens to the network and it can obtain all the messages that the federated learning parties exchange during a computation. These messages, which are the model coefficients, were encrypted by a node with its secret encryption key. Following the protocol presented in this section, the only way that the adversary has to decrypt these ciphertexts is to get all the others messages from the others nodes of the group, sum them and decrypt the aggregated value with the aggregator's private key.

Now, we assume that our protocol is insecure. Then we can assume that there is an adversary that may decrypt each message it intercepts in the network (without knowing the secret key). So, the adversary can decrypt every message exchanged during the machine learning computation. We start from the fact that an encrypted message with our protocol is equal to $c = E(p_i, m) = E((n, g, r_i), m) = g^m * g^{r_i} * r^n \mod n^2$, and, if we set $ri = 0$ we obtain $c = E(p_i, m) = E((n, g), m) = g^m * r^n \mod n^2$ that is equal to a ciphertext encrypted with the Paillier standard protocol. Given this fact and taking into account an adversary with the previously described power, we can conclude that an attacker that can easily decrypt a message encrypted with our protocol can easily decrypt a message encrypted with the standard Paillier protocol. Thus, an adversary that uses the procedure for breaking our protocol as a block-box for breaking the Paillier scheme.

In conclusion, if we consider [3], where the authors prove that Paillier's encryption scheme is semantically secure, we can assume that our protocol is also semantically secure.

## 4  Experimental Evaluation

In this section, we describe how we modified the algorithm presented in Sect. 2 to make it more secure, i.e., to avoid that a node can infer sensible information from data shared by other participants in the computation. We also present how we evaluated the impact of our protocol on the algorithm, considering both the time used to train the model and the performance of classification obtained in tests.

To develop the secure version of cPDS we use the *phe* Python3 library [5] that implements the Paillier partially homomorphic encryption. This library is composed of some functions that allow us to generate a different set of keys, encrypt some values, and decrypt the ciphertexts. It also contains a function to sum two ciphertexts and one to multiply a ciphertext with a scalar. We modified this library to adapt it to our requirements; in particular, we added a new function that allows us to generate a new set of keys following the protocol that we previously described. We also adapted the encryption and decryption functions to work correctly with the new version of the keys. Algorithm 2 illustrates the details about these functions.

Finally, we apply to the cPDS algorithm, the adapted functions of the *phe* library, to encrypt the computed coefficients, sum them and decrypt the aggregated values that the nodes composing the system exchange during algorithm execution.

## 4.1  Settings

To test the cPDS algorithm in a distributed way we considered different environment setups. In particular, we took into account the number of nodes that compose the system and the topology of the network that includes all these nodes.

To test the algorithm in a realistic scenario we vary the number of nodes that want to participate in the computation. In the healthcare scenario, this number represents the number of hospitals that own part of the data used to train the model. To emulate a real environment we range this number from 5 to 30. We observed these different numbers of clients in some business settings where solutions like [14].

In a real scenario, it is not sure that all nodes are communicating with each other. To take into account all the different possibilities we choose to test the secure version of the cPDS algorithm considering different network topologies. We run different tests, and before each test, we generate a graph that represents the topology of the network using the *Erdős - Rényi* model. To generate the graph we use three different levels of connection between nodes, in this way we have (i) a low connected graph where the edges of the nodes are as lower as possible, (ii) a partially connected graph where the nodes are on average connected and (iii) a fully connected graph where all the nodes are connected. To define more formally these three types we take into account the degree property of a network [13], that is the number of edges that a node has. This way, define $n$ as the number of nodes present in the network, the expected number of a node's edges is equal to $n * p$ [9,20]. Given this property, we define (i) a low connected graph as a network where nodes have an average degree equal to $n * 0.2$, (ii) a partial connected graph as a network with an average degree of $n * 0.5$ and finally (iii) a fully connected graph where the average degree is $n * 1$.

When varying the topology of the network, and/or the number of nodes, the number of the edges that connect the nodes between them also varies, and, as a consequence, the number of messages circulating on the network increases or decreases. This allows us to study - if and how much - the different number of messages and the different number of nodes impact the times and the accuracy of the model.

## 4.2  Datasource

To evaluate our protocol we train the cPDS algorithm considering three different datasets. The first dataset is a synthetic dataset generated in three different versions that vary in the number of features: the first one has $15,000$ instances and 5 features, the second one has $15,000$ instances and 10 features, and the

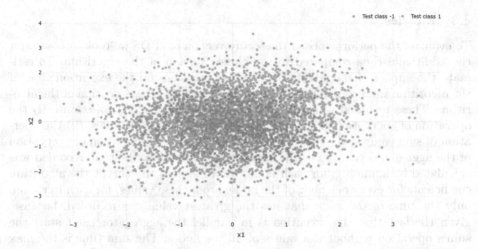

**Fig. 2.** Synthetic test dataset's classes.

third one has $15,000$ instances and 20 features. All of these synthetic datasets were generated randomly following a Multivariate Gaussian Distribution [11]. We choose to vary these datasets based on the number of features because, in this way, we can study how the time to encrypt the coefficients of the cPDS algorithm increases as the number of features increases. We show an example of this synthetic dataset in Fig. 2.

To evaluate our protocol in a real-world scenario with a dataset based on real data, we use the *"Heart Disease"* dataset [7]. This set is composed of different subsets of data, where each of these sets describes a heart disease study on a different location. In particular, we choose to use the dataset describing the Cleveland population, which is the only one that has been used by machine learning researchers and practitioners. This because it is the only dataset that has a very small percentage of *NaN* values and it is the one that has the highest number of instances. This dataset describes different health situations of patients, and the purpose is to find the presence, or not, of heart disease in a patient. The database has 76 raw features, but we used the *pre-processed* version, which is the version used by all the published experiments that use this dataset where the unimportant attributes are dropped and only the important ones are considered [22], that are only 14; the set has 303 instances. Finally, given the low number of data of the previous set, we choose to test the cPDS algorithm with another medical database, based on real data, that has more instances. The dataset that we choose to use is a subset of the Framingham database that is available on Kaggle [1,6]. This set of data includes 15 features and more than $4,000$ instances. This set is a study of cardiovascular disease conducted in the town of Framingham, Massachusetts, on over 5000 citizens. The data, as the previous one, describes different health situations of patients, and the purpose is to find the presence, or not, of cardiovascular disease in a patient.

## 4.3   Metrics

To evaluate the performance of the secure version of cPDS we took into account the additional time compared to the classic version of the algorithm. To estimate the impact of the adapted *phe* secure functions on the execution time of the algorithm we recorded three different times during the execution of the algorithm. These recorded values are the times that were added to execute (i) the operation of encryption of the algorithm coefficients by the nodes, (ii) the operation of sum computed by the aggregators, and (iii) the operation of decryption of the aggregated values. For the encryption's operation, the time recorded was calculated by summing, for each node, the time used to encrypt the algorithm coefficients for every neighbor of the node. From these values, for each iteration, only the time of the node that has the greatest value was recorded, because, given the fact that the execution is in parallel the aggregator can't start the sum's operation without the values of all the nodes. The sum time is the max time that a node used to sum all the values that it receives from all its neighbors. The aggregator starts the operation only when it has received all the values from all its neighbors. Taking into account the fact that each node is both a simple node and an aggregator, when a node finishes the sum's operation it can start to decrypt the aggregated values. The decryption time was taken from each node and is the time that a node used to decrypt its aggregated coefficients. Then a new iteration can start immediately with the new values used to compute a new set of coefficients. Finally, to evaluate the performance of classification, we took into account, the Receiver Operating Characteristic Curve (AUC), obtained in the test of the model. We investigated - if and how much - our secure version of the algorithm impacted the precision of the model compared with the one that is not secure.

## 5   Results

In this section, we present the conducted tests and the results that we obtained, for both the added time to the computation and the performance of the trained models. We executed different tests to evaluate the secure version of the cPDS algorithm. These tests vary based on the dataset considered, the number of nodes, and the topology of the network that connected the nodes.

For each dataset, we run three different tests, one for each graph topology, and for each of these, we run four other tests, with a different number of nodes. We executed these tests one time for the secure version of cPDS algorithm and one time for the standard version. The results for the synthetic datasets are presented in Fig. 3a. These three graphs differ based on the number of features that are present in the dataset. Each of these graphs represents the total time per iteration that we added to the computation of the secure version of cPDS compared to the non-secure version, as a function of the number of nodes that participate in the machine learning computation. The total time is the sum of the time used, by each node, to execute the three secure functions, the encryption, the sum, and the decryption ones, presented in Sect. 4.3. We consider the maximum time

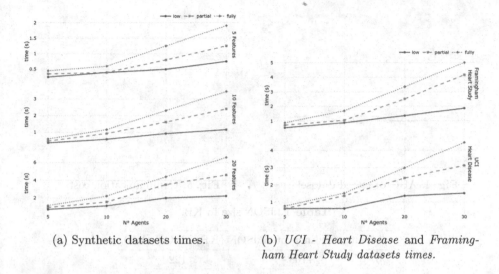

(a) Synthetic datasets times.    (b) *UCI - Heart Disease* and *Framingham Heart Study datasets times.*

**Fig. 3.** Max time per iteration.

of each of these functions because, taking into account the fact that they are executed in parallel, a node must wait for the values from other nodes before start a new iteration. In each of these graphs, we present the total time based also on the topology of the network taking into account the number of edges that connect the nodes. In Fig. 3b we show the results obtained from the executed tests for the other two datasets, the *"UCI - Heart Disease"* and the *"Framingham Heart Study"*. These two datasets are based on real data and regards the study of heart diseases. They have 13 and 15 features respectively. As in the previous case, we present the total time as a function of the number of nodes. We consider also the topology of the network.

We present in Fig. 4 the AUC that we obtained from the tests that we executed with *"UCI - Heart Disease"* and the *"Framingham Heart Study"* datasets. In this graph, we inserted only one value per test, given the fact that the values obtained from the executed tests with the secure version of cPDS are exactly the same as the values obtained from the non-secure version. To be able to compare the AUC obtained in tests between the two cPDS versions, we used the same parameters and the same network configuration between the nodes. In this way, we could see - if and how much - the added functions to make the algorithm secure impacted the performance of the trained model. In this graph is possible to see the AUC of the model in the setting where the protocol variation is applicable. These cases are the ones where we have 5 and 10 nodes with a lower connected graph, and so we have the highest probability to find a node with only one neighbor. To have a better understanding of this fact, we also show in this graph the AUC obtained from tests executed removing the protocol variation. These tests are executed with the same setting, but given the fact that some

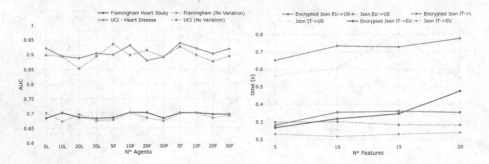

**Fig. 4.** AUC of tested datasets.          **Fig. 5.** Communication cost.

**Table 1.** JSON size in KB.

| # Features | Encrypted JSON (KB) | JSON (KB) |
|---|---|---|
| 5 | 7768 | 122 |
| 10 | 14243 | 227 |
| 15 | 20715 | 332 |
| 20 | 27194 | 435 |

cPDS parameters are randomly initialized, the obtained AUCs are not perfectly the same.

Finally, we tested the communication costs, taking into account the time that two nodes use to exchange a message and the size of this message. We consider the different number of features, given the fact that a message corresponds to a serialized version of the coefficients computed by a node, and these coefficients are equal in number to the feature of the data, as required by cPDS. We present the communication time based on different server locations in Fig. 5 and based on the message sizes in Table 1. To test the time we have created two different servers on the *Heroku* platform, the first one is located in *EU* region, and the second one in the *US* region and we exchange messages with our server located in *Italy*. This time includes the time to serialize a message in JSON format, send it from a server to another, and deserialize the JSON object. We recorded the times with both messages that include encrypted values and messages with clear values.

## 6    Discussion

Below, we discuss the results presented in the previous section. We also highlight the limits that our solution presents.

In Fig. 3a we present the total time that we obtain from the tests with the synthetic datasets. From these three graphs, we show how the time that we add to the execution, to make it secure, depends on the number of features. This is given by the fact that the coefficient vector of cPDS is as long as the number of features that are present in the dataset. This implies that each node has to encrypt more values, so the time increase. In fact, from this Figure, we can notice that the time increases linearly based on the number of features. We observe the same dependence considering not only the number of features but also the number of nodes and how much these nodes are connected between them. As we show in Fig. 3a we note that, taking into account the three graph topologies independently, how the time slightly increases as the number of nodes increases. This is given by the fact that the more nodes we have, and the more they are connected, the more encrypted values each node has to sum. If we also consider the number of edges that connect the nodes we notice how the time increases as the connections between the nodes increase. This is motivated by the fact that each node must encrypt its coefficient several times, with different keys, that strictly depends on the number of nodes, as presented in Sect. 3.2. We also note that the number of instances of a dataset does not impact the added time to the secure cPDS. We observe the same dependencies in Fig. 3b where we show the results obtained from the tests with *"UCI - Heart Disease"* and the *"Framingham Heart Study"* datasets.

In Fig. 6 we split the total time that we add to an iteration of the tests with the *"Framingham Heart Study"* dataset in its three components, the encryption, the sum, and the decryption time. We present, how the encryption time, that is the time that a node used to encrypt all the values in a single iteration, is around 96–98% of the total time that we added to make the cPDS secure. We observe the same relation in all the others sets. From the above analysis, we can conclude that our solution performs well in presence of datasets with a restricted number of features, regardless of the number of instances. We also notice that our solution could be considered too expensive in the presence of a large number of participants in the computation that are all connected because this could fall into an expensive time-consuming.

Regarding Fig. 4, one can observe that, for the two datasets considered, the obtained AUC is the same for both the secure version of cPDS and the non-secure version. This implies that our solution has no impact on the classification performance of the machine learning model. Moreover, we observe that the error introduced by the conversion from floating-point coefficients to integer during the encryption process is negligible in all the configurations, as shown in Fig. 7. The AUC is also constant for all the settings that we have presented in Sect. 4.1. We also note how the obtained values do not vary too much in the settings where the protocol variation is applicable compared to the others. We conclude that the protocol variation does not impact the performance of the model, where applicable.

Finally, in Fig. 5, where we show the communication cost, we observe that the time that two nodes used to serialize, send and deserialize an encrypted JSON is slightly higher than the not encrypted version, for all the servers considered. This is given by the fact that in a JSON file of the encrypted version are stored the encrypted coefficients, where each coefficient has a length of 2048 bits.

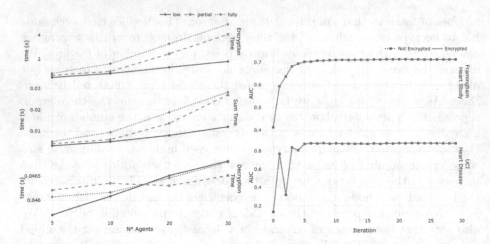

**Fig. 6.** Framingham components.    **Fig. 7.** Training AUC in a setting with 10 nodes partially connected.

In the not encrypted version, these coefficients have a length equal to a double-precision floating-point length, which is 64 bits in our Python implementation. This has an impact also in the size of the JSON as showed in Table 1.

## 7    Conclusions and Future Work

In this work, we presented an extension of the cPDS algorithm based on the Paillier Homomorphic encryption scheme. Our solution allows hospitals to compute a machine learning model in a distributed way without sharing their private data, preserving their patients' privacy from inference attacks. Our work added a secure layer to protect the cPDS model's coefficient from Honest-but-Curious adversaries and we proved that SHSP is semantically secure assuming that Paillier's encryption scheme is semantically secure.

We evaluated our solution with different datasets, with both synthetic data and medical data, that vary according to the number of features and the number of instances. We showed how the time that we added to preserve the privacy of the data depends on the number of features that are present in the data and it does not on the number of instances. We considered also the topology of the network that connects the participants to the computation and we showed that this time depends also on the number of clients that participate in the computation and the number of edges that connect these nodes. We also demonstrated that our solution preserves the accuracy of the model, compared to the non-secure version, without any loss. However, we noted how our solution does not work well in all the settings that we considered. In fact, we noticed how the time that we added could be considered too high in the presence of a higher number of features and also in the settings where are present a lot of nodes with a high degree value.

Further analysis can be conducted to improve the time of our solution, for example reducing the number of encryptions that a node must do before sharing its coefficients with the other nodes. This would greatly reduce the time each node uses to encrypt the values, making our solution much more efficient. A potential future research direction could also be to investigate how we can protect the cPDS from other types of attacks, like membership inference attack.

**Acknowledgement.** Stefano Braghin and Theodora Brisimi are partially funded from the European Union's Horizon 2020 research and innovation programme under grant agreement No. 824988. https://musketeer.eu/

# References

1. Ajmera, A.: Framingham heart study dataset (2018). Data Accessed from Kaggle. https://www.kaggle.com/amanajmera1/framingham-heart-study-dataset
2. Brisimi, T.S., Chen, R., Mela, T., Olshevsky, A., Paschalidis, I.C., Shi, W.: Federated learning of predictive models from federated electronic health records. Int. J. Med. Inform. **112**, 59–67 (2018)
3. Catalano, D., Gennaro, R., Howgrave-Graham, N.: The bit security of Paillier's encryption scheme and its applications. In: Pfitzmann, B. (ed.) EUROCRYPT 2001. LNCS, vol. 2045, pp. 229–243. Springer, Heidelberg (2001). https://doi.org/10.1007/3-540-44987-6_15
4. Chen, H., Dai, W., Kim, M., Song, Y.: Efficient multi-key homomorphic encryption with packed ciphertexts with application to oblivious neural network inference. Cryptology ePrint Archive, Report 2019/524 (2019). https://eprint.iacr.org/2019/524
5. CSIRO Data61: Python Paillier Library (2013). https://github.com/data61/python-paillier
6. Dawber, T.R., Meadors, G.F., Moore, F.E.: Epidemiological approaches to heart disease: the Framingham Study. Am. J. Public Health Nations Health **41**(3), 279–286 (1951)
7. Detrano, R., et al.: International application of a new probability algorithm for the diagnosis of coronary artery disease. Am. J. Cardiol. **64**(5), 304–310 (1989)
8. Du, W., Han, Y.S., Chen, S.: Privacy-preserving multivariate statistical analysis: linear regression and classification. In: Berry, M.W., Dayal, U., Kamath, C., Skillicorn, D.B. (eds.) Proceedings of the Fourth SIAM International Conference on Data Mining, Lake Buena Vista, Florida, USA, 22–24 April 2004, pp. 222–233. SIAM (2004)
9. Erdős, P., Rényi, A.: On random graphs I. Publicationes Math. Debrecen **6**, 290 (1959)
10. Fang, H., Qian, Q.: Privacy preserving machine learning with homomorphic encryption and federated learning. Future Internet **13**(4), 94 (2021)
11. Flury, B.: The multivariate normal distribution. In: Flury, B. (ed.) A First Course in Multivariate Statistics. STS, pp. 171–207. Springer, New York (1997). https://doi.org/10.1007/978-1-4757-2765-4_3
12. Guo, J., Liu, Z., Lam, K., Zhao, J., Chen, Y., Xing, C.: Secure weighted aggregation in federated learning. CoRR abs/2010.08730 (2020)

13. Kantarci, B., Labatut, V.: Classification of complex networks based on topological properties. In: 2013 International Conference on Cloud and Green Computing, Karlsruhe, Germany, 30 September–2 October 2013, pp. 297–304. IEEE Computer Society (2013)
14. Ludwig, H., et al.: IBM federated learning: an enterprise framework. White Paper V0.1 (2020)
15. Lyu, L., et al.: Privacy and robustness in federated learning: attacks and defenses. CoRR abs/2012.06337 (2020)
16. Ma, J., Naas, S.A., Sigg, S., Lyu, X.: Privacy-preserving federated learning based on multi-key homomorphic encryption (2021)
17. Mammen, P.M.: Federated learning: opportunities and challenges. CoRR abs/2101.05428 (2021)
18. McMahan, H.B., Moore, E., Ramage, D., Hampson, S., Arcas, B.A.: Communication-efficient learning of deep networks from decentralized data (2017)
19. Melis, L., Song, C., Cristofaro, E.D., Shmatikov, V.: Exploiting unintended feature leakage in collaborative learning. In: 2019 IEEE Symposium on Security and Privacy, SP 2019, San Francisco, CA, USA, 19–23 May 2019, pp. 691–706. IEEE (2019)
20. Newman, M.E.J.: Random graphs as models of networks, pp. 35–68. Wiley (2002)
21. Paillier, P.: Public-key cryptosystems based on composite degree residuosity classes. In: Stern, J. (ed.) EUROCRYPT 1999. LNCS, vol. 1592, pp. 223–238. Springer, Heidelberg (1999). https://doi.org/10.1007/3-540-48910-X_16
22. Patel, J., Tejalupadhyay, S., Patel, S.: Heart disease prediction using machine learning and data mining technique, March 2016
23. Truex, S., et al.: A hybrid approach to privacy-preserving federated learning. In: Cavallaro, L., et al. (eds.) Proceedings of the 12th ACM Workshop on Artificial Intelligence and Security, AISec@CCS 2019, London, UK, 15 November 2019, pp. 1–11. ACM (2019)
24. Xu, R., Baracaldo, N., Zhou, Y., Anwar, A., Ludwig, H.: Hybridalpha: an efficient approach for privacy-preserving federated learning. In: Cavallaro, L., et al. (eds.) Proceedings of the 12th ACM Workshop on Artificial Intelligence and Security, AISec@CCS 2019, London, UK, 15 November 2019, pp. 13–23. ACM (2019)
25. Yang, Q., Liu, Y., Chen, T., Tong, Y.: Federated machine learning: concept and applications. ACM Trans. Intell. Syst. Technol. 10(2), 12:1–12:19 (2019)
26. Yin, L., Feng, J., Xun, H., Sun, Z., Cheng, X.: A privacy-preserving federated learning for multiparty data sharing in social IoTs. IEEE Trans. Netw. Sci. Eng. 8(3), 2706–2718 (2021)
27. Zhang, C., Li, S., Xia, J., Wang, W., Yan, F., Liu, Y.: BatchCrypt: efficient homomorphic encryption for cross-silo federated learning. In: Gavrilovska, A., Zadok, E. (eds.) 2020 USENIX Annual Technical Conference, USENIX ATC 2020, 15–17 July 2020, pp. 493–506. USENIX Association (2020)

# Benchmarking Multi-instance Learning
# for Multivariate Time Series Analysis

Rufat Babayev[✉][iD] and Lena Wiese[iD]

Fraunhofer ITEM, Nikolai-Fuchs-Strasse 1, 30625 Hannover, Germany
{rufat.babayev,lena.wiese}@item.fraunhofer.de

**Abstract.** Successful incorporation of Electronic Health Records to the data mining tools created new frontiers in digital clinical data analysis. One of the well-known applications of clinical data analysis is the mortality prediction of patients in intensive care units (ICUs). One important aspect of mortality prediction is the analysis of multivariate time series of observations after 24 or 48 h of ICU admission. Recent mortality prediction models for ICU patients are based on either recurrent neural networks or traditional machine learning algorithms using statistical summaries of timestamped observations. Instead of using complex neural network architectures and statistical summaries, we transform multivariate time series into multi-instance representation by keeping the expressiveness of the original observations. We then perform mortality prediction using multi-instance machine learning algorithms. Our empirical study shows that multi-instance representation achieves comparable or better (in some configurations) performance in various experiments.

**Keywords:** Multi-instance learning · Multivariate time series analysis · Machine learning using statistical summaries · Descriptive statistics · Ensemble methods

## 1 Introduction

Electronic Health Records (EHRs) contain an electronic medical history of different patients collected over time, namely, the key clinical data related to the health routine of patients. Clinicians need to examine these data and prepare treatment options for patients in a short period of time [21, 22, 37]. A fast diagnosis and treatment is especially important for the patients staying in intensive care units (ICUs), because they are admitted to these units in extreme situations. Hospitals and health care providers are also interested in a status of patients in intensive care units such as how long a patient is going to stay in ICU, whether or not a patient is going to die after certain number of hours (e.g. 24 or 48 h after ICU admission). With this grounding, they are able to organize future actions to save time, cost and other resources required for each patient.

This work was supported by the Fraunhofer Internal Programs under Grant No. Attract 042-601000.

© Springer Nature Switzerland AG 2021
E. K. Rezig et al. (Eds.): Poly 2021/DMAH 2021, LNCS 12921, pp. 103–120, 2021.
https://doi.org/10.1007/978-3-030-93663-1_9

To determine future patient status, monitoring data are utilized. These data are mostly collected as multivariate time series containing values for each key health indicator (e.g. heart rate, respiratory rate, Creatinine level, etc.) in a temporal order. In our study, we focus on mortality prediction after 48 h of ICU admission through multivariate time series classification.

A lot of research has been carried out for multivariate time series analysis of health monitoring data [3,8,19,32,40]. In their experiments, the authors either use deep neural networks (especially recurrent neural networks) for sequence/temporal modeling or create feature spaces from time series variables digested by traditional machine learning algorithms such as random forests, logistic regression classifiers, support vector machines, etc. Recurrent neural networks are useful tools to learn sequential or temporal relationships from time series data [32]. However, there are still some open questions remaining about the possible effectiveness of deep learning models for health care data. For example, the size of the data in health care applications is often modest relative to the complexity of deep learning models [19]. More specifically, these models can easily overfit on small-scale data. Moreover, complex architectures and parameter configurations need to be maintained for training. In contrast, traditional machine learning algorithms are not as complex as deep neural networks, however, the vast majority of them are not designed in a way that they can handle sequential/temporal data. To cope with this issue, the straightforward approach is to map multivariate time series data to the data with a single instance (or a propositional) feature space. As an example, assume that a multivariate time series contains $T$ observations of $D$ variables in a temporal order. One can generate the following statistical summaries for each variable $d \in \{1, \ldots, D\}$ from that time series by considering all $T$ observations; *Maximum, Minimum, Mean, Median, Mode, Standard deviation, Variance, Range, Geometric center, Kurtosis, Skewness, Averaged power, Energy spectral density* [35]. Then a feature space can be generated by all of these summaries or a subset of them. Now assume that the *Maximum* and *Minimum* are selected, then a single instance obtained from the respective time series becomes a part of *Minimax* feature space containing $2 \cdot D$ variables (features). In this approach, the time order is not considered and instead of using raw features and their values, generated features and their corresponding values are applied for training machine learning models. This kind of approach does indeed show decent predictive performance [3,8,19,35]. In our work, we focus on using as many raw features as possible to keep the expressiveness of the original dataset. To do so, we represent multivariate time series data as multi-instance data in the context of an MIL (Multi-Instance Learning) framework. In this representation, each observation of variables in a time series is considered as one instance and a collection of such instances is denoted as a *bag* with a corresponding class label. Finally, we benchmark multivariate time series classification by classifying bags with multi-instance versions of traditional machine learning algorithms in the MIL framework. Our results show that the multi-instance representation yields comparable or sometimes better (in some configurations) performance as compared to the statistical summary representation.

## 2   Related Work

Multi-Instance Learning (MIL) is a notable topic in machine learning proposed in 1997 [9] as a variation of supervised learning (weakly supervised) for drug activity prediction. Since then, MIL frameworks are adapted for many other areas. For instance, [2] incorporated SVM (support vector machines) to the MIL framework and proposed MISVM to generate instance-level and bag-level predictions effectively. The work by [45] expanded multi-instance SVM approaches through MIMLSVM (multi-instance multi-label SVM) for solving multi-label classification tasks. MIGraph [46] is proposed to model multi-instance bag structures. Generative mixture models – MIMM (multi-instance mixture model) [11], and DPMIL (dirichlet process mixture of gaussians) [27] are adapted to tackle binary multiple-instance classification problems. Deep multi-instance learning methods are also introduced in an MIL setting [23,30,31,42,44,47]. In-depth surveys of MIL frameworks are given in works such as [1,7,20,39]. Time series analysis is adopted into the MIL framework by [17] which utilizes an autoregressive hidden markov model for an activity recognition in time series data. The work by [36] proposes a multi-instance learning method for a sound event detection from time series. Multi-instance learning approach based on the time series modeling for EEG (Electroencephalogram) identification is proposed by [24].

Despite some applications, we have not noticed any work which benchmarks multi-instance learning on multivariate time series data. The goal of our work is to achieve this in the context of multivariate time series classification.

## 3   Preliminaries

In this section, we present mathematical notations for a multivariate (multi-dimensional) time series and briefly discuss background for the multi-instance learning in this context.

Following the notations from [8], we specify a multivariate time series with $D$ variables (also known as a $D$-dimensional time series) of length $T$ as $X = (x_1, x_2, \ldots, x_T)^\mathsf{T} \in \mathbb{R}^{T \times D}$, where $\forall t = \{1, 2, \ldots, T\}$, $x_t \in \mathbb{R}^D$ is a vector which represents the $t$-th measurements (observations) of all variables and $x_t^d$ is the observation of $d$-th variable of $x_t$. In this paper, we focus on time series classification to predict a label $l_n \in \{1, \ldots, L\}$ for each of $N$ multivariate time series collected in a dataset $\mathcal{D}$, where $\mathcal{D} = \{(X_n)\}_{n=1}^N$ and $X_n = \left[ x_1^{(n)}, x_2^{(n)}, \ldots, x_{T_n}^{(n)} \right]$.

### 3.1   Multi-instance Learning

Multi-instance learning (MIL) is a type of supervised learning where the data points are collected in multisets called bags, and the entire bag has a label – either discrete or real-valued. The data points of each bag are called instances. The main purpose is to learn a model from the instances of the bag and the label of the bag such that bag-level and instance-level predictions can be generated. Our focus in this work is a classification task (i.e. discrete-valued labels), more specifically binary classification. In general, there are two types of assumptions that can be used to model relationships between the bag label and labels of instances inside the bag. The first assumption is called the *standard MI assumption* [9]. In this assumption, the bag label is considered negative if all instances inside the bag are negative and it is considered positive if at least one instance inside the bag has a positive label. We follow the notations provided by [7] to explain the assumptions. Let $B$ be a bag of $M$ instances with static features (a.k.a propositional instances or feature vector instances), namely, $B = \{z_1, z_2, \ldots, z_M\}$. Assume that $\forall m \in \{1, \ldots, M\}$, an instance $z_m$ in a feature space $\mathcal{Z}$ is mapped to a class by some imaginary function $f : \mathcal{Z} \to \Omega$, where $\Omega = \{0, 1\}$, and where 0 and 1 represent negative and positive labels correspondingly. Then, the bag classifier (a.k.a the aggregator function), $g(B)$ is given by:

$$g(B) = \begin{cases} 1 & \text{if } \exists z \in B : f(z) = 1 \\ 0 & \text{otherwise} \end{cases} \tag{1}$$

This standard assumption might be viewed as too strict for some cases where positive bags cannot be determined by a single instance of a bag. Therefore, this assumption is relaxed to the *collective MI assumption* [10,43] which treats the contribution of each instance to the bag label separately. In contrast to the standard assumption, the collective assumption considers a bag $B$ as a distribution $P(z|B)$ (the probability of an instance $z$ given a bag $B$) over the feature space $\mathcal{Z}$, and similarly considers labels as a distribution $P(c|z)$ over instances, where $c \in \Omega = \{0, 1\}$. The collective assumption then models the distribution

$$P(c|B) = \int_{\mathcal{Z}} P(c|z)P(z|B)dz. \tag{2}$$

To calculate this, the probability distribution $P(z|B)$ for the bag must be known. Generally, this probability distribution is not known in practice; hence, an empirical version over the instances in the bag is calculated instead:

$$\hat{P}(c|B) = \frac{1}{M_B} \sum_{m=1}^{M_B} P(c|z_m), \tag{3}$$

where $M_B$ is the number of instances inside the bag $B$. Since $P(c|z_m)$, $\forall m = \{1, \ldots, M_B\}$ is also unknown, most methods based on the collective assumption learn this distribution as in a single-instance dataset [10,43]. The probability distribution in (3) is also called an *arithmetic average of posterior probabilities* of instances in the bag. In this probability distribution, the instance-level class label is modeled by $P(c|z_m)$ for each $m \in \{1, \ldots, M_B\}$ for the bag $B$. It can also be modeled by a logit transformation, namely, the log-odds function

$\log \dfrac{P(c=1|z_m)}{P(c=0|z_m)}$ [10]. When the logit transformation is substituted in (3), the following equation is obtained:

$$\log \frac{P(c=1|B)}{P(c=0|B)} = \frac{1}{M_B} \sum_{m=1}^{M_B} \log \frac{P(c=1|z_m)}{P(c=0|z_m)}$$

$$= \frac{1}{M_B} \log \left[ \frac{P(c=1|z_1)}{P(c=0|z_1)} \cdot \ldots \cdot \frac{P(c=1|z_{M_B})}{P(c=0|z_{M_B})} \right]$$

$$\Rightarrow \frac{1 - P(c=0|B)}{P(c=0|B)} = \frac{[\prod_{m=1}^{M_B} P(c=1|z_m)]^{1/M_B}}{[\prod_{m=1}^{M_B} P(c=0|z_m)]^{1/M_B}}$$

$$\Rightarrow \begin{cases} P(c=1|B) \\ \quad = \dfrac{[\prod_{m=1}^{M_B} P(c=1|z_m)]^{1/M_B}}{[\prod_{m=1}^{M_B} P(c=1|z_m)]^{1/M_B} + [\prod_{m=1}^{M_B} P(c=0|z_m)]^{1/M_B}} \\[2ex] P(c=0|B) \\ \quad = \dfrac{[\prod_{m=1}^{M_B} P(c=0|z_m)]^{1/M_B}}{[\prod_{m=1}^{M_B} P(c=1|z_m)]^{1/M_B} + [\prod_{m=1}^{M_B} P(c=0|z_m)]^{1/M_B}} \end{cases} \quad (4)$$

Equation (4) is called a (normalized) *geometric average of posterior probabilities* (or an arithmetic mean of log-posterior) [10] of instances in the bag.

The collective assumption weights every instance inside a bag equally. The paper [12] presents a collective assumption with instance weights. It is called the (arithmetic) *weighted collective MI assumption* and simply utilizes weights of instances inside a bag to calculate the probability distribution

$$\check{P}(c|B) = \frac{1}{w_B} \sum_{m=1}^{M_B} w(z_m) \cdot P(c|z_m), \quad (5)$$

where $w : \mathcal{Z} \rightarrow \mathbb{R}^+$ is a weight function over instances and $w_B = \frac{1}{M_B} \sum_{z \in B} w(z)$ [10]. The probability distribution for a geometric weighted collective assumption can be calculated similarly. Finally, an aggregator function for the collective assumptions can be defined as follows:

$$g(B) = \begin{cases} 1 & \text{if } P(c=1|B) \geq P(c=0|B) \\ 0 & \text{otherwise} \end{cases}. \quad (6)$$

### 3.2  Multivariate Time Series in the MIL Framework

We incorporated multivariate time series into the MIL framework as follows; we consider $\forall n = \{1, \ldots, N\}$ a multivariate time series $X_n$ as one bag, and the observations of all $D$ variables at each time step $t \in \{1, \ldots, T_n\}$ as an instance of this bag. More formally, the bag $B_n$ of $X_n$ is defined as $B_n = \{x_1^{(n)}, x_2^{(n)}, \ldots, x_{T_n}^{(n)}\}$, where the class label of $X_n$ becomes the bag label of $B_n$. With this in mind, various multivariate time series having different lengths can be considered inside their own encapsulating bags, so that the expressiveness of the original values is maintained without rescaling the time series data.

## 4    Empirical Evaluation

### 4.1    Dataset and Task Description

We evaluate the performance of a classification in the MIL framework on multivariate time series data using several robust machine learning approaches specifically used for this kind of classification tasks. We evaluate our models for different settings such as for the data obtained by different imputations methods, by boosting and bagging.

*PhysioNet Challenge 2012 Dataset (PhysioNet).* This dataset is from PhysioNet Challenge 2012 [38] which is a publicly available[1] collection of multivariate clinical time series records of 12000 intensive care unit (ICU) patients. Each record is a multivariate time series of 48 h after ICU admission of a corresponding patient and contains 36 variables such as *mean arterial blood pressure, heart rate, respiratory rate,* etc. The dataset is divided into three sets (Set-A, Set-B, Set-C) each having 4000 multivariate time series. Set-C is designated for the reviews of the challenge, so we did not use it. We used Set-A and Set-B in our experiments. We perform the mortality prediction task on this dataset to predict whether a patient dies in a hospital after 48 h. We designate the class of death as a positive class (with the label of 1) and the class of survival as a negative class (with the label of 0). This is a binary classification task. There are 554 positively labeled multivariate time series, and 3446 negatively labeled multivariate time series in Set-A. For Set-B and Set-C, these numbers are 568–3432, and 585–3415 respectively. The class imbalance for each of these sets is roughly 14% (positive)– 86% (negative). We test different approaches to handle the class imbalance, i.e. through undersampling or oversampling.

Because the PhysioNet dataset is collected from Electronic Health Records, it has missing values. We replace missing values with **Mean** and **Forward** methods. Apart from that (similarly to [8]), we combine the invasive blood pressure variables DiasABP (diastolic arterial blood pressure), SysABP (systolic arterial blood pressure) and MAP (mean arterial blood pressure) with noninvasive ones, i.e., NIDiasABP, NISysABP and NIMAP respectively which effectively reduces the number of variables to 33. The combination of variables enables us to reduce the number of missing values as well. More formally, it is possible to obtain one value from the other using the following formula [6]:

$$MAP = \frac{(2 \cdot DiasABP + SysABP)}{3}. \tag{7}$$

---

[1] https://physionet.org/content/challenge-2012/.

In this case, if a MAP value is not present for some time step, then it can be calculated from the existing DiasABP and SysABP value of that time step. The similar approach is also used for missing DiasABP and SysABP values. After that, it is possible to replace missing values with the computed values. The main benefit here is the replacement of missing values with the real values, instead of imputed ones. During the combination, if there are existing values for invasive and noninvasive counterparts for the same time step, then we prefer an invasive measurement instead of noninvasive one [33]. Our combination of variables differs from [8] in a few more nuances. For example, instead of using raw timestamps in each multivariate time series, they take hourly samples of observations. Moreover, they perform forwarding through hourly/2-hourly samples in their forward imputation method. In terms of expressiveness, we do not apply such stages.

## 4.2   Machine Learning Approaches

To benchmark the multivariate time series classification in the MIL framework, we used different multi-instance learners from the WEKA machine learning workbench (version 3.7.2) [18]. The multi-instance learners are available under the *weka.classifiers.mi* package. We explicitly tested the following learners:

- *weka.classifiers.mi.MILR* uses either the standard or collective multi-instance assumption, but within a logistic regression. We picked the collective assumption with the geometric average of posterior probabilities which outperformed other assumptions for this learner.
- *weka.classifiers.mi.MIWrapper* [13] is a simple Wrapper class for applying standard propositional (feature vector) learners to multi-instance data. As the first step, MIWrapper gathers instances from all bags, and labels each instance with the label of its bag. This step creates a propositional (i.e. single-instance) version of the multi-instance dataset. Then, it weights all instances such that each bag has equal cumulative total weight. Different weighting schemes are available; we used unit weighting for propositional instances. After weighting, a single-instance (feature vector) learner is utilized for this propositional dataset. During the learning phase, the single-instance learner estimates class probabilities for all instances inside the bag for which the bag label should be generated. The generated bag label is simply the mean (arithmetic or geometric) of the estimated class probabilities of the corresponding instances [10]. For MIWrapper, we selected
  - *weka.classifiers.trees.RandomForest*
  - *weka.classifiers.functions.Logistic*
  as propositional learners and used the collective assumption with the geometric average which performed better than other collective assumptions. The latter class refers to the logistic regression (LR). Both LR and the random forest (RF) are widely used in health care applications [3,8,19,40].
- *weka.classifiers.mi.SimpleMI* reduces multi-instance data into single-instance data by taking an arithmetic or geometric average of variable (feature) values of instances or by creating a minimax feature space from instances

inside each bag. After reducing each bag into a single instance or feature vector, single-instance learners such as the random forest or the logistic regression can be used for modeling. In our experiments, we make use of the arithmetic average of variable values which provides higher performance. This scheme is equivalent to the feature space obtained by *Mean* statistical summary having the same number of variables (features) as of multi-instance data (see Sect. 1).

- *weka.classifiers.meta.RealAdaBoost* is a class for boosting a binary classifier using the Real Adaboost method [16]. We utilized this class to boost binary classifiers which are wrapped by MIWrapper and SimpleMI.
- *weka.classifiers.meta.Bagging* [5] is a class for bagging a classifier to reduce variance. It can perform a classification and regression depending on the base learner. We used this class as a meta learner for MILR and for the logistic regression wrapped by SimpleMI.

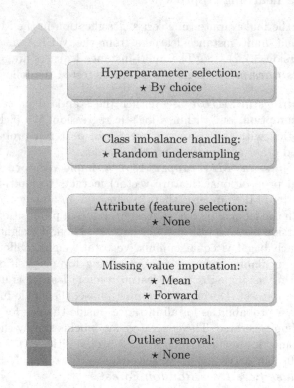

**Fig. 1.** Multi-instance learning pipeline

Remember that a bagging (**b**ootstrap **aggregating**) [5] and boosting are ensemble machine learning methods to enhance base classifiers for a better predictive performance. Thus, there is a clear distinction between an ensemble method *bagging* and bags used in the MIL setting where each bag is a multiset instance.

In our study, we compare the performance of learners in the multi-instance context with the learners using the data obtained by SimpleMI (i.e. statistical summary representation). We use short names of learners for the demonstration of results such as SMI for SimpleMI, MIW for MIWrapper, RB for RealAdaBoost, BG for Bagging, RF for random forest and LR for logistic regression.

### 4.3 Multi-instance Learning Pipeline

To make the data ready for multi-instance learners, the data preprocessing is performed through the pipeline presented in Fig. 1. More comprehensively:

– Physionet dataset is a dataset containing the first 48 h of recordings after ICU admission. After 48 h, either a patient died or survived. Patients are admitted to the intensive care unit (ICU) in extreme circumstances. In this case, their health recordings may contain values deviating from the rest of the population in the ICU. However, these values are still valid and might not be taken as outliers. From the statistical point of view, traditional outlier removal methods (e.g. standard deviation based or median absolute deviation based) can easily strip out this information from the patients' data. For the sake of expressiveness, we do not explicitly perform outlier removal. We also observed that the authors of Physionet dataset successfully removed the medically implausible values during the dataset creation [25].
– For imputing missing values we used mean and forward methods which show decent results [8,32].
  • **Mean** (shortly M) [8] – a mean value for each of 33 variables is computed from the existing measurements in all multivariate time series in Set-A. Then, missing values for each variable in Set-A and Set-B are replaced by the corresponding mean value.
  • **Forward** (shortly F) [32] – in this strategy, we impute the missing value $x_d^t$ of a variable $d$ at a time step $t$ as follows; if there is at least one measurement which is recorded previously for a variable $d$ at a time $t' < t$, we perform a forward imputation by $x_d^t \leftarrow x_d^{t'}$. If there is no measurement that is recorded previously (or if the variable is completely empty), then we compute the median over all existing measurements in Set-A and replace the missing values by the respective median in both Set-A and Set-B.
– We do not perform an attribute selection for Physionet dataset. Our purpose is to make the version of the dataset comparable to the dataset used in [8] which also applies a variable combination we explained in Sect. 4.1.
– The class imbalance for each subset (Set-A, Set-B, Set-C) of Physionet dataset is around 14% (positive)–86% (negative). To handle this problem, we make use of SpreadSubsample class (shortly SS) from the package *weka.filters.supervised.instance* with a distribution 1.0 which is a random undersampling effectively reducing the negative class to the size of the positive class (a class imbalance of 50%-50%). We also checked random oversampling of the positive class to the size of negative class using the respective

WEKA class. However, this caused higher false negatives in our experiments. Oversampling is a data generation process and we think that more sophisticated oversampling strategy is required to mimic the existing multivariate time series data (especially for the health-related data).

– Finally, we set hyperparameters for machine learning algorithms by choice. For instance, for the RF, we set the number of trees to 100 (which demonstrated better performance and is tolerable in terms of runtime). For boosting algorithms, the number of boosting iterations is selected to be 10. For runtime constraints, we do not apply hyperparameter tuning through the cross-validation (CV) or grid search, because the learners are wrapped by classes where each wrapper has its own parameters. The other parameters of learners are WEKA defaults.

### 4.4   Experimental Setup

In our experiments, two different setups are tested. For each setup, an AUROC value of the classification is reported. The AUROC is a standard metric for evaluating the performance of classifiers. The *weka.classifiers.Evaluation* class is applied for the evaluation.

1. Learners are trained on Set-A and tested on Set-B in 10 runs. In each run, Set-A is randomly shuffled with a different random seed and then a train/test procedure applied. Finally, the results are averaged.
2. Predictive models are built using a stratified CV on Set-A and then an average AUROC is reported. Some papers [8] only used this setup, since at their time of writing, class labels were not available for Set-B and Set-C.

### 4.5   Interpretation of Results

Results are generated for different configurations. Each configuration is titled by the short names of learners and short names of pipeline stages. For instance, RB-MIW-RF-M-SS means that the data are mean imputed (M), a class imbalance is handled by SpreadSubsample (SS) (undersampled) and the resulting data are learned by the random forest (RF) which is wrapped by MIWrapper (MIW) and boosted by RealAdaBoost (RB). For BG-SMI-LR-F-SS, the data are forward imputed (F), a class imbalance is handled by SpreadSubsample (SS) (undersampled), then the data are transformed into a single-instance format (using *Mean* statistical summary) by SimpleMI (SMI), and the resulting data are learned by LR which is enhanced by Bagging (BG). The other configurations can be understood similarly.

The bagging is a technique to reduce the complexity of models that overfit during training, whereas boosting is used to increase the complexity of models subject to high bias, thus, handles underfitting during training. We observe that the RF is better enhanced by RealAdaBoost and LR is by Bagging through systematically testing different meta learners that WEKA provides. These boosting and bagging combinations yield more balanced learners for our experiments where we compare them to non-bagged and non-boosted variants. In this manner, the RF is boosted by RealAdaBoost in both multi-instance and propositional settings. MILR and the propositional logistic regression (SMI-LR) are enhanced by Bagging. The only exception is a logistic regression in the multi-instance setting which is wrapped by MIWrapper; we find that RealAdaBoost improves the base learner better than Bagging (especially for the mean imputation) so that we provide the results for the former meta learner. The main benefit of RealAdaBoost is that it improves the base learner by adapting predicted class probabilities of instances [34] which is useful in a multi-instance setting – a bag label is determined collectively by the probability distribution of labels of its instances.

**Table 1.** Model performances measured by average AUROC score for mortality prediction. The weight of each instance in a bag is 1. After propositional conversion unit-weighting for each single instance is still maintained. The results are generated by train/test procedure through 10 runs.

| Mortality prediction on PhysioNet dataset | | | |
|---|---|---|---|
| MILR | | BG-MILR | |
| MILR-M-SS | 0.8051 | BG-MILR-M-SS | 0.8075 |
| MILR-F-SS | 0.8094 | BG-MILR-F-SS | 0.8098 |
| MIW-RF | | MIW-LR | |
| MIW-RF-M-SS | 0.7736 | MIW-LR-M-SS | 0.7645 |
| MIW-RF-F-SS | 0.8146 | MIW-LR-F-SS | 0.8094 |
| RB-MIW-RF | | RB-MIW-LR | |
| RB-MIW-RF-M-SS | 0.7808 | RB-MIW-LR-M-SS | 0.8035 |
| RB-MIW-RF-F-SS | **0.8190** | RB-MIW-LR-F-SS | 0.8044 |
| SMI-RF | | SMI-LR | |
| SMI-RF-M-SS | 0.8212 | SMI-LR-M-SS | 0.8051 |
| SMI-RF-F-SS | 0.8224 | SMI-LR-F-SS | 0.8094 |
| RB-SMI-RF | | BG-SMI-LR | |
| RB-SMI-RF-M-SS | 0.8301 | BG-SMI-LR-M-SS | 0.8075 |
| RB-SMI-RF-F-SS | **0.8313** | BG-SMI-LR-F-SS | 0.8098 |

In Table 1, we report the results of the first experimental setup (train/test) and in Table 2, we show the results for the second setup (stratified CV). In both tables, we tested all configurations for unweighted instances in the bag, namely the weight of every instance is 1 in each bag. In the experiments, a unit weighting is also maintained after propositional conversion. In multi-instance configurations, bags are also unit-weighted.

We observe that the settings we set for MILR, BG-MILR and SMI-LR, BG-SMI-LR respectively, resulted in a similar predictive performance. MILR and BIG-MILR applies a geometric average of posterior probabilities of instances inside a bag to obtain a bag label, however, SMI-LR and BG-SMI-LR uses *Mean* statistical summary of instances inside a bag during training. We notice that a bagging slightly improves MILR and SMI-LR performances for both setups.

As compared to MILR (in MILR-M-SS), MIW-LR demonstrates slightly lower performance for the mean imputation (MIW-LR-M-SS). The MIWrapper (MIW) performs a propositional conversion and generates a bag label from the estimated class probabilities of bag's instances. Remember that the mean imputation replaces all missing values with the corresponding mean value. Thus, it inherently causes the creation of more similar propositional instances (after conversion) from each bag and across the bags as compared to the forward imputation which in turn negatively affects the performance of a bag label prediction from the class probabilities of respective instances for the LR. The similar phenomenon also occurs for MIW-RF with the mean imputation (namely, MIW-RF-M-SS). The forward imputation enables MIW-RF (in MIW-RF-F-SS) and MIW-LR (in MIW-LR-F-SS) to show similar or better performance than MILR (i.e. MILR-F-SS).

**Table 2.** Model performances measured by average AUROC score for mortality prediction. The weight of each instance in a bag is 1. After propositional conversion unit-weighting for each single instance is still maintained. The results are generated by 10-fold CV on Set-A.

| Mortality prediction on PhysioNet dataset | | | |
|---|---|---|---|
| MILR | | BG-MILR | |
| MILR-M-SS | 0.7540 | BG-MILR-M-SS | 0.7583 |
| MILR-F-SS | 0.7679 | BG-MILR-F-SS | 0.7685 |
| MIW-RF | | MIW-LR | |
| MIW-RF-M-SS | 0.7537 | MIW-LR-M-SS | 0.7274 |
| MIW-RF-F-SS | 0.7917 | MIW-LR-F-SS | 0.7685 |
| RB-MIW-RF | | RB-MIW-LR | |
| RB-MIW-RF-M-SS | 0.7563 | RB-MIW-LR-M-SS | 0.7518 |
| RB-MIW-RF-F-SS | **0.7977** | RB-MIW-LR-F-SS | 0.7639 |
| SMI-RF | | SMI-LR | |
| SMI-RF-M-SS | 0.8113 | SMI-LR-M-SS | 0.7540 |
| SMI-RF-F-SS | 0.7939 | SMI-LR-F-SS | 0.7679 |
| RB-SMI-RF | | BG-SMI-LR | |
| RB-SMI-RF-M-SS | **0.8159** | BG-SMI-LR-M-SS | 0.7583 |
| RB-SMI-RF-F-SS | 0.8101 | BG-SMI-LR-F-SS | 0.7685 |

The variants of MIWrapper (MIW) with RealAdaBoost, namely, RB-MIW-RF and RB-MIW-LR improves the performance of MIW-RF and MIW-LR respectively (except for MIW-LR-F-SS). Remember that 10 runs/folds used in both experimental setups averages the predictive performance of the boosted variants (where each variant internally does 10 iterations). Thus, even an averaging in our setups enables boosted variants enhance their non-boosted counterparts.

The multi-instance configuration with the highest performance in Table 1 is RB-MIW-RF-F-SS with **0.8190** average AUROC which improves upon MIW-RF-F-SS having 0.8146 average AUROC. We observe the similar case in Table 2.

In Table 1, the single-instance configuration with *Mean* statistical summary shows the highest performance in RB-SMI-RF-F-SS with **0.8313** average AUROC. In our tests, it is even higher than *Geometric Center* and *Minimax* statistical summaries that SimpleMI class provides for the same configuration. It seems that *Mean* statistical summary better reflects original data points than the other summaries. In our experiments, we utilize *Mean* statistical summary for all configurations containing SimpleMI (SMI).

The single-instance configuration with *Mean* statistical summary showing the highest performance is RB-SMI-RF-M-SS having **0.8159** average AUROC in Table 2. In general, the CV (Table 2) does not yield higher results as compared to the train/test setup in Table 1. The main reason of that is the number of instances used in both setups. The train/test setup has more instances to learn/test (since it trains on Set-A and tests on Set-B) than the CV setup (which does a stratified CV on Set-A). In both setups, the forward imputation generally yields better results as compared to the mean imputation.

Our experimental setups show that the multi-instance learners are capable of performing multivariate time series classification in a decent level. We expect that they can show even higher performance after more careful data preparation and in more sophisticated parameter configurations.

## 5   Discussion

### 5.1   The Other Multi-instance Learners

In our tests, we comparably examined different multi-instance learners from the ***weka.classifiers.mi*** package in terms of their heuristics, hyperparameter space and predictive performance with respect to the learners presented in Sect. 4.2. For some of them, the implementation is not relevant for a multivariate time series representation. For the others, they either need many hyperparameters to be adjusted or do not provide an adequate predictive performance in their default settings. For instance:

– ***weka.classifiers.mi.MIBoost*** is a multiple instance AdaBoost method which considers the geometric average of posteriors of instances in the bag and takes the expectation for a bag inside the loss function [15]. Analogous to MIWrapper, it is possible to wrap RF and LR by MIBoost. The default number of boosting iterations is set to 10 by WEKA.
  • The one drawback of this method is that AdaBoost adapts itself according to the amount of error on predicted classes of instances [34] rather than class probabilities of instances like RealAdaBoost. Thus, it may not be effective in a multi-instance setting.

- Another drawback is that it internally converts all instances in the bag to the propositional format and weights each propositional instance by *total number of propositional instances after conversion*/(*total number of bags * total number of instances in the corresponding bag*). This weighting scheme is not appropriate for a multivariate time series representation and we indeed obtained relatively low predictive performance in the tests with respect to our chosen learners (i.e. MILR, MIW-LR, MIW-RF and their boosted/bagged variants).

– *weka.classifiers.mi.MISVM* is a class which implements MISVM [2] (Maximum pattern Margin Formulation of MIL). It internally applies the algorithm called *weka.classifiers.functions.SMO* [28] to solve multiple instance problem.

- We observed that its predictive performance was relatively low (in default settings) as compared to the chosen learners. Moreover, many hyperparameter configurations need to be maintained (such as a kernel type, a complexity constant, a cache size, a usage of lower order terms, etc.) [2].

Our findings showed that the learners we chose in our experimental setups were suitable for the multivariate time series representation in the MIL setting, required less hyperparameter space to adjust and displayed a decent classification performance in a straightforward comparison.

## 5.2  Hyperparameters

We investigated different hyperparameters for our learners to find the proper ones. In WEKA (version 3.7.2), the RF implementation has 10 trees by default. Instead, we used 100 trees in our experiments. We additionally observed that 1000 trees slightly improved the performance of configurations containing the RF in Sect. 4.5. However, this number brought additional runtime overhead (i.e. for the configurations which also employed RealAdaBoost).

Both MILR and the original LR have a parameter to set the ridge in the log-likelihood. The former used $10^{-6}$ and the latter used $10^{-8}$ as its ridge parameter which resulted in an adequate performance both in multi-instance and single-instance settings.

As a multi-instance hyperparameter, our selected multi-instance learners employed the collective assumption with the geometric average of posteriors in all experiments which outperformed the other assumptions including the standard assumption and the collective assumption with the arithmetic average.

## 5.3  Future Work

In this section, we discuss the future insights to improve the predictive capabilities of multi-instance learners for multivariate time series analysis.

**Weighting Instances in the Bag.** When a multivariate time series is represented in the MIL framework, each instance in a bag is treated equally without a time order (similarly to statistical summaries where the time order is also discarded). In this case, every instance in each bag has a weight of 1 by default. To incorporate the temporal order to the multi-instance learning, we checked weighted inner bag instances in one of our tests. Our weighting scheme is straightforward. In Physionet dataset every time step of a multivariate time series has its own timestamp value. That value is in $hh{:}mm$ format, namely, numbers of hours and number of minutes after ICU admission. We converted each timestamp value to minutes. More formally, for each multivariate time series $X_n$, $\forall n \in \{1, \ldots, N\}$ in $\mathcal{D}$, all respective timestamp minutes are summed up. Then for each $t$-th observations of $D$ variables, i.e. $x_t \in X_n$, $\forall t \in \{1, \ldots, T_n\}$, $x_t$ is weighted as the ratio of its timestamp minutes divided by the corresponding sum. Finally, the weighted instances are put to the respective bag $B_n$. In this weighting scheme, instances close to the 48-h threshold gain more weight in the temporal order. For this scheme, the weighted collective assumption of the MIL framework can be utilized for generating class labels of bags (see (Eq. 5)). Our findings and future proposals for this and other custom weighting schemes are given in the next two paragraphs.

We observed that a WEKA implementation of multi-instance learners does not support such a weighting scheme. We discovered that our weighting scheme is supported by SimpleMI (which performs a single-instance transformation) where *Mean* statistical summary also averages the weights of inner bag instances so that after transformation by SimpleMI (SMI), propositional instances gain different weights. In fact, this weighting scheme improved the performance of the configurations using SMI-LR, SMI-RF, BG-SMI-LR and RB-SMI-RF presented in Sect. 4.5. It is because the original Logistic and RandomForest class from WEKA can handle weighted instances. The highest performance is obtained in RB-SMI-RF-F-SS configuration with the average AUROC performance of **0.8427** (in the train/test setup) which is a decent improvement over the unweighted configuration which displays 0.8313. This insight augments our expectations that the multi-instance learners supporting such custom weighting schemes can get a similar performance improvement.

As a future work, one can port custom weighting schemes to multi-instance learners (e.g. MILR and MIWrapper) by modifying WEKA source code. Then, the similar tests from Sect. 4.5 can be performed to reveal the effectiveness.

**Propositionalisation of Multivariate Time Series Data by Sophisticated Approaches.** Remember that SimpleMI class is designed to generate three different statistical summaries, namely *Geometric Center, Mean* and *Minimax* from the multi-instance representation of multivariate time series data. There are also approaches to propositionalise multi-instance data by decision trees [41] and more ingeniously by random forests [14]. These approaches can create more advanced feature spaces from the multi-instance representation in contrast to the statistical summaries. As a future work, every multivariate time series can be propositionalised by one of these approaches in its MIL format and then the resulting data can be fed to traditional ML algorithms for classification.

# 6   Conclusion

In this paper, we benchmarked multi-instance learning for clinical multivariate time series classification (on the mortality prediction task). We utilized different multi-instance learners to study the time series data in multi-instance format and then used multi-instance assumptions of the MIL framework to generate class labels for each multivariate time series. We evaluated the multi-instance learners in different experimental setups and configurations using the well-known metric named AUROC in both multi-instance and propositional settings. We compared their performance to the performance of traditional machine learning algorithms using statistical summaries. Despite the fact that we focused on the mortality prediction using time series data collected in intensive care units, we believe that the multi-instance representation will be also useful for other tasks such as a length-of-stay prediction, phenotype classification, and psychological decompensation prediction. It will be also interesting to see the generalization of multi-instance learners on the other healthcare datasets such as MIMIC-III [26], EEG database dataset [4] and ICU dataset [29].

## 6.1   Code Availability

For the sake of reproducing the results obtained in this work, all our source code is published in a public repository[2].

# References

1. Amores, J.: Multiple instance classification: review, taxonomy and comparative study. Artif. Intell. **201**, 81–105 (2013)
2. Andrews, S., Tsochantaridis, I., Hofmann, T.: Support vector machines for multiple-instance learning. In: Advances in Neural Information Processing Systems, vol. 15, pp. 561–568. MIT Press (2003)
3. Awad, A., Bader-El-Den, M., McNicholas, J., Briggs, J., El-Sonbaty, Y.: Predicting hospital mortality for intensive care unit patients: time-series analysis. Health Inform. J. **26**(2), 1043–1059 (2019). https://doi.org/10.1177/1460458219850323
4. Begleiter, H.: UCI machine learning repository: EEG database data set (1999). https://archive.ics.uci.edu/ml/datasets/eeg+database
5. Breiman, L.: Bagging predictors. Mach. Learn. **24**(2), 123–140 (1996). https://doi.org/10.1007/BF00058655
6. Brunner, L.S.: Brunner & Suddarth's Textbook of Medical-Surgical Nursing, vol. 1. Lippincott Williams & Wilkins (2010)
7. Carbonneau, M.A., Cheplygina, V., Granger, E., Gagnon, G.: Multiple instance learning: a survey of problem characteristics and applications. Pattern Recogn. **77**, 329–353 (2018)
8. Che, Z., Purushotham, S., Cho, K., Sontag, D., Liu, Y.: Recurrent neural networks for multivariate time series with missing values. Sci. Rep. **8**(1), 1–12 (2018)
9. Dietterich, T.G., Lathrop, R.H., Lozano-Pérez, T.: Solving the multiple instance problem with axis-parallel rectangles. Artif. Intell. **89**(1–2), 31–71 (1997)

---

[2] https://github.com/CavaJ/time-series-analysis.

10. Foulds, J., Frank, E.: A review of multi-instance learning assumptions. Knowl. Eng. Rev. **25**(1), 1–25 (2010)
11. Foulds, J., Smyth, P.: Multi-instance mixture models and semi-supervised learning. In: Proceedings of the 2011 SIAM International Conference on Data Mining, pp. 606–617. SIAM (2011)
12. Foulds, J.R.: Learning instance weights in multi-instance learning. Ph.D. thesis, The University of Waikato (2008)
13. Frank, E.T., Xu, X.: Applying propositional learning algorithms to multi-instance data. Technical report, University of Waikato, Department of Computer Science, Hamilton, NZ, June 2003
14. Frank, E., Pfahringer, B.: Propositionalisation of multi-instance data using random forests. In: Cranefield, S., Nayak, A. (eds.) AI 2013. LNCS (LNAI), vol. 8272, pp. 362–373. Springer, Cham (2013). https://doi.org/10.1007/978-3-319-03680-9_37
15. Freund, Y., Schapire, R.E.: Experiments with a new boosting algorithm. In: Thirteenth International Conference on Machine Learning, pp. 148–156. Morgan Kaufmann, San Francisco (1996)
16. Friedman, J., Hastie, T., Tibshirani, R.: Additive logistic regression: a statistical view of boosting. Ann. Stat. **95**(2), 337–407 (2000)
17. Guan, X., Raich, R., Wong, W.K.: Efficient multi-instance learning for activity recognition from time series data using an auto-regressive hidden Markov model. In: International Conference on Machine Learning, pp. 2330–2339 (2016)
18. Hall, M., Frank, E., Holmes, G., Pfahringer, B., Reutemann, P., Witten, I.H.: The WEKA data mining software: an update. SIGKDD Explor. **11**(1), 10–18 (2009)
19. Harutyunyan, H., Khachatrian, H., Kale, D.C., Steeg, G.V., Galstyan, A.: Multitask learning and benchmarking with clinical time series data. arXiv preprint arXiv:1703.07771 (2017)
20. Herrera, F., et al.: Multiple instance learning. In: Herrera, F., et al. (eds.) Multiple Instance Learning, pp. 17–33. Springer, Cham (2016). https://doi.org/10.1007/978-3-319-47759-6_2
21. Hesse, B.W., Ahern, D., Beckjord, E.: Oncology Informatics: Using Health Information Technology to Improve Processes and Outcomes in Cancer. Academic Press, Cambridge (2016)
22. Howie, J.G., Heaney, D.J., Maxwell, M., Walker, J.J., Freeman, G.K., Rai, H.: Quality at general practice consultations: cross sectional survey. BMJ **319**(7212), 738–743 (1999)
23. Huang, Y., Wang, W., Wang, L., Tan, T.: Multi-task deep neural network for multi-label learning. In: 2013 IEEE International Conference on Image Processing, pp. 2897–2900. IEEE (2013)
24. Jafari, A., Gandhi, S., Konuru, S.H., Hairston, W.D., Oates, T., Mohsenin, T.: An EEG artifact identification embedded system using ICA and multi-instance learning. In: 2017 IEEE International Symposium on Circuits and Systems (ISCAS), pp. 1–4. IEEE (2017)
25. Johnson, A.E., Dunkley, N., Mayaud, L., Tsanas, A., Kramer, A.A., Clifford, G.D.: Patient specific predictions in the intensive care unit using a Bayesian ensemble. In: 2012 Computing in Cardiology, pp. 249–252. IEEE (2012)
26. Johnson, A.E., et al.: MIMIC-III, a freely accessible critical care database. Sci. Data **3**, 1–9 (2016)
27. Kandemir, M., Hamprecht, F.A.: Instance label prediction by Dirichlet process multiple instance learning. In: UAI, pp. 380–389 (2014)
28. Keerthi, S., Shevade, S., Bhattacharyya, C., Murthy, K.: Improvements to Platt's SMO algorithm for SVM classifier design. Neural Comput. **13**(3), 637–649 (2001)

29. Kohane, I.: UCI machine learning repository: ICU data set (1994). https://archive.ics.uci.edu/ml/datasets/ICU
30. Kotzias, D., Denil, M., Blunsom, P., de Freitas, N.: Deep multi-instance transfer learning. arXiv preprint arXiv:1411.3128 (2014)
31. Kraus, O.Z., Ba, J.L., Frey, B.J.: Classifying and segmenting microscopy images with deep multiple instance learning. Bioinformatics **32**(12), i52–i59 (2016)
32. Lipton, Z.C., Kale, D.C., Wetzel, R.: Modeling missing data in clinical time series with RNNs. arXiv preprint arXiv:1606.04130 (2016)
33. McMahon, N., Hogg, L., Corfield, A., Exton, A.: Comparison of non-invasive and invasive blood pressure in aeromedical care. Anaesthesia **67**(12), 1343–1347 (2012)
34. Nock, R., Nielsen, F.: A real generalization of discrete AdaBoost. Artif. Intell. **171**(1), 25–41 (2007)
35. Sadeghi, R., Banerjee, T., Romine, W.: Early hospital mortality prediction using vital signals. Smart Health **9**, 265–274 (2018)
36. Salamon, J., McFee, B., Li, P., Bello, J.P.: DCASE 2017 submission: multiple instance learning for sound event detection. In: Detection and Classification of Acoustic Scenes and Events 2017 (2017)
37. Sandberg, J.G., Johnson, L.N., Robia, M., Miller, R.B.: Clinician identified barriers to clinical research. J. Marital Fam. Ther. **28**(1), 61–67 (2002)
38. Silva, I., Moody, G., Scott, D.J., Celi, L.A., Mark, R.G.: Predicting in-hospital mortality of ICU patients: the PhysioNet/computing in cardiology challenge 2012. In: 2012 Computing in Cardiology, pp. 245–248. IEEE (2012)
39. Soleimani, H., Miller, D.J.: Semisupervised, multilabel, multi-instance learning for structured data. Neural Comput. **29**(4), 1053–1102 (2017)
40. Song, H., Rajan, D., Thiagarajan, J.J., Spanias, A.: Attend and diagnose: clinical time series analysis using attention models. In: Thirty-Second AAAI Conference on Artificial Intelligence (2018)
41. Weidmann, N., Frank, E., Pfahringer, B.: A two-level learning method for generalized multi-instance problems. In: Lavrač, N., Gamberger, D., Blockeel, H., Todorovski, L. (eds.) ECML 2003. LNCS (LNAI), vol. 2837, pp. 468–479. Springer, Heidelberg (2003). https://doi.org/10.1007/978-3-540-39857-8_42
42. Wu, J., Yu, Y., Huang, C., Yu, K.: Deep multiple instance learning for image classification and auto-annotation. In: Proceedings of the IEEE Conference on Computer Vision and Pattern Recognition, pp. 3460–3469 (2015)
43. Xu, X.: Statistical learning in multiple instance problems. Ph.D. thesis, The University of Waikato (2003)
44. Yan, Z., et al.: Multi-instance deep learning: discover discriminative local anatomies for bodypart recognition. IEEE Trans. Med. Imaging **35**(5), 1332–1343 (2016)
45. Zhang, Z.L., Zhang, M.L.: Multi-instance multi-label learning with application to scene classification. In: Advances in Neural Information Processing Systems, pp. 1609–1616 (2007)
46. Zhou, Z.H., Sun, Y.Y., Li, Y.F.: Multi-instance learning by treating instances as non-IID samples. In: Proceedings of the 26th Annual International Conference on Machine Learning, pp. 1249–1256 (2009)
47. Zhu, W., Lou, Q., Vang, Y.S., Xie, X.: Deep multi-instance networks with sparse label assignment for whole mammogram classification. In: Descoteaux, M., Maier-Hein, L., Franz, A., Jannin, P., Collins, D.L., Duchesne, S. (eds.) MICCAI 2017. LNCS, vol. 10435, pp. 603–611. Springer, Cham (2017). https://doi.org/10.1007/978-3-319-66179-7_69

# A Cloud-Native NGS Data Processing and Annotation Platform

Giannis Mouchakis[1], Babis Kostopoulos[1], Stasinos Konstantopoulos[1(✉)] [iD],
Ilias Kanellos[2], Anargiros Tzerefos[2], Thanasis Vergoulis[2],
and Thodoris Dalamagas[2]

[1] Institute and Informatics and Telecommunications, NCSR 'Demokritos',
Ag. Paraskevi, Greece
{gmouchakis,kostbabis,konstant}@iit.demokritos.gr

[2] Information Management Systems Institute, ATHENA RC, Marousi, Greece
{ilias.kanellos,tzerefos,vergoulis,dalamag}@athenarc.gr

**Abstract.** Low-cost and widely available Next-Generation Sequencing
(NGS) is revolutionizing clinical practice, paving the way for the realization of precision medicine. Applying NGS to clinical practice requires
establishing a complex loop involving sample collection and sequencing,
computational processing of the NGS outputs to identify variants, and
the interpretation of the variants to establish their significance for the
condition being treated. The computational tools that perform variant
calling have been extensively used in bioinformatics, but there are few
attempts to integrate them in a comprehensive, production-grade, Cloud-
native infrastructure able to scale to national levels. Furthermore, there
are no established interfaces for closing the loop between NGS machines,
computational infrastructure, and variant interpretation experts.

We present here the platform developed for the Greek National Precision Medicine Network for Oncology. The platform integrates bioinformatics tools and their orchestration, makes provisions for both experimental and clinical usage of variant calling pipelines, provides programmatic interfaces for integration with NGS machines and for analytics,
and provides user interfaces for supporting variant interpretation. We
also present benchmarking results and discuss how these results confirm
the soundness of our architectural and implementation choices.

**Keywords:** NGS data · Variant calling · Variant annotation ·
Cloud-native

## 1 Introduction

Low-cost and widely available *Next-Generation Sequencing (NGS)* is revolutionizing clinical practice and paves the way for the realization of precision medicine.

The work described here has received funding from the Greek General Secretariat for
Research and Innovation in the context of the Hellenic Network of Precision Medicine
on Cancer. See also https://oncopmnet.gr for more details.

E. K. Rezig et al. (Eds.): Poly 2021/DMAH 2021, LNCS 12921, pp. 121–132, 2021.
https://doi.org/10.1007/978-3-030-93663-1_10

Applying NGS to clinical practice requires establishing a complex loop involving sample collection and sequencing, *variant calling*, the computational processing of the NGS outputs to identify variants, and *variant annotation*, the interpretation of the variants to establish their significance for the condition being treated.

Computational tools for variant calling are computationally challenging processes, developed with parallelisation being a major design consideration. Both multi-threading of individual processes and the Map/Reduce paradigm have been extensively explored [1]. The advent of Cloud computing has also seen the appearance of specialized omics Cloud services that offer flexible scalability by porting these tools to remote infrastructures. Such service include those offered by the European ELIXIR project,[1] commercial services such as DNAnexus,[2] and services provided by the manufacturers of NGS engines such as Illumina.[3] Each of these services emphasises different aspects and features, ranging from open interfaces and software, ability to extend the bioinformatics toolset with custom tools, to tracking the lineage and provenance of data and experiments, and integrating with variant annotation databases and environments.

But there are few attempts to integrate a comprehensive, production-grade infrastructure able to scale to national levels. Furthermore, there are no established interfaces for closing the loop between NGS machines, computational infrastructure, and variant interpretation experts. Even more so, when one want to also include in the loop secondary medical research usage of the data produced by clinical usage.

In this paper we present an architecture that integrates bioinformatics tools and their orchestration, makes provisions for both experimental and clinical usage of variant calling pipelines, provides programmatic interfaces for integration with NGS machines and for medical analytics, and provides user interfaces for supporting variant interpretation.

We also present the implementation of this architecture as the end-to-end variant calling and annotation platform developed for the Greek National Precision Medicine Network for Oncology, and is in the final stages before entering productive clinical use.

## 2    Use Case-Driven Platform Design

The design of our platform was based on common processes followed by labs that support NGS processing for Precision Medicine applications. Our analysis for the distinct user roles in this context has identified the following user profiles and service needs:

- *Clinicians* have access to samples and NGS machines and need to get the NGS data processed by executing a *variant calling* workflow in order to get a VCF data structure that represents all variants found in the sample's DNA along

---

[1] Cf. https://www.elixir-europe.org.
[2] Cf. https://www.dnanexus.com.
[3] Cf. https://basespace.illumina.com.

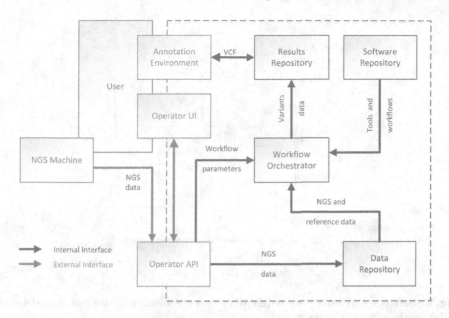

**Fig. 1.** Services and interfaces required in clinical use.

with useful metadata (e.g., coverage, statistical significance). Subsequently, they *annotate* each variant according to its clinical significance.

– *Bioinformaticians* provide the definition of the variant calling processing. In particular, they determine and configure the steps of the workflows and then test them by applying them on benchmark datasets and/or on the inputs from past clinical usage. They evaluate alternative tools and workflows on both their *efficacy* in correctly calling variants and their *computational efficiency*.

– *Medical researchers* seek to correlate variants, diseases, treatments, and outcomes and, in general, to perform data analytics queries on the repository of results of the platform. They provide access to the clinical data the need to join with the VCF data computed using this platform.

Based on these user profiles, in the next paragraphs, we will present use cases and the relevant requirements for our precision medicine platform.

In clinical usage (Fig. 1), the user needs to load the outputs of the NGS machine into the platform and select among parameter presets, such as the clinical purpose of the processing. The platform is pre-configured with the appropriate processing and the clinician cannot affect the workflows and tools used. This is facilitated by an *Operator API* through which the desktop computer directly attached to the NGS machine can upload inputs to the platform and the user can select and initiate the processing. A minimal *Operator UI* also provides a graphical environment for this usage.

When processing terminates, the infrastructure adds the resulting VCF data to the *Results Repository* that constitutes the clinical usage record of the

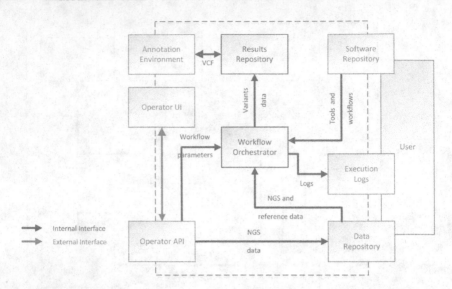

**Fig. 2.** Services and interfaces required to execute bioinformatics benchmarks and maintain the clinical pipelines.

infrastructure and also makes them available for annotation in a *Variant Annotation Environment*. These environments initialize the annotation by accessing databases of variants known to be significant for the specific condition and allow the user to edit these initial annotations. These manual annotations are also added to the Results Repository, available both for reporting and for medical research.

Bioinformatics usage (Fig. 2) ensures the efficacy and efficiency of the pre-configured processing made available to clinicians. Following standard practice in bioinformatics, this processing is organized as the application to the input data of a *workflow* that is the composition of several tools. A *Workflow Orchestrator* reads the definition of the workflow and then ensures that each tool referenced in the definition is given as input the output of the previous step in the pipeline and is appropriately parameterized and invoked. The software that implements each step is retrieved from a *Software Repository* and inputs and outputs are retrieved from and stored to a *Data Repository*.

Bioinformaticians update and evaluate *reference data* (effectively, inputs that are the same for all runs), bioinformatics tools, and workflows. Testing is performed by applying alternative workflows on benchmark data and on previous clinical data, so the infrastructure needs to clearly distinguish between clinical and experimental workflow execution. The former are restricted to the pre-configured workflow and write their output to the Results Repository; There is only one such output associated with each input. The latter are unrestricted computational experiments, are not meant to be used for any medical purposes, and there will be multiple runs and outputs for each input.

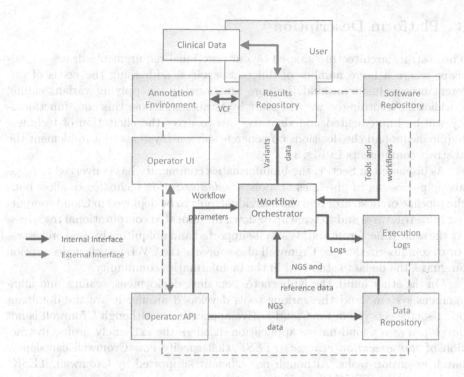

**Fig. 3.** Services and interfaces required for medical research.

Bioinformaticians have access to several components that are internal from the perspective of clinicians: They can directly access the data repository to provide benchmark and reference data, they can add and update the bioinformatics tools and workflows in the Software Repository, and they can read detailed *Operational Logs* from the execution of workflows so that they can debug and benchmark tools and workflows.

It should be noted at this point that the data in the platform does not constitute *personally identifiable information (PII)* either by itself or when combined with other information: The number of variants needed for precision medicine purposes is too small to identify individuals. Furthermore, NGS data, VCF data, and annotations are internally linked by a unique key, but this key is created by infrastructure and unrelated to any external PII or key.

Medical research users need to combine access to external data with access to the platform's Results Repository to extract statistics about how variants correlate with clinical and, possibly, other data (Fig. 3). This is facilitated by foreseeing linking the internal index used by the platform with an external index, such as a medical exam referral number. Medical research users who are authorized to access clinical and other sensitive PII can use this link to join variants with the clinical or personal data, without having to store PII in this platform.

# 3    Platform Description

The abstract architecture shaped by our functional requirements draws a landscape where a large number of different services, addressing the needs of different users, cluster around the core functionality of applying variant calling workflows. Accordingly, we will start by establishing how this core functionality will be implemented and then use this to drive the elicitation of technical requirements and the decisions on concrete software systems that implement the abstract components in Fig. 3.

As discussed in Sect. 1, the bioinformatics community has converged to organizing processing in pipelines of tools. *Containerization* technologies allow both the pipeline orchestrator and the individual tools to be deployed in Cloud computing infrastructures and to scale up or down the allocated computational resources. At the same time, Cromwell[4] is a well-supported and ubiquitously-used orchestrator of containerized tools. Cromwell also supports the CWL workflow description language, the de facto standard in the bioinformatics community.

On the other hand, the Kubernetes container deployment, scaling, and management system[5] and the various tools developed around it are the dominant open-source ecosystem for Cloud-native applications. Although Cromwell is not developed as a Cloud-native application, it offers the extremely useful abstraction of *task execution schemas (TES)*[6] that specify how Cromwell can deploy batch execution tasks. Although not officially supported by Cromwell, TESK[7] implements the TES API on Kubernetes.

## 3.1    Variant Calling

The entry point of the Variant Calling sub-system is the REST API. Through this API a user can submit pipelines, either provided by the system and stored in platform's software repository or custom pipelines defined by them. Either way the pipelines should be defined in CWL. The REST API is also the interface of the metadata subsystem so users can be informed about the status of pipelines submitted by them or their group and retrieve other pipeline metadata such as the exact pipeline inputs, the location of the output files in the object store, and pipelines logs.

Upon pipeline submission, the REST API submits the pipeline to Cromwell which handles the workflow orchestration. The orchestrator reads the CWL definition and starts the execution of every job defined there. Cromwell monitors the health of every job and handles job failures by retrying failed jobs whenever appropriate. It also ensures that each job is given the appropriate inputs from previous job outputs if needed. The metadata sub-system polls Cromwell to

---

[4] Cf. https://cromwell.readthedocs.io.
[5] cf. https://kubernetes.io.
[6] https://github.com/ga4gh/task-execution-schemas.
[7] Cf. https://github.com/elixir-cloud-aai/TESK.

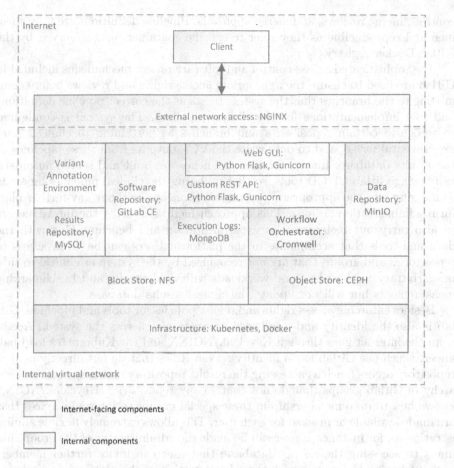

**Fig. 4.** Systems and components integrated to realize the architecture.

retrieve information about the status of the workflow, workflow logs and output files location in the object store (Fig. 4).

Task execution is handled by TESK. A task defines a set of input files, a set of (Docker) containers and commands to run, a set of output files, and some other logging and metadata. TESK implements TES on Kubernetes backends so each task is executed in a Kubernetes pod. It handles task execution, failure recovery, task resource assignments (CPU, RAM, block disk size), and housekeeping. Every task is scheduled by Kubernetes on nodes with available resources, is assigned block storage from NFS for temporary file storage and retrieves input files and stores output files in the system's object store.

Finally, we use an instance of Gitlab installed on our Kubernetes infrastructure[8] as our software repository and identity server. By storing the platform's predefined pipelines on a Git server we support version control, branch access

---

[8] Cf. https://docs.gitlab.com/charts.

controls, merge reviews, and merge approvals. Pipeline definitions are fully specified and reproducible as they refer to specific container images, served by the Gitlab Docker registry.

The sophisticated access control and software review mechanisms included in Gitlab are used to ensure the appropriate access rights and reviews before committing to the branches that the system trusts as the correct pipeline definitions and tool implementations for the clinical pipelines. The system is configured to recognize certain repositories and branches as pertaining to clinical, non-experimental usage, and to only write the VCF outputs from these pipelines to the results database. Images for these branches are built and served automatically using Gitlab CI/CD tools, so that updating the clinical pipelines amounts to merging into the appropriate (protected) branches, without any further platform administration actions. This approach facilitates using the infrastructure to also carry out bioinformatics experimentation and benchmarking with the data and tools that accumulate in the platform: Users can be given access to repositories and groups that are *not* recognized by the system as clinical to submit arbitrary workloads; these workloads will yield results and benchmarking measurements but will *not* update the clinical results database.

Besides enforcing access rights and review policies for tools and pipelines, Gitlab is also the identity and role-based access service across the system. Access from the internet goes through Keycloak/NGINX and the Kubernetes load balancer, which use Gitlab as an identity server. Roles that do not directly map to repository access (such as accessing the results repository) are mapped to a hierarchy of Gitlab groups that do not contain any repositories. Keycloak/NGINX knows how to map membership in these special groups to internal services that are made available or masked for each user. This allows extremely flexible administration as, for instance, a user can be made the administrator of the group that maps to accessing the results database; that user can invite further members without having to interact with the administration of the platform as a whole.

## 3.2   Variant Annotation

The Variant Annotation component of our platform automates and facilitates gathering genomic annotation data from external databases and combining them with VCF data coming from the Variant Calling step of the platform (Sect. 3.1). The integrated results are then stored in the platform's data space and they are ready to be used both for the production of patient reports and for answering research questions posed by medical researchers (see also Sect. 3.3).

In the core of this component, lies a deployment of the open-source Ensembl Variant Effect Predictor (VEP) software [3]. This tool can be configured to make use of data gathered from a set of desired external databases to analyse, annotate, and prioritize genomic variants in coding and non-coding regions. In our case, VEP is run with the default configuration that includes a variety of variant (e.g., COSMIC, dbSNP), protein (UniProt), algorithmic variant effect prediction (e.g., SIFT, Polyphen), variant allele frequency (e.g. gnomAD), clinical significance

(ClinVar), and scientific literature (PubMed) databases.[9] Further, we include data from the LOVD variation database (using VEP's LOVD plugin),[10] as well as variant nomenclature from HGVS. For efficiency reasons, the data of each source are stored locally in our platform's data space in the form of a collection of annotation database cache files, which can optionally be installed alongside VEP itself.

It is worth mentioning that for clinicians it is very crucial to have access to the most recent information; the results of new research may identify previously unknown variants or reveal and correct data for already studied ones. To make sure that the most recent information is used during the annotation step, we have developed a custom module which, at runtime, examines if the information gathered from important external databases (like ClinVar) is up-to-date. This module compares the cached version of the respective database to the most recently published one and loads the more recent version in the platform's data space, if needed.

By default, the output of VEP is given in the form of an annotated VCF file which contains integrated information from the input VCF and the selected external databases. This file is stored by itself in the Results Repository, however, to better support basic functionalities of the Variant Annotation component the same information is also loaded into a relational database schema. This database schema is a custom extension of LOVD [2], particularly tailored to accommodate storing and indexing VCF annotation data. This is achieved by the extension, modification, and addition of tables to the schema. For example, tables storing individual patient data in the original LOVD schema, only store referral numbers which correspond to particular NGS analyses in our version of LOVD (as per the requirements of Sect. 2 regarding PII data). Further, our schema extends LOVD with additional tables, e.g., for recording data from ClinVar, data gathered from clinical analysis report forms, filled out by clinicians during variant interpretation, etc.

The Variant Annotation component offers a functionality to browse the annotated data through a basic user interface that retrieves data from the aforementioned database and displays them in a tabular form. This interface allows the user to identify any variants of interest that should reported in the context of the investigation of the case of a particular patient. Finally, the users are also able to report newly identified links between variants and phenotypes, diseases, treatments, etc. These special-purpose contributions are very important since they may be related to particularities of the population being investigated by the lab that owns the platform and may be a very valuable addition for investigating research questions by medical researchers (see Sect. 3.3).

---

[9] An exhaustive list of annotation databases used with VEP's default configuration can be found here:
https://www.ensembl.org/info/docs/tools/vep/script/VEP_script_documentation.pdf.

[10] This plugin retrieves LOVD variation data from http://www.lovd.nl.

## 3.3   Knowledge Base

Our platform offers a Knowledge Base component which consists of the Results Repository along with a graphical UI-enabled analytics query engine. This knowledge base is intended for medical researchers and, hence, should not require familiarity with any database and/or respective query language. To facilitate this requirement, our platform uses metabase[11] running on top of mariaDB.

Metabase is an open source tool that allows for querying databases through user friendly UIs and without requiring users to be familiar with database query languages, or the underlying database schemas. It offers automatic explorations of the tables of databases it connects to, and allows for performing and saving queries on their data. It is particularly tailored to performing statistical queries, offering a variety of visualization options for the results, such as bar charts, pie charts, etc. Metabase supports connecting to a variety of different database management systems, such as MySQL, PostgreSQL, MongoDB, and others.

In the case of our platform's knowledge base, we use MariaDB as the underlying RDBMS. The core of this database is a collection of clinical variant interpretation data collected in a single table, alongside their connection to external exam referral data links (see Sect. 2). The clinical interpretation data stored originate from the Variant Annotation system of the platform, in particular, data from clinical interpretation result forms provided by the tool. These data concern the characterization of variants detected using the platform's workflow (i.e., pathogenic, uncertain/unknown significance), the genes on which they were found, alongside data pertaining to the particular analysis (i.e., the frequency and coverage of the variants).

Registered users of the platform may access the knowledge base through a web interface provided by metabase. The web interface facilitates access to the underlying database tables through an intuitive UI, through which users can ask simple questions by applying filters on values of the selected table's columns, and summarizations (i.e., aggregation queries and/or grouping) on the data by clicking on buttons provided for each of these functions. Further options are provided with regards to the display format of the results. By default these are shown in table format, but users may choose more appropriate visualizations, such as bar charts, or chronological time series, which are additionally customizable in terms of display (user can change display colors, types of axes, texts in legends, etc.).

Researchers querying the data are given the option to save each performed query. Saved queries, alongside their resulting visualizations, can be added to dashboards, which are readily available to users when accessing metabase. Various dashboards can focus on particular aspects of the data (e.g., statistical data of variants based on each gene they were found on), allowing for a fine grained organization and real time monitoring of the summary statistics recorded in the knowledge base. Finally, the various dashboards and saved questions make up a powerful tool that enables the sharing of results among different users of the platform.

---

[11] https://www.metabase.com.

## 4 Scalability Experiments and Discussion

In order to test the scalability of the platform, we collected execution time measurements from two different pipelines, with a different number of pipeline instances (runs) executing concurrently. The experiment was carried out on an installation of the system with 26 nodes. Each node has sufficient resources to execute two tasks (pipeline steps) where each task is allocated 8 CPU threads and 16 Gb RAM. Regarding storage, 8 nodes with a total of 36 Gb RAM are used to serve 6 Tb of disk space, split between transient NFS space and longer-term CEPH S3 space.

These resources suffice to execute the number of concurrent runs we show in Table 1 without scheduling and without deploying multiple runs on the same node. These execution times show that there is relatively small deviation between execution times and, consequently, it does not make sense to invest in migrating still-executing tasks to nodes where processing has finished and, in general, in more dynamic scheduling.

We also observe that processing times scale well, and bigger batches do not require linearly longer execution times. As discussed in the introduction, processing takes place in batches of roughly identical runs as soon as FASTQ inputs become available from an NGS engine. This motivates our approach of parallelizing the execution of multiple, independent of each other, runs. Furthermore, bioinformatics pipelines are computationally challenging and, subsequently, most of the execution time is consumed in actual computation rather than network and disk transfers. Having relatively small network and disk overhead means that we expect (and actually observe in Table 1) a sub-linear relationship between the number of runs in a batch and execution time for the batch.

However, some non-constant overhead and some noticeable execution time deviation is still visible in the results. This is due to the fact that input files are large and in our experiments (as foreseen by the use case) all runs are loaded at the same time, so that network and hard disk access becomes a temporary bottleneck at the beginning of the execution of each batch. The phenomenon

**Table 1.** Execution times (average, standard deviation, and maximum) for pipeline runs executing concurrently. Batch size gives the number of concurrently executing runs.

| Pipeline | Batch size | Input size | Execution time (min) | | |
| --- | --- | --- | --- | --- | --- |
| | | | Avg | Std dev | Max |
| Solid tumors | 2 | 970 Mb | 137 | 8 | 142 |
| | 4 | | 138 | 2 | 141 |
| | 8 | | 161 | 7 | 170 |
| Hematologic tum. | 2 | 675 Mb | 68 | 3 | 62 |
| | 4 | | 63 | 3 | 66 |
| | 8 | | 70 | 2 | 78 |

dampens after the first step, as it is highly unlikely that all runs terminate their steps at exactly the same time. This observation motivated our devoting to storage the considerable resources mentioned above.

## 5    Conclusions and Future Work

We presented the architecture and implementation of the end-to-end precision medicine platform developed for the Greek National Precision Medicine Network for Oncology. The architecture describes the platform as an ecosystem of Cloud-native applications offering services over a backbone that executes variant calling workflows. The platform is implemented using the Cromwell orchestrator and the Kubernetes container deployment, scaling, and management system. Our tests confirm that our architecture and our choices on which systems to integrate in order to materialize the architecture are sound, and fit well with our use cases and with the nature of bioinformatics pipelines.

Besides the focus on scalable Cloud deployment, another innovation is using an internal Gitlab instance as the provider not only of container images, but also of identity services and access right management. This maximally exploits the flexibility of the Gitlab role-based access control system and its UI for managing users and roles.

Future work includes defining a digital artifact that combines reference to specific container image tags, reference data versions, and outputs. Such an artifact will constitute a fully specified experiment that can be reliably reproduced on any instance of our architecture.

Further work will look into interesting integrations with client applications and external resources. This includes developing higher-level analytics interfaces, such as in R or as Python Notebooks. Another useful integration is with clinical databases that follow standard schemas such as the OHDSI Common Data Model,[12] facilitating the processing of medical research queries and analyses.

## References

1. Fjukstad, B., Bongo, L.A.: A review of scalable bioinformatics pipelines. Data Sci. Eng. **2**, 245–251 (2017)
2. Fokkema, I.F., Taschner, P.E., Schaafsma, G.C., Celli, J., Laros, J.F., den Dunnen, J.T.: LOVD v.2.0: the next generation in gene variant databases. Hum. Mutat. **32**(5), 557–563 (2011)
3. McLaren, W., et al.: The ensembl variant effect predictor. Genome Biol. **17**(1), 1–14 (2016)

---

[12] Cf. https://www.ohdsi.org/data-standardization.

# Administrative Health Data Representation for Mortality and High Utilization Prediction

Negin Asadzadehzanjani[(⊠)] and Janusz Wojtusiak

George Mason University, Fairfax, VA 22030, USA
{nasadzad, jwojtusi}@gmu.edu

**Abstract.** Administrative data, including medical claims, are frequently used to train machine learning-based models used for predicting patient outcomes. Despite many efforts in using administrative data, little systematic work has been done in understanding how the codes in such data should be represented before model construction. Traditionally, the presence/absence of codes representing diagnoses or procedures (Binary representation) over a fixed period (typically one year) is used. More recently, some studies included temporal information into data representation, such as counting, calculating time from diagnosis, and using multiple time windows. This paper investigates different methods of administrative data representation and more specifically diagnoses extracted from claims data before applying machine learning algorithms. Then the study compares two data representations (Binary and Temporal Min-Max) using two classification problems: one-year mortality prediction and high utilization of medical services prediction. The results indicated that Temporal Min-Max representation outperforms Binary representation in both predictive models. It was shown that the optimal way of representing the data is problem-dependent, thus optimization of representation parameters is required as part of the modeling.

**Keywords:** Medical claims · Data preprocessing · Supervised learning · Temporal machine learning

## 1 Introduction

Administrative data is a broad term referring to data that is used to process and document the registration and transactions for service delivery. Administrative data are collected to document a variety of services including education, healthcare, housing, taxation, etc. [1]. In healthcare, the most frequently used type of administrative data is medical claims. Often the terms administrative data and claims data are used interchangeably. Claims are essentially bills for provided medical services and include information required for the healthcare providers to receive payment. Therefore, the information included in claims data is limited to what is required by payers and typically corresponds to specific forms, such as CMS-1450 or CMS-1500 used by in the United States by Medicare [2]. Health claims databases keep records of interactions that occurred between healthcare providers and patients which include all the billing information provided by hospitals, nursing homes, clinics, pharmacies, public and

© Springer Nature Switzerland AG 2021
E. K. Rezig et al. (Eds.): Poly 2021/DMAH 2021, LNCS 12921, pp. 133–150, 2021.
https://doi.org/10.1007/978-3-030-93663-1_11

private insurance organizations such as Medicare/Medicaid and Blue Cross Blue Shield [3]. Claims data are typically generated at every encounter of the patient, which could be a procedure, a visit to doctors' office, admission to a hospital, or prescription [4].

For most patients, claims span longitudinally and provide a comprehensive summary of provided services when integrated by one payer. However, in certain situations, claims are incomplete, i.e., for dual- or triple-eligible patients. For example, Medicare beneficiaries may be also eligible for Medicaid and receive certain services from the Veteran's Affairs Health System for a military service-related disability. For research purposes, claims data are typically acquired from a single payer. For example, Medicare claims can be used to study populations 65 years and older in the United States. Private-pay claims data are typically used to study populations covered by a single insurer. In addition, it is sometimes possible to obtain integrated datasets from multiple payers (so-called all-payer data), but such data are often very costly and come with other types of limitations. Another reason for potential incompleteness of claims data is the inclusion of only billable items, i.e., those tied to reimbursement, which may miss additional services provided or the diagnosis that is not covered by insurance. In contrast to claims used for billing purposes, the Electronic Health Record (EHR) data are developed to store patient's information for clinical documentation and healthcare delivery. EHRs provide details not available in claims (i.e., lab values, vitals, clinical notes), but are limited to a single provider such as practice or health system [5]. Therefore, in applications that require integrated longitudinal data, medical claims are often the best choice in studying healthcare delivery and cost. Many studies have focused on using claims data to predict health outcomes including but not limited to mortality, readmissions, high utilization of services, disabilities. Depending on the specific application and population considered, the quality of these models varies. For example, the area under the Receiver-operator Curve (AUC) of the models for predicting mortality varies from 0.54 to 0.82 in different studies [6–8]. In predicting hospital readmissions and utilization of healthcare services, the AUC varied from 0.5 to 0.79 [9–11] and from 0.78 to 0.88 [12–14], respectively. Among the most frequently used methods to model outcomes from claims data are Random Forest, Logistic Regression, Gradient Boosting, Support Vector Machines, and Neural Networks. Beyond the prediction of outcomes, claims are frequently used in policy population-level studies, typically using traditional statistical methods [15–18].

The presented study focuses on data preprocessing steps applied to transform raw claims data into a final analytic file using ML methods. It is the authors' experience that data preprocessing and construction of the final analytic file is more important than algorithm hyperparameter tuning or selection of specific ML methods. In fact, this work considers data preprocessing steps as part of model tuning: the way data are represented affects the performance of specific types of models. For example, the representation of diagnoses not present in patient's record affects the performance of specific types of methods, but is irrelevant for other methods.

# 2  Methods

## 2.1  Claims Data Preprocessing

Due to high-dimensionality, heterogeneity, noise, incompleteness, sparseness, and errors in the data, modeling of health data, including claims, is difficult [19]. Therefore, data preprocessing as an essential step in developing ML-based models is the remedy to this problem. The reliability of the preprocessed data should be checked before training the model as any errors made in constructing the data would impact the accuracy of the models [20]. Data preprocessing refers to a number of steps required to transform raw data into the appropriate format for analysis [21]. In another definition, data preprocessing refers to the methods including constructing new attributes (attribute construction), removing irrelevant attributes (attribute selection) and modifying the attributes in which the initial representation space is improved [22]. In data preprocessing, the goal is to reduce the complexity of the data and extract the relevant attributes from the data, which can subsequently be used for analysis [23].

The types of information in claims data vary across different databases, but almost all claims datasets include date of service, diagnosis and procedure codes, provider information, site of service, charges and cost of healthcare delivery. They typically include demographic information including age (or date of birth), sex, race, and ethnicity, and sometimes education and income [24]. The claims databases usually provide a list of all variables in a dictionary, yet the information is often vague and requires good understanding of coding systems and healthcare processes to correctly analyze data. Claims data have information in the forms of code, date, text, symbols etc. each of which requires special preprocessing steps for use in developing models. Claims data are typically structured, meaning that the data are stored in organized format, with little or no information provided as free text. This makes them suitable for data analysis and interpretation. In this structured data, there are standard healthcare coding systems (administrative codes) that are either universally or locally utilized by the healthcare systems. These include International Classification of Diseases (ICD-9 or ICD-10) codes, Current Procedural Terminology (CPT), Healthcare Common Procedure Coding System (HCPCS) codes, etc. These codes refer to procedure or diagnosis codes that are used to report diagnoses, encounters, injuries, morbidities etc. withing the healthcare system. Diagnosis and procedure codes assigned to medical claims are known to contain errors and inaccuracies. Despite these errors, they are popular source of information in predictive modeling and there are many successful applications of these administrative codes in predicting health outcomes. This manuscript focuses on the preprocessing of these administrative codes.

Figure 1 shows how the raw claims data are transformed into an "analytic file" for training and testing of classification and regression models. Claims data usually consist of tables from multiple sources including inpatient files, outpatient files, carrier files etc. collected over many years and stored in separate files. Different files/tables correspond to types of claims and are separated because they include different fields. Depending on the application, relevant information including administrative codes, demographic information, patient IDs, claim IDs, various dates etc. is first extracted from claims. Then one or more inclusion/exclusion criteria are applied to construct the targeted cohort from data. After defining the prediction time, the observation and prediction windows are defined in which input and output attributes are constructed, respectively. The attributes are then processed in multiple steps including aggregation, discretization, normalization, and handling missing and integrated if needed, resulting in creation of the final analytic file. The analytic files are in the matrix format where rows represent instances and columns represent constructed attributes in the data. A wide variety of steps are defined for data preprocessing in the literature and depending on the application and needs, some or all are used to prepare the final analytic table.

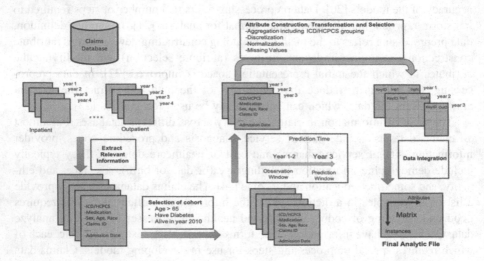

**Fig. 1.** An example process of transforming raw claims data into the final analytic file.

## 2.2    Methods of Representing Claims Data

Claims data, can be viewed as a sequence of claims that include one or more diagnosis codes recorded over time. They are irregularity spaced in time. The data are also potentially censored on both sides because of benefit eligibility and events such as death. Since most machine learning (ML) algorithms cannot handle records with variable number of attributes, some summary functions including Boolean representation and counting the occurrence of each event are used to aggregate the data and remove temporality before applying ML algorithms. This is not different from other health data such as EHRs.

The following sections describe increasingly complex approaches for representing diagnoses extracted from claims data. While these sections focus on diagnoses, the same methods can be applied to procedure codes.

**Binary Representation.** The simplest and most frequently used method is to represent presence/absence of diagnosis codes with a set of binary attributes (dummies). Let $Code_i$ be the administrative code representing a diagnosis code and C be the claim in the patient's record prior to the prediction time. Sometimes, the presence of codes within a certain time window is used instead of entire patient record. Either looking into entire records or a specific time frame, the frame is called the observation window. The administrative code ($Code_i$) associated with "C" is represented as 1 if the $Code_i$ belongs to claim C, 0 otherwise. The equation is given as follows:

$$Code_i = \begin{cases} 1 & \exists C \qquad : Code_i \in C \\ 0 & Otherwise \end{cases} \tag{1}$$

The above method however has the risk of information loss. Most health data collected during patient care are longitudinal, meaning that the patients are observed over a course of time. The health data have time-stamped entities, meaning that much of the information such as emergency visit, hospitalization or blood test are recorded with time. Moreover, the time each patient is tracked varies across all patients [25]. Also, the sequences of the events are highly correlated; for instance, a diagnosis could be made after a blood test result comes back [26]. The above Binary representation method cannot capture the heterogeneity and hidden temporal information in the data i.e., the severity of illness or the changes in prognosis of the disease over time. Therefore, there has been a growing interest to leverage such information in constructing the analytic file. Studies have shown that the incorporation of temporal information would improve the performance of the predictive models [27, 28]. Google has recently proposed a method to learn temporal attributes from all attributes in EHRs using long short-term memory (LSTM) and could improve the AUC of three health outcomes (mortality, readmission and long hospital stay) by 10% [29]. Below, several methods used in the literature to introduce temporal information into data representation are explained.

**Binary Representation with Multiple Time Bins.** Another standard method to capture temporal attributes is to divide the observation window into multiple time bins and apply binary representation for each bin separately. Assume "w" is the bin in an observation window and $t(C)$ is the time of claim. As shown, the administrative code ($Code_i$) associated with "C" at time window (bin) "w" is represented as 1 if the code belongs to claim $C$ and $t(C)$ falls in bin "w", 0 otherwise. The method works as follows:

$$Code_i^w = \begin{cases} 1 & \exists C \qquad : Code_i \in C \ \wedge t(C) \in w \\ 0 & Otherwise \end{cases} \tag{2}$$

The advantage of such representation is that the approximate time of an event is incorporated into the coding system and model. Such method was used in a study, in which equal time intervals (yearly, quarterly, monthly) were constructed to predict the number of hospitalization days in the upcoming year. It was observed that using smaller bins would add more temporal information to the models and the yearly model had significantly worse performance compared to other models [27].

Figure 2 graphically compares how the Binary representation method is applied when single and multiple time bins are used. In single observation window, diagnosis codes are extracted from raw data and then Binary representation is applied to create separate column of each code shown as $Code_1$, $Code_2$, ... , $Code_N$. The table shows six records associated with three patients. The data is then aggregated resulting in the final file with three records of three patients. However, when multiple time bins are used, the observation window is divided into multiple time bins (w bins) and within each bin, the Binary representation is applied. Therefore, the total number of attributes in the final analytic file is "w" times more than the single window. It should be noted that these time bins can have overlap or can be disjoint.

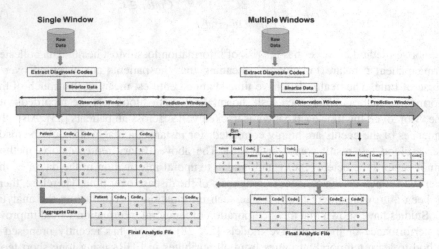

**Fig. 2.** Comparison of single vs. multiple time bins in Binary representation.

**Enumeration Representation.** Enumeration is another method in representing the administrative codes. In this method, the number of times a code is present in patient's medical history within a predefined time window is counted. Therefore, instead of using binary indicators, the present/non-present codes could be replaced by the number of times they occurred. The formula to create these codes are given below. As shown, each code ($Code_i^{cnt}$) is represented as sum of present codes specific to claim C.

$$Code_i^{cnt} = \sum_{c \in claims} \begin{cases} 1 & \exists C \text{ if code } i \text{ present on claim } c \\ 0 & Otherwise \end{cases} \tag{3}$$

This method of representing data clearly captures more information than simple Binary representation. However, one needs to carefully plan for the specific type of classifier to construct models, and specifically how to represent diagnoses that are not present in patient's record (see more discussion in Temporal Min-Max Representation section). This approach was used to create a set of independent attributes that represent the total number of admissions, and the total number of each CPT and diagnosis codes in predicting readmissions [9]. In another study and in predicting high healthcare cost, the number of comorbidities as well as diagnoses were used in developing models [30].

**Temporal Min-Max Representation.** Another approach to represent diagnoses is to explicitly use time from when the diagnosis happened for the first time and most recently [31]. This is possible as records in claims data are time-stamped helping us to understand when an event occurred. The diagnoses codes could be represented by calculating the number of days from the first known occurrence of the i-th, diagnosis code at time ($t_i$) to the time of prediction ($t_p$), named as $Code_i^{max}$, as well as last recorded occurrence of the diagnosis code relative to the time of prediction, named as $Code_i^{min}$. Using this approach, two copies of each administrative code is created and represented by the number of days. Formulas used to generate these codes are given below:

$$Code_i^{max} = \max_{t_i}(t_p - t_i) \qquad (4)$$

$$Code_i^{min} = \min_{t_i}(t_p - t_i) \qquad (5)$$

This method provides information about how long a patient has a health condition, which is important for chronic conditions. Also, it gives information about the last time the condition was present in patient's history, which is important for acute conditions that affect patient's health temporarily.

As the codes are represented using the number of days, special values need to be assigned to indicate diagnoses that are not present in patients' records. It is incorrect to simply represent non-present diagnoses with "0". One assumption to indicate non-present codes is to use a relatively large value to represent the infinity in time. Therefore, these codes could be represented with a very large positive and negative values, like ±999999.0 (denoted as 6_9), ±99999.0 (denoted as 5_9), and ±9999.0 (denoted as 4_9) etc. Here, $10^n-1$ is represented as n_9, where 'n' is the number of '9's. Also, positive and negative numbers are selected to represent the positive (max columns) and negative (min columns) correlation between the number of days and predicted outcome. The main reason for selecting $10^n-1$ as special values is that these numbers are easily visible when performing manual inspection of the data. Also, previous research indicated that the choice of value replacing these non-present codes could have impact on the performance of the model and depends on the algorithm being used [31].

Our group developed this method for the first time when predicting Activity of Daily Living (ADL)s using patients' diagnosis codes collected over ten years and demographic factors. In the study, non-present codes were replaced with ±999999.0 (6_9) and the models were constructed using different algorithms including Random Forest, Logistic Regression, Decision Tree and Naïve Bayes. It was shown that the method had an overall better performance compared with Binary representation [31].

**Additional Information and Derived Attributes.** In addition to the methods that represent individual attributes, combinations of multiple attributes are often derived from the data. For example, the total number of claims within a time window, time between hospitalizations, and the number of emergency care visits can be extracted from claims data. Further, individual and derived attributes can be modified by applying numerical transformations. For example, instead of considering time from the onset of a chronic condition, one may consider log(time) to emphasize recent changes and downplay small changes in distant past. Finally, global transformations such as those based on kernel methods or principal component can be used to transform all attributes in the space. These methods are beyond the scope of this paper, which focuses on representation of individual attributes.

To the best of our knowledge, the above methods are being used in limited settings and in some cases on a limited set of administrative codes. There is not any study that has done systematic investigation of administrative code representation. It is our understanding that the method of representing data could be impacted by many factors including the type of algorithm, outcome, size of observation window, the type of administrative code etc. In the next section, the Temporal Min-Max and simple Binary representation methods are compared and evaluated using two classification problems. In this study, the focus is on diagnosis codes grouped into 282 categories using AHRQ's Clinical Classification Software (CCS) [32]. This grouping is because the total number of CCS codes are large enough to provide sufficient information about patient's medical history and small enough to prevent overfitting the models.

### 2.3    Evaluation of Claims Data Representation

**Datasets and Prediction Problems.** Two classification problems were defined for predicting one-year mortality (Model 1) and predicting high utilization of medical services (Model 2) defined as $90^{th}$ percentile of the number of claims. In both models, the outcomes were calculated in year 2013, and all inputs were calculated from data prior to 2013. The data used to construct the models were 5% sample of Medicare beneficiaries from the Surveillance, Epidemiology, and End Results (SEER)-Medicare dataset between years 1995 and 2013. In this study, noncancer individuals who served as the control group in SEER-Medicare files were used to construct the models. Despite its limitations (i.e., data from SEER regions, male patients only), this dataset is sufficient for the purpose of investigating data representation. The patient cohort included those alive and at least 70 years old on January 1st, 2013. Excluding patients younger than 70 years guarantees that there are at least 5 years of data available prior to the prediction time as Medicare eligibility generally starts at 65.

For Model 1, a binary output/outcome was created with value 1 indicating that the patient died in 2013, and value 0 showing that patient was alive at the end of 2013. In Model 2, a binary output attribute was created to indicate high utilization in 2013. For this purpose, a simple approach was used in which the patients were classified as high utilizers when their total number of claims was above 90-th percentile in 2013.

In addition to the diagnosis codes that are the focus of this work, patient age and race were included in the analysis. The ICD-9 diagnosis codes were combined from multiple tables in the dataset: Medicare provider analysis and review (MedPAR), outpatient, durable medical equipment (DME), carrier (NCH), home health agency (HHA) and hospice. The ICD-9 codes were transformed into 282 AHRQ's CCS codes. The representation methods discussed in earlier sections were applied to the data, resulting in 282 diagnosis codes for Binary representation and 564 codes for Temporal Min-Max representation. The codes that were not present in medical history were replaced with $\pm999999.0$ (6_9).

The prediction time ($t_0$) was January $1^{st}$, 2013 and a fixed one-year prediction window was defined to construct the output attributes ending on December $31^{st}$, 2013. The diagnosis codes were extracted in multiple time windows up to 1 year, 2 years, … 12 years as well as 18 years prior to the prediction time to allow for investigating the impact of the amount of clinical information on model performance (see Fig. 3).

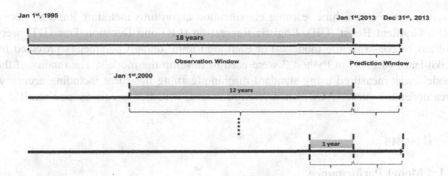

**Fig. 3.** Illustration of temporality in diagnosis codes extraction.

Table 1 shows the characteristics of the data in the study population. The unit of analysis in the two models was patient and the final dataset included 83,590 patients. The distribution of the data within each outcome is also shown. As it can be seen, about 7% of the cohort died in 2013 and about 10% of the population were high healthcare utilizers. Most patients were white and the average age in the cohort was about 80 years old.

When the observation window size was 18 years, the average number of days to the time of prediction across all CCS codes ($CCS^{total}$) was about 1846. The average number of days across all CCS codes (both $CCS^{min}$ and $CCS^{max}$ attributes) was smaller among positive examples (i.e., died or high utilizers). In addition, the average number of present diagnosis codes in the cohort was about 48. It was also shown that the number of present codes was higher among "Death" and "High Utilization" groups.

**Table 1.** Characteristics of the study population.

| | | Total | Model 1 | | Model 2 | |
| --- | --- | --- | --- | --- | --- | --- |
| | | | Death | No death | High Ut | No high Ut |
| N | | 83590 | 6111 | 77477 | 8401 | 75189 |
| % | | | 7.32% | 92.68% | 10.05% | 89.95% |
| Race | White | 82.67% | 82.06% | 82.71% | 82.68% | 82.67% |
| | Black | 6.96% | 8.49% | 6.84% | 8.56% | 6.87% |
| | Asian | 4.09% | 4.02% | 4.1% | 3.58% | 4.15% |
| | Native | 0.39% | 0.54% | 0.38% | 0.39% | 0.39% |
| | Hispanic | 2.83% | 2.45% | 2.86% | 2.61% | 2.85% |
| | Unknown | 3.05% | 2.43% | 3.1% | 2.17% | 3.15% |
| Age | | 79.72 | 82.6 | 79.5 | 80.3 | 79.7 |
| $CCS^{total}$ | | 1846.2 | 1693.9 | 1858 | 1612.7 | 1872.6 |
| $CCS^{max}$ | | 2312.4 | 2230.8 | 2318.8 | 2252.5 | 2319.3 |
| $CCS^{min}$ | | 1379.88 | 1157.0 | 1397.2 | 971.9 | 1426 |
| # Code | | 47.76 | 57.2 | 47.0 | 70.8 | 45.2 |

The models were developed using the standard model construction methodology. The data was first split into 90% training set and 10% testing set. Ten-fold cross validation within the training data was used to tune the models.

A number of machine learning classification algorithms including Random Forest (RF), Gradient Boost (GB), Logistic Regression (LR) and Decision Tree (DT) were utilized to construct the models. For each algorithm, default parameters provided by scikit-learn (0.21.3) in Python 3 were used to develop the models. The quality of the models was measured using standard machine learning measures including accuracy, area under the curve (AUC; often referred to as C-statistic), precision, and recall.

## 3 Results

### 3.1 Model Performance

The first set of experiments was to compare the quality of the models when diagnoses were constructed using standard Binary and Temporal Min-Max representations. For this purpose, the observation window size was set to 18 years. Table 2 presents a summary of the performance of the models in terms of AUC, accuracy (Acc), precision (Prec), and recall (Rec). Two tailed t-test was used to determine the level of significance ($p < 0.05$). As summarized, the performance of Temporal Min-Max representation was statistically significantly higher than Binary representation ($p < 0.05$) for almost all four criteria except for accuracy and precision of LR algorithm in predicting mortality and precision of LR in predicting high utilization, for which the difference was not significant. From among the different types of algorithms in predicting mortality, GB achieved the highest performance with the average AUC of 0.79. In predicting high utilization, the highest AUC of 0.85 was achieved in RF and GB-based models. As shown, recall was low in the models due to imbalanced data. However, it should be mentioned that the purpose of this study was not to develop the best models with optimized parameters, but to systematically compare different diagnosis representation methods for supervised learning. It is also possible that adding more attributes to the data (i.e., provider information) could improve the results.

**Table 2.** Average AUC, accuracy, precision and recall of the two tested models.

| Alg | Temporal | | | | Binary | | | |
|-----|------|------|------|------|------|------|------|------|
| | AUC | Acc | Prec | Rec | AUC | Acc | Prec | Rec |
| *Model 1 – Mortality* | | | | | | | | |
| RF | .767* | .927* | .605* | .025* | .735 | .926 | .312 | .003 |
| GB | .794* | .928* | .579* | .084* | .767 | .927 | .467 | .014 |
| LR | .765* | .926 | .436 | .032* | .759 | .926 | .415 | .021 |
| DT | .575* | .874* | .183* | .208* | .550 | .865 | .140 | .164 |
| *Model 2 – High Utilization* | | | | | | | | |
| RF | .845* | .911* | .748* | .179* | .787 | .902 | .656 | .060 |
| GB | .853* | .914* | .682* | .263* | .803 | .903 | .603 | .115 |
| LR | .821* | .905* | .595 | .160* | .801 | .903 | .578 | .118 |
| DT | .628* | .859* | .315* | .344* | .574 | .836 | .221 | .250 |

* Indicates significance ($p < 0.05$) of Temporal vs. Binary representation.

The following experiments aim at understanding individual differences between the data representations. For this purpose, a detailed comparison was made on the actual output probabilities of the models. Firstly, the average output probability was compared from instances that are correctly classified by Temporal vs. Binary representation methods. Then the probabilities were calculated when classified by true classes. As shown in Table 3, the average output probability among Temporal Min-Max representation cases is significantly higher than Binary representation across all algorithms and for two predictive models, resulting in overall higher recall. When comparing based on true classes, it was observed that the output probability was larger for Temporal representation among true positive cases (Death and High Utilization) and smaller among true negative cases (No Death and No High Utilization) for GB and LR algorithms. For other algorithms, the results were only significant among true positive cases (high utilization) using RF. Overall, the results suggest that Temporal representation methods are more likely to correctly classify positive cases across the two models. In other words, Temporal representation of diagnoses allows the algorithms to pick more positive cases that are missed in Binary representation method.

**Table 3.** Comparison of output probability for Temporal Min-Max (Tem) vs. Binary (Bin) representation. The results indicate higher probabilities for Temporal representation.

| | Model 1 – Mortality | | | | | | Model 2 – High Utilization | | | | | |
|---|---|---|---|---|---|---|---|---|---|---|---|---|
| | All | | Death | | No death | | All | | High Ut | | No high Ut | |
| Alg | Tem | Bin | Tem | Bin | Tem | Bin | Tem | Bin | Tem | Bin | Tem | Bin |
| RF | .54* | .34 | .56 | .71 | .32 | .30 | .56* | .39 | .60* | .55 | .34 | .35 |
| GB | .61* | .31 | .66* | .58 | .21* | .28 | .59* | .36 | .69* | .60 | .25* | .30 |
| LR | .47* | .42 | .57* | .54 | .35* | .40 | .51* | .45 | .58* | .56 | .37* | .41 |
| DT | .16* | .13 | 1.0 | 1.0 | .00 | .00 | .24* | .18 | 1.0 | 1.0 | .00 | .00 |

*Indicates significance ($p < 0.05$) of Temporal vs. Binary representation.

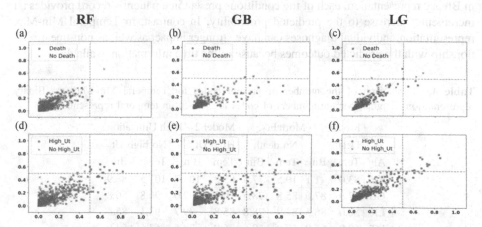

**Fig. 4.** Comparison of the output probability of Temporal vs. Binary representation that shows weak correlation. Vertical and horizontal axis show Binary and Temporal representation, respectively. Plots (a), (b) and (c) are for Model 1 and plots (d), (e), (f) for Model 2.

The data summarized in Table 3 are also shown graphically in Fig. 4 using scatterplots from 1000 randomly selected patients from the test set. Green points represent negative cases (no death or no high utilization) and red represent positives (death or high utilization) according to real labels. Values on axes represent output probabilities from models (vertical Binary, horizontal Temporal Min-Max). The plots were created for RF, GB, and LR algorithms which give outputs in the form of probabilities, thus are not applicable to DT which is a symbolic classification method. The models showed an overall medium or weak agreement between Binary and Temporal representations. While overall agreement on negative cases (lower left part of the plots) was very high ($R2 \approx 1$), there was little agreement within positive cases ($R2 = 0.2$ for Model 1 and $R2 = 0.1$ for Model 2). For RF and GB models, there was a clear shift of values to the right of the plots, indicating that the Temporal models output overall higher values.

Further, to determine how the number of present diagnosis codes impacts the prediction, the average number of present CCS codes was compared for cases correctly classified by the two representation methods. The comparison was made based on true class of each model and the results were shown in Table 4. In general, the number of codes was larger or smaller depending on what is being predicted, algorithm, and true class. In Model 1, the average number of CCS codes was significantly larger for Temporal representation using RF and DT algorithms among true positive cases (Death) and smaller among true negative cases (No Death). When analyzing true negative cases in GB and LR models, the average number of codes was significantly larger for Temporal representation. In Model 2, the number of codes was significantly larger for Binary representation among true positive cases and smaller for true negative cases except for DT algorithm. The results were more consistent in Model 2. Therefore, the larger number of present codes in predicting true positive cases of Model 2 suggests that sicker patients (more diagnosis codes) are better predicted with Binary representation. Conversely, sicker patients are better captured with Temporal representation in predicting true negative cases. These results can be interpreted as when using the Binary representation in predicting true positive cases, patients need to be more severely sick with larger number of conditions present. In general, in Binary representation, each of the conditions present in a patient's record provides an incremental increase to the predicted probability. In contrast, in Temporal Min-Max representation, individual diagnoses can have stronger impact as well as non-linear relationship with the predicted outcomes because of the time information available.

**Table 4.** Comparison of the number of present codes for Temporal Min-Max vs. Binary representations. Higher average numbers of codes are present in temporal representation.

| | Model 1 – Mortality | | | | Model 2 – High Utilization | | | |
| | Death | | No death | | High Ut | | No high Ut | |
| Alg | Tem | Bin | Tem | Bin | Tem | Bin | Tem | Bin |
|---|---|---|---|---|---|---|---|---|
| RF | 83.0* | 1.1 | 10.5* | 77.3 | 85.3* | 103.7 | 101.5* | 88.9 |
| GB | 77.9 | 87.0 | 85.8* | 78.5 | 79.7* | 97.0 | 96.8* | 80.8 |
| LR | 80.0 | 86.5 | 84.9* | 78.8 | 85.8* | 99.7 | 98.1* | 85.6 |
| DT | 68.9* | 65.0 | 57.8* | 59.5 | 76.9* | 78.6 | 63.6* | 64.0 |

* Indicates significance ($p < 0.05$) of Temporal vs. Binary representation.

A similar experiment was conducted to compare the average number of days between diagnosis occurrence and prediction time across all diagnosis codes between Temporal and Binary representations. As shown in Table 5, the average number of days was smaller for Temporal representation among true positive cases and larger among true negative cases. The results were significant except for RF and GB used for mortality prediction. This suggests that Temporal representation tends to correctly classify positive cases who had health issues for a shorter period, while it tends to correctly predict true negative cases who were sick longer. This is further investigated in Sect. 3.2 in which the relationship between observation window sizes (history length) and model performance is examined.

**Table 5.** Comparison of the average number of days for Temporal Min-Max vs. Binary representations. Lower average numbers of days are present in temporal representation.

| | Model 1 – Mortality | | | | Model 2 – High Utilization | | | |
|---|---|---|---|---|---|---|---|---|
| | Death | | No feath | | High Ut | | No high Ut | |
| Alg | Tem | Bin | Tem | Bin | Tem | Bin | Tem | Bin |
| RF | 1259.6 | 2599.1 | 2405.3* | 1243.4 | 1432.5* | 1913.5 | 2070.2* | 1555.0 |
| GB | 1353.6 | 1413.3 | 1898.0* | 1380.5 | 1468.2* | 1754.1 | 1834.7* | 1525.5 |
| LR | 1181.7* | 1906.9 | 2608.1* | 1193.3 | 1184.2* | 2195.7 | 2362.4* | 1213.2 |
| DT | 1595.1* | 1680.8 | 1981.4* | 1838.6 | 1579.9* | 1669.6 | 1944.5* | 1754.2 |

* Indicates significance ($p < 0.05$) of Temporal vs. Binary representation.

### 3.2 History Length (Back Window Size)

The second set of experiments was to investigate the impact of the observation window size (length of patient history in constructing diagnoses) on the quality of models when applying the Binary and Temporal Min-Max representations. Intuitively, longer windows allow for inclusion of more diagnosis codes present in the patients' history. However, when Binary representation is used, large window size causes inclusion of codes that are no longer relevant (i.e., acute conditions). In contrast, when Temporal Min-Max representation is used, data with irrelevant timeframe can be adjusted by the model itself. The presented work assumes fixed window size across all diagnoses. However, initial results (out of scope of this paper) have shown that this assumption is an over-simplification since period of relevance depends on specific diagnoses.

Figure 5 graphically shows the performance of the two constructed models across different algorithms. The vertical axis refers to the AUC of the models and horizontal axis represents the size of the observation window ranging from 18 years to 1 year. Similar plots were generated for accuracy, precision, and recall, but they are not included here due to space limitation. Red and black lines correspond to the changes in AUC for Temporal vs. Binary methods. An interesting observation was that the changes in observation window size affect the quality differently across the two models, four algorithms and two representation methods. The results suggest that one needs to carefully pick the optimal size of observation window with respect to the algorithm, outcome, and the representation method to improve the quality of the models.

The AUC of Model 1 varies between about 0.53 to 0.76, while it changes between 0.54 to 0.85 in Model 2.

In general, it was observed that Temporal Min-Max method outperforms Binary method in most observation window sizes. The AUC change pattern was similar for RF and GB across the two models. In predicting mortality, the accuracy of temporal-based models increased with more amount of data achieving the highest AUC when the window size was 18 years (the longest that can be constructed from available data). This suggests that in predicting mortality, it is important to know what happened in patient's medical history long time ago and that "Max" columns should be more important. In Model 2 however, it was observed that the accuracy of the models does not depend on the amount of data as it was almost constant over the course of 18 years, suggesting that the most recent diagnoses or "Min" columns should be more important. Using Binary representation for these algorithms, the performance of the models increased with less amount of data achieving the best performance by having about three years of data in Model 1 and only one year in Model 2. Also, there was no difference in the AUC of two representations with window size of 1 year in Model 1. Using LR to predict mortality, the accuracy of each method increased with less amount of data before reaching the peak between 2 to 4 years depending on the representation method. In this model, Temporal representation outperformed Binary representation when the observation window size ranged between 18 to 10.5 years after which the trend was reversed. In predicting high utilization though, the AUC of Temporal representation was higher than Binary representation up to 2 years after which there was not difference between the two methods. For Decision Tree (DT), the accuracy dropped with less amount of data for both Temporal and Binary representations. The decrease was more consistent in Model 1, in which the AUC was constant from 18 to 5 years before starting to decrease.

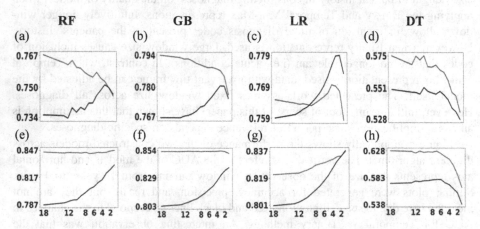

**Fig. 5.** Comparison of the Temporal (red) vs. Binary representation (black) for the two models. Vertical and horizontal axis show AUC and observation window size, respectively. Plots (a), (b), (c) and (d) correspond to Model 1 and plots (e), (f), (g) and (h) refer to Model 2. Different scales on the sub-plots are irrelevant because the focus was on presenting shapes of the curves. (Color figure online)

### 3.3     Diagnosis Groupers

The original diagnoses are stored in claims data as ICD-9 or ICD-10 codes. When modeling, these codes are often grouped to larger categories such as CCS, Elixhauser [33] Charlson [34] etc. to reduce dimensionality of the representation space. This experiment addresses the question that if the results described above are specific to CCS codes or are generalizable to other coding systems (code groupings). More specifically, a version of Elixhauser (Elix) code (version 3.0 or AHRQ-web ICD-9-CM Elixhauser code) [35] was applied to map ICD-9 codes into 30 categories. Specifically, CCS codes were mapped to Elix codes resulted in a total of 30 attributes for Binary and 60 attributes for Temporal Min-Max representation. The models were reconstructed using Elix grouping and compared with CCS-based models discussed earlier in this paper.

Figure 6 compares the AUC of the two models constructed using CCS and Elix codes. The AUC of the models constructed on the Elix codes was lower than the CCS-based models across all algorithms. This is reasonable as some information is lost when mapping CCS codes to Elix grouper codes with smaller number of categories, resulting in lower performance. A key observation was that the change in the AUC is independent of the coding systems in both Temporal and Binary representations, which suggests potential generalizability of the findings to other groupers.

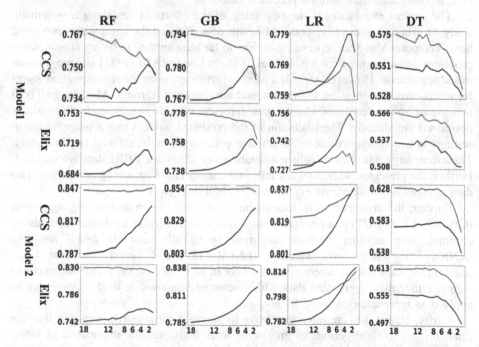

**Fig. 6.** Comparison of the AUC of models on two different coding systems. Red and black lines indicate Temporal vs. Binary representations, respectively. Shape of the curves indicate that model performance depends on data representation but not on diagnosis groupers used. (Color figure online)

# 4 Conclusion

The problem of representing data before applying machine learning methods has significant impact on quality of the models applied in patient care and management of health systems, as well as health policy and payment. It was previously observed that ML methods perform similarly on health-related applications, specifically when claims data are used [36]. The real difference in the model quality is in the extraction of appropriate information from raw data, followed by the construction of proper representation space. Despite wide use of administrative codes in predicting health outcomes, the representation of these codes has not been systematically studied and the literature provides only solution to ad-hoc modeling problems. The presented work provided a partial remedy for this situation and benefit all modeling efforts that rely on the use of medical claims and health data.

This manuscript evaluated and compared Temporal Min-Max and Binary representation methods using a large-scale experimental evaluation. In this study, more sophisticated representation schemas were used. These methods were applied on two classification problems: predicting mortality and predicting high utilization of medical services. The results indicated that Temporal Min-Max representation outperforms Binary representation in most cases. However, the optimal data representation is highly dependent on the classification problem, observation window size, model representation, learning algorithm and the predicted outcome.

The current manuscript is the beginning of the efforts in designing a systematic study of using administrative codes in health data. Beyond the comparison presented here, Temporal Min-Max representation has so far been applied to binary classification problems including predicting Activities of Daily Living (ADLs) [31] and progression of kidney disease. However, there is a need to further examine the representation issues for multi-class classification, regression, and unsupervised learning. Also, the goal is to investigate more details of claims data representation in which each diagnosis is optimized individually. The limitation of the presented work is that it is applicable in settings in which longitudinal information of patients are collected over multiple years. Therefore, large and well-established databases of claims or EHRs data are required. Further, the presented work does not take into consideration censoring of data based on data availability (multiple payers, insurance eligibility, etc.).

Further, the presented work focuses on "traditional" machine learning algorithms (GB, RF, LR and DT) and results are most likely generalizable to similar methods. In contrast, deep learning methods and more specifically recurrent neural networks (RNN), Long Short-Term Memory (LSTM) [37] and Gated Recurrent Units (GRU) [38] are attractive alternatives. RNNs can be trained on the actual sequences of claims rather than aggregated data within selected windows. It is also interesting to apply data representation using RNNs.

Lastly, claims data are often expensive to purchase for research purposes, thus are often limited to short periods of time. This work highlights the importance of longitudinal data to create high quality models. It is the authors' opinion that it is more beneficial to use data collected over longer periods of time (even with smaller sample sizes) when limited resources are available.

# References

1. Connelly, R., Playford, C., Gayle, V., Dibben, C.: The role of administrative data in the big data revolution in social science research. Soc. Sci. Res. **59**, 1–12 (2016)
2. CMS Forms List. https://www.cms.gov/Medicare/CMS-Forms/CMS-Forms/CMS-Forms-List
3. Ferver, K., Burton, B., Jesilow, P.: The use of claims data in healthcare research. Open Public Health J. **2**, 11–24 (2009)
4. Cadarette, S.M., Wong, L.: An introduction to health care administrative data. Can. J. Hosp. Pharm. **68**, 232 (2015)
5. Wilson, J., Bock, A.: https://www.optum.com/content/dam/optum/resources/whitePapers/Benefits-of-using-both-claims-and-EMR-data-in-HC-analysis-WhitePaper-ACS.pdf
6. Berg, G.D., Gurley, V.F.: Development and validation of 15-month mortality prediction models: a retrospective observational comparison of machine-learning techniques in a national sample of Medicare recipients. BMJ Open **9**, 7 (2019)
7. Makar, M., et al.: Short-term mortality prediction for elderly patients using medicare claims data. Int. J. Mach. Learn. Comput. **5**(3), 192–197 (2015)
8. Desai, R.J., et al.: Comparison of machine learning methods with traditional models for use of administrative claims with electronic medical records to predict heart failure outcomes. JAMA Netw. Open **3**, 1 (2020)
9. He, D., et al.: Mining high-dimensional administrative claims data to predict early hospital readmissions. J. Am. Med. Inform. Assoc. **21**(2), 272–279 (2014)
10. Min, X., Yu, B., Wang, F.: Predictive modeling of the hospital readmission risk from patients' claims data using machine learning: a case study on COPD. Sci. Rep. **9**, 1–10 (2019)
11. Morel, D., et al.: Predicting hospital readmission in patients with mental or substance use disorders: a machine learning approach. Int. J. Med. Inform. **139**, 104136 (2020)
12. Osawa, I., et al.: Machine-learning-based prediction models for high-need high-cost patients using nationwide clinical and claims data. NPJ Digit. Med. **3**, 1 (2020)
13. Luo, L., et al.: Using machine learning approaches to predict high-cost chronic obstructive pulmonary disease patients in China. Health Informatics J. **26**(3), 1577–1598 (2019)
14. Chen, S., et al.: Using applied machine learning to predict healthcare utilization based on socioeconomic determinants of care. Am. J. Manag. Care **26**(1), 26–31 (2020)
15. Davis, M.M., et al.: Geographic and population-level disparities in colorectal cancer testing: a multilevel analysis of Medicaid and commercial claims data. Prev. Med. **101**, 44–52 (2017)
16. Singh, J.A., et al.: Trends in and disparities for acute myocardial infarction: an analysis of Medicare claims data from 1992 to 2010. BMC Med. **12**, 1 (2014)
17. Inguva, S., et al.: Factors influencing Human papillomavirus (HPV) vaccination series completion in Mississippi Medicaid. Vaccine **38**(8), 2051–2057 (2020)
18. Gray, S.E., et al.: Association between workers' compensation claim processing times and work disability duration: analysis of population level claims data. Health Policy **123**(10), 982–991 (2019)
19. Miotto, R., et al.: Deep patient: an unsupervised representation to predict the future of patients from the electronic health records. Sci. Rep. **6**, 1 (2016)
20. Ngiam, K.Y., Khor, I.W.: Big data and machine learning algorithms for health-care delivery. Lancet Oncol. **20**, 5 (2019)

21. Malley, B., Ramazzotti, D., Wu, J.: Data prerocessing. In: Secondary Analysis of Electronic Health Records, pp. 115–141. Springer, Cham (2016). https://doi.org/10.1007/978-3-319-43742-2_12
22. Wojtusiak, J.: Data-driven constructive induction in the learnable evolution model. In: Proceedings of the 16th International Conference Intelligent Information Systems (2008)
23. Castillo, S., et al.: Algorithms and tools for the preprocessing of LC–MS metabolomics data. Chemom. Intell. Lab. Syst. **108**(1), 23–32 (2011)
24. Stein, J.D., Lum, F., Lee, P.P., Rich, W.L., Coleman, A.L.: Use of health care claims data to study patients with ophthalmologic conditions. Ophthalmology **121**, 1134–1141 (2014)
25. Tran, T., et al.: A framework for feature extraction from hospital medical data with applications in risk prediction. BMC Bioinform. **15**, 1 (2014)
26. Liu, L., et al.: Learning the joint representation of heterogeneous temporal events for clinical endpoint prediction, https://arxiv.org/abs/1803.04837
27. Xie, Y., et al.: Analyzing health insurance claims on different timescales to predict days in hospital. J. Biomed. Inform. **60**, 187–196 (2016)
28. Singh, A., et al.: Incorporating temporal EHR data in predictive models for risk stratification of renal function deterioration. J. Biomed. Inform. **53**, 220–228 (2015)
29. Rajkomar, A., et al.: Scalable and accurate deep learning with electronic health records. NPJ Digit. Med. **1**(1), 1–10 (2018)
30. Kim, Y.J., Park, H.: Improving prediction of high-cost health care users with medical check-up data. Big Data. **7**(3), 163–175 (2019)
31. Wojtusiak, J., et al.: Computational Barthel Index: an automated tool for assessing and predicting activities of daily living among nursing home patients. BMC Med. Inform. Decis. Mak. **21**, 1 (2021)
32. Clinical Classifications Software (CCS) for ICD-9-CM. https://www.hcup-us.ahrq.gov/toolssoftware/ccs/ccs.jsp. Accessed 14 May 2021
33. Elixhauser, A., et al.: Comorbidity measures for use with administrative data. Med. Care **36**(1), 8–27 (1998)
34. Charlson, M.E., et al.: A new method of classifying prognostic comorbidity in longitudinal studies: development and validation. J. Chronic Dis. **40**(5), 373–383 (1987)
35. Quan, H., et al.: Coding algorithms for defining comorbidities in ICD-9-CM and ICD-10 administrative data. Med. Care **43**, 1130–1139 (2005)
36. Lynam, A.L., et al.: Logistic regression has similar performance to optimised machine learning algorithms in a clinical setting: application to the discrimination between type 1 and type 2 diabetes in young adults. Diagn. Progn. Res. **4**, 1 (2020)
37. Hochreiter, S., Schmidhuber, J.: Long short-term memory. Neural Comput. **9**, 8 (1997)
38. Cho, K., et al.: Learning phrase representations using RNN encoder-decoder for statistical machine translation (2014)

**Invited Paper**

# Generating Longitudinal Synthetic EHR Data with Recurrent Autoencoders and Generative Adversarial Networks

Siao Sun[1]([✉]), Fusheng Wang[2,3], Sina Rashidian[2], Tahsin Kurc[3],
Kayley Abell-Hart[3], Janos Hajagos[3], Wei Zhu[1], Mary Saltz[3],
and Joel Saltz[3]

[1] Department of Applied Mathematics and Statistics, Stony Brook University,
Stony Brook, NY, USA
siao.sun@stonybrook.edu
[2] Department of Computer Science, Stony Brook University,
Stony Brook, NY, USA
[3] Department of Biomedical Informatics, Renaissance School of Medicine
at Stony Brook University, Stony Brook, NY, USA

**Abstract.** Synthetic electronic health records (EHR) can facilitate effective use
of clinical data in software development, medical education, and medical
research without the concerns of data privacy. We propose a novel Generative
Adversarial Network (GAN) approach, called Longitudinal GAN (LongGAN),
that can generate synthetic longitudinal EHR data. LongGAN employs a
recurrent autoencoder and the Wasserstein GAN Gradient Penalty (WGAN-GP)
architecture with conditional inputs. We evaluate LongGAN with the task of
generating training data for machine/deep learning methods. Our experiments
show that predictive models trained with synthetic data from LongGAN achieve
comparable performance to those trained with real data. Moreover, these models
have up to 0.27 higher AUROC and up to 0.21 higher AUPRC values than
models trained with synthetic data from RCGAN and TimeGAN, the two most
relevant methods for longitudinal data generation. We also demonstrate that
LongGAN is able to preserve patient privacy in a given attribute disclosure
attack setting.

**Keywords:** Deep learning · Machine learning · Electronic health records ·
Generative models · Synthetic data generation

## 1 Introduction

Electronic health record (EHR) systems capture vast amounts of digital data about
patients' health status, their medical and treatment histories, and clinical outcomes.
These data provide opportunities to improve healthcare delivery, reduce medical costs
and, when integrated with genomic and imaging data, can enable the development of
strategies for personalized medicine. However, the use of EHR data in medical research
and software development is often impeded by the complexities of regulatory over-
sight. Because electronic health records contain patients' information, data access and

© Springer Nature Switzerland AG 2021
E. K. Rezig et al. (Eds.): Poly 2021/DMAH 2021, LNCS 12921, pp. 153–165, 2021.
https://doi.org/10.1007/978-3-030-93663-1_12

sharing are strictly controlled by rules and processes to protect patient privacy. Getting approvals for access to de-identified clinical data can be time consuming. Approvals are generally granted for specific subsets of data (new approvals are required, if a study later needs additional data subsets) with limits on how the data can be shared within and among research teams. Higher security requirements on computing and storage infrastructure put additional burden on EHR based medical and informatics research. The process of data de-identification is also time consuming and expensive, especially for large EHR datasets. Moreover, de-identified data can still pose privacy and security risks [1].

Realistic synthetic datasets that maintain the statistical properties of real datasets can mitigate the complexities of clinical data access by eliminating (or significantly reducing) privacy and security risks and can complement de-identified real clinical data in informatics and medical research [2–11]. For instance, synthetic datasets can be used for data analysis3 and cohort identification tasks [2]. They can also replace or augment real data for a more efficient development and evaluation of computerized analysis methods [4, 5]. Realistic synthetic EHR data can, in particular, benefit deep learning analysis workflows, which often require large volumes of data to train accurate and robust models. Large longitudinal EHR datasets, for example, are critical to the development of reliable predictive models, which are generally based on recurrent neural networks (RNN), such as long short-term memory [12] (LSTM) architectures. However, there are challenges in generating realistic synthetic datasets. Data heterogeneity, large numbers of data elements and types, irregularities in data, and missing values make it arduous to implement efficient methods that can produce realistic synthetic data.

We propose a novel deep learning method, coined as Longitudinal GAN (Long-GAN), for generating longitudinal synthetic EHR data. A trained LongGAN model generates high-quality clinical data containing continuous laboratory and medication values for given diseases for a time period of 72 h. It can be applied to any continuous-valued longitudinal data for any reasonable time range given.

Deep learning has in recent years become the preferred method for data analysis in a wide range of applications including analysis of clinical data for identification of disease risk, outcome prediction, and the extraction and classification of clinical information. For example, deep learning methods have been used to analyze EHR data to identify the risk of opioid use disorder [13] and opioid overdose [14] in population studies and to detect miscoded diabetes diagnosis codes for quality improvement [15]. Deep learning methods have also been successfully applied to synthetic data generation in many application domains, such as text-to-image synthesis [16], video generation [17], and music generation18. Most synthetic data methods employ the Generative Adversarial Network [19] (GAN) architecture, which consists of a generator component and a discriminator (or a critic) component. The generator produces synthetic data, whereas the discriminator distinguishes between real and synthetic data. The adversarial relationship between the generator and the discriminator forces the generator to learn to produce realistic synthetic data. Several recent projects have employed GANs for synthetic EHR data generation [20–27]. Medical Generative Adversarial Network (MedGAN) [20] implements a method for generating discrete data elements (medication codes and diagnosis codes). SMOOTH-GAN [21] demonstrated GANs would generate more realistic synthetic data when binary labels are converted to continuous values by using imperfect machine learning models as heuristic functions for generating laboratory values and medications as a snapshot of patients' records. However, most of the previous efforts have focused on producing non-longitudinal synthetic data that represent a snapshot of a patient's medical history. Applications of GANs for synthetic time-series clinical data remain scarce, owing mainly to the fact that generating sequences requires the generated data to have not only similar overall distribution of attributes, but also similar temporal dynamics to the real sequences. Some recent efforts have resulted in methods for generating longitudinal synthetic data. Recurrent Conditional Generative Adversarial Networks (RCGAN) [22] used a RNN architecture for both the generator and the discriminator and took conditional input at each time step. The authors evaluated the performance on the eICU Collaborative Research Database with four selected regularly sampled features. Time-series Generative Adversarial Networks (TimeGAN) [23] introduced supervised loss to enforce temporal dynamic preservation and trained the generator and the discriminator in embedded space. The authors of TimeGAN measured its success on a discrete-valued lung cancer dataset. Dual Adversarial Autoencoder (DAAE) [24] made use of an inner GAN and an outer GAN to learn set-valued sequences of medical entities such as diagnosis codes.

LongGAN takes advantage of recurrent autoencoders and the Wasserstein Generative Adversarial Network with Gradient Penalty [28] (WGAN-GP) architecture. Recurrent autoencoders have been successfully applied to multivariate time series analysis such as forecasting [29] and anomaly detection [30]. They can learn useful representations of sequences while preserving temporal dynamics during the reconstruction. LongGAN leverages this property of recurrent autoencoders and adapts it to train an autoencoder model to generate realistic sequences. Our work differs from the previous work as follows: 1) Unlike regularly sampled bedside data, our data are irregularly sampled with many missing values. 2) Our data contains many features, rather than only a few handcrafted features. 3) Conditions are combined to generate realistic longitudinal data.

We evaluated the performance of LongGAN by training a logistic regression model, a random forest model, and a two-layer long short-term memory (LSTM) network model to predict acute kidney injury (AKI). These models represent examples of linear models, nonlinear models, and deep learning models, respectively. The experimental results show that predictive models trained with synthetic data from LongGAN achieve comparable Area Under the Receiver Operating Characteristics (AUROC) and Area Under the Precision Recall Curve (AUPRC) values to models trained with real data. In addition, synthetic datasets from LongGAN lead to much better models, with up to 0.27 higher AUROC and up to 0.21 higher AUPRC values, compared with synthetic data from RCGAN and TimeGAN, the two most relevant GAN-based methods for synthetic longitudinal data generation.

Beyond the realisticness of synthetic data, a key concern is protecting patient privacy (i.e., an attacker should not be able to discover the identities of patients from a synthetic dataset). We examined this aspect of LongGAN in the context of attribute disclosure attacks. The experimental results show that an attacker, who has a subset of attributes from the real dataset, could achieve a mean accuracy of 20% in predicting missing attributes with k-nearest neighbors (KNN) estimation using the synthetic dataset generated by LongGAN. This value is lower than the mean accuracy of 26% that the attacker could achieve without access to the synthetic dataset using a population median method.

## 2  Methods

### 2.1  Architecture of LongGAN

The proposed method consists of a recurrent autoencoder network and a GAN network as is shown in Fig. 1. A recurrent autoencoder is a neural network trained to copy its input sequence to its output sequence31. More specifically, it can be viewed as having two parts: the encoder Enc takes sequential data X and maps it to a dense representation h, then the decoder Dec takes h and tries to reconstruct the input from it. Here, $X = (s_1, s_2, \ldots, s_T)$ is a time-ordered sequence of vectors. Each vector $s_i = (s_i^1, s_i^2, \ldots, s_i^C), 1 \leq i \leq T$ represents C features at the time point$i$. In our implementation, the encoder and decoder both have three LSTM layers. We aim to minimize the reconstruction loss, which is:

$$\sum_{X \in D} ||X - X'||^2$$

where D is the dataset, and $X' = Dec(h) = Dec(Enc)(X)$ is the reconstruction of X.

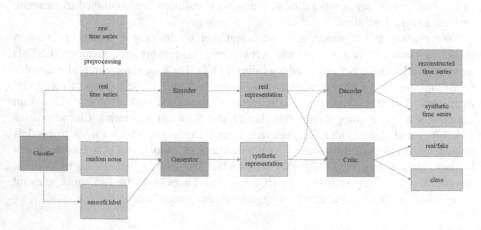

**Fig. 1.**   Architecture of the proposed LongGAN model.

The GAN network is based on the WGAN-GP architecture with conditional inputs. A GAN consists of two components: a generator $G(z; \theta_g)$ and a discriminator $D(h; \theta_d)$. The generator takes random noise and tries to generate samples that follow the same distribution of the real data. Meanwhile, the discriminator receives both real and generated data, and tries to detect whether a sample is real or fake. Ideally, the optimal generator $G^*$ would generate samples that are indistinguishable from real samples, and the discriminator would be forced to make a random guess. Conditional GANs [32] (cGANs) are extensions of GANs where the generator takes not only random noise but also some auxiliary information such as labels, to help with the generation. The objective of a conditional GAN is:

$$min_G max_D V(\theta_g, \theta_d) = E_{h \sim P_h}[\log(D(h|y))] + E_{z \sim P_z}[\log(1 - D(G(z|y)))]$$

Here $h$ is the output of the pre-trained encoder, i.e. representation of real longitudinal data, $P_h$ represents the distribution of real representation, $P_z$ is the distribution of random noise (here we used Gaussian distribution), and y is the conditional input. WGAN-GP is an extension of the basic GAN architecture that improves the stability when training the model. Compared to the original GAN, it uses the Wasserstein distance instead of the Jenson-Shannon (JS) divergence, replaces the discriminator with a critic that scores the realness or fakeness of a given sample, and adds gradient penalty to enforce Lipschitz constraints on the critic. The objective function of WGAN-GP is:

$$L = E_{\tilde{h} \sim P_g}[D(\tilde{h})] - E_{h \sim P_h}[D(h)] + \lambda E_{\hat{h} \sim P_{\hat{h}}}[(\|\nabla_{\hat{h}} D(\hat{h})\|_2 - 1)^2]$$

The synthetic representation $\tilde{h}$ was fed to the pre-trained encoder to generate synthetic longitudinal data:

$$\tilde{X} = Dec(\tilde{h}) = Dec(G(z|y))$$

In our method, the generator has two leakyRelu hidden layers with $\alpha = 0.2$, each followed by a batch normalization layer, and the output layer is tanh. The critic has two leakyRelu hidden layers with $\alpha = 0.2$. The output layer is linear.

## 2.2 Training LongGAN

We extracted inpatient encounter data for adults (18+) from the Cerner Health Facts database [33–35], a large multi-institutional de-identified database derived from EHRs and administrative systems. The extracted data were mapped to the OHDSI Common Data Model (version 5.3) and vocabulary release (2/10/2018) [36]. We randomly chose two facilities (131 and 143) from the 10 highest volume inpatient facilities and extracted encounters from 1/1/2016 to 12/31/2017 for the experimental evaluation of the proposed method.

Medications and laboratory tests with no less than 5% appearance rate by encounter in both facilities were extracted, and the raw values were converted to quantiles. We further extracted encounters with length of stay no less than 72 h and sampled one medication/laboratory test per hour. If there were more than one measurement in an hour, medians were computed. Diagnosis codes were mapped from the International Classification of Diseases (ICD) codes to Systematized Nomenclature of Medicine Clinical Terms (SNOMED CT). SNOMED codes and the descendant codes for Acute Kidney Injury (AKI) were combined and used as labels for our study.

The extracted datasets were extremely sparse because not all patients have measurements of all medications/laboratory tests every hour, and thus imputation was necessary. There are many approaches to impute time-series data. Here we used the interpolation part of the Interpolation-Prediction Network [37]. The Interpolation-Prediction Network is a semi-parametric network designed for irregularly sampled multivariate time series, taking into account correlations across all time series from different dimensions.

After the preprocessing, we obtained multidimensional longitudinal data for every patient, where each dimension represents the trajectory of a specific medication/laboratory test measurement from the first 72 h of hospitalization. We then trained a classifier to get smooth labels [21, 38] of AKI. More specifically, we trained a random forest model on the training set of real longitudinal EHR data with AKI as labels to assign probabilities of patients' developing AKI, and then adjusted these probabilities to obtain smooth labels. The adjustment is done as follows:

$$\text{SmoothLabel}(X_{prob}, X_{label}) = \begin{cases} 0.49, & \text{if } X_{prob} > 0.5 \text{ and } X_{label} == 0 \\ 0.51, & \text{if } X_{prob} < 0.5 \text{ and } X_{label} == 1 \\ X_{prob}, & \text{otherwise} \end{cases}$$

Here X_prob is the probability of getting AKI assigned by the trained classifier, and X_label is the original binary valued label for AKI.

To train a synthetic data generation model, we first pre-trained the encoder and decoder with the real EHR data with reconstruction loss. We then took the output of the encoder, i.e., the representation of the input data, and trained the WGAN-GP to produce synthetic representations. The smooth labels of AKI were used as conditional input for both the generator and the discriminator. Finally, the generated representations were input into the trained decoder to obtain synthetic longitudinal data.

The method was implemented in Python v3.6. The random forest and logistic regression method were implemented using the scikit-learn package [39]. The recurrent encoder network and the GAN network were developed using Tensorflow [40]. Other libraries used include Python Numpy41, Python Pandas [42], and Python Scipy [43]. Training was performed on an NVIDIA Tesla V100 (16 GB RAM).

# 3 Results

## 3.1 Evaluation of Realism

We have evaluated the performance of LongGAN by training traditional machine learning models and RNNs to predict whether or not a patient will develop AKI based on the medication and laboratory results from the first 72 h of hospitalization. In our experiments we used logistic regression, random forest, and a two-layer LSTM network as examples of linear models, nonlinear models, and neural networks, respectively. In each case we trained two models, one using the real training dataset and the other using the synthetic dataset, and then evaluated both models on a real test dataset. This approach, called Train on Synthetic and Test on Real (TSTR), is a common mechanism with which to evaluate the realism of synthetic data [21, 22]. Since logistic regression and random forest are not designed for time-series data, we flattened the sequence along the time dimension as input for these two algorithms. We measured the performances of the models with AUROC and AUPRC as they are commonly used metrics for TSTR [21, 22].

We compared our method with RCGAN and TimeGAN. Since TimeGAN is not designed for conditional generation, we trained two TimeGAN models on positive cases and negative cases separately to generate synthetic data with both cases. Table 1 shows the experimental evaluation results. Our results demonstrate that the models trained on synthetic datasets generated by LongGAN have performances closer to those trained on real datasets than other synthetic datasets generated by RCGAN and TimeGAN. Models trained with synthetic data from LongGAN achieved up to 0.27 higher AUROC and up to 0.21 higher AUPRC values than models trained with data from RCGAN and TimeGAN.

**Table 1.** Performance of trained predictive models on real and synthetic datasets.

| Predictive model | Metric | Real | RCGAN | TimeGAN | LongGAN |
|---|---|---|---|---|---|
| Logistic regression | AUROC | 0.80 | 0.57 | 0.61 | 0.74 |
|  | AUPRC | 0.57 | 0.34 | 0.36 | 0.51 |
| Random forest | AUROC | 0.86 | 0.50 | 0.71 | 0.77 |
|  | AUPRC | 0.70 | 0.29 | 0.50 | 0.51 |
| LSTM network | AUROC | 0.83 | 0.63 | 0.67 | 0.77 |
|  | AUPRC | 0.67 | 0.39 | 0.45 | 0.52 |

In the next set of experiments, we examined whether models trained with the synthetic dataset selected a similar set of features for prediction compared with models trained with the real dataset. To this end, we extracted the top 15 most important features of the random forest models trained with the real and synthetic datasets. Table 2 shows the list of features from each random forest model. Our experiments show that 10 features overlap between the two models.

**Table 2.** Top 15 most important features of random forest model trained on real/synthetic datasets.

| Top 15 features from random forest model trained on the real dataset | Top 15 features from random forest model trained on the synthetic dataset |
|---|---|
| Creatinine [Mass/volume] in Serum or Plasma | Creatinine [Mass/volume] in Serum or Plasma |
| Creatinine [Mass/volume] in Urine | Neutrophils/100 leukocytes in Blood by Automated count |
| Chloride [Moles/volume] in Serum or Plasma | Aspartate aminotransferase [Enzymatic activity/volume] in Serum or Plasma |
| Ferritin [Mass/volume] in Serum or Plasma | Respiratory rate |
| Phosphate [Mass/volume] in Serum or Plasma | Phosphate [Mass/volume] in Serum or Plasma |
| Respiratory rate | Eosinophils/100 leukocytes in Blood by Automated count |
| Sodium [Moles/volume] in Serum or Plasma | Chloride [Moles/volume] in Serum or Plasma |
| Iron [Mass/volume] in Serum or Plasma | Ferritin [Mass/volume] in Serum or Plasma |
| Glasgow coma scale | Protein [Mass/volume] in Serum or Plasma |
| Aspartate aminotransferase [Enzymatic activity/volume] in Serum or Plasma | Diastolic blood pressure |
| Basophils/100 leukocytes in Blood by Automated count | paracetamol |
| Glucose [Mass/volume] in Serum or Plasma | Creatinine [Mass/volume] in Urine |
| Potassium [Moles/volume] in Serum or Plasma | Iron [Mass/volume] in Serum or Plasma |
| Mean blood pressure | Glucose [Mass/volume] in Serum or Plasma |
| Cholesterol [Mass/volume] in Serum or Plasma | Basophils/100 leukocytes in Blood by Automated count |

### 3.2    Evaluation of Privacy Preservation

A critical requirement for a synthetic EHR data generator is that it must preserve patient privacy. In this section we evaluate this aspect of our method with respect to attribute disclosure attacks. Attribute disclosure occurs when attackers can derive target attributes about a patient based on key attributes that they already know about the patient [8, 44]. This is a prominent issue for synthetic datasets as attackers might gain sensitive knowledge of real patients based on similar records in a given synthetic dataset.

We assume the attacker has full access to the synthetic dataset and partial access to the real dataset. This is a commonly adopted setting for evaluating the attribute disclosure risk [20, 45]. More specifically, we randomly sampled 1% of patients from the real training set as the compromised records, flattened them along the time dimension, and randomly masked 10% of the attributes as the set of target attributes that are unknown to the attacker.

While there are different potential attack methods for synthetic dataset [20, 46, 47], in this paper, due to space limitation, we focused on KNN estimation, a common method considered for privacy preserving evaluation. For each compromised record, we retrieved its k-nearest neighbors in the synthetic dataset based on the key attributes and estimated the target attribute using the median of corresponding attributes of these k neighbors. We call an estimation accurate, if the relative error of the estimation is below 5%. We used a dummy baseline where the attacker simply guesses the median value in the population. Here it is 0.5 since our data are in quantile. This simulates the attacker's behavior when they have no knowledge of the original dataset or the synthetic dataset and have to make estimations uniformly at random [46].

The idea is that a privacy-preserving synthetic dataset should avoid providing the attacker with additional knowledge for better estimation of target attributes, in order to minimize the risk of attribute disclosure. We repeated the experiment for 30 times, with different records of patients randomly selected and different attributes randomly masked and mean accuracy computed for all masked attributes. The experiments showed that with the KNN estimation the attacker on average achieved a mean accuracy of 20%, while with the estimation of the population median the mean accuracy was 26%. The paired samples t-test of the mean accuracies from different experiments resulted in a p-value of $7.12e-23$. This indicates that the mean accuracy from the KNN estimation was significantly smaller than that of random guess, suggesting that in the given scenario, an attacker using KNN estimation cannot do better than random guess.

## 4  Discussion

Generating synthetic clinical data has great potential for researchers to conduct competitive and reproducible research with electronic health records without privacy concerns. However, very few works have tackled the problems of generating continuous time-series clinical data. We have proposed a model that combines a recurrent autoencoder and WGAN-GP to generate realistic time-series data containing continuous laboratory and medication values for given diseases. While we focused on a specific disease (AKI) in our experimental evaluation, the methodology is universal and can be applied in the context of other diseases.

### 4.1  Comparison with Previous Work

In Esteban's work on RCGAN, they used RNNs (LSTM) as the generator and the discriminator, and the labels were fed to the generator and the discriminator at every time step [22]. In Yoon's work on TimeGAN, they used RNNs as embedding and recovery functions to provide mappings between feature space and latent space, and then trained the GAN within the latent space [23]. The GAN aspect of TimeGAN also utilized the RNNs as both the generator and the discriminator. In addition, another RNN (called supervisor in the paper) was added to enforce the generated longitudinal data having similar temporal relationships to the real longitudinal data.

GANs and RNNs can both be hard to train [28, 48], and using the RNN structure in GANs would intuitively introduce instability in training. Compared with previous studies, the key difference of our study is that we managed to bypass the RNN structure in the GAN. We accomplished this by taking advantage of a pre-trained recurrent autoencoder and transformed the problem of generating sequences to the problem of generating dense representations of sequences. Since the generated representations are input to the decoder, which was trained on real longitudinal data, the generated longitudinal data would maintain similar temporal dynamics to the real dataset. Our model also differs from previous work in that we took advantage of WGAN-GP and smooth labels, which made the training more stable. Moreover, our model requires minimal domain knowledge to make hand-crafted features, rendering it more generalizable.

Our model achieved much better AUROC and AUPRC values than the baseline models in predictive modeling tasks. The significant overlap of top features between models trained with synthetic data and those trained with real data suggests LongGAN can generate realistic synthetic data which can in turn be used to complement or replace real data for training machine learning models. The experiments on attribute disclosure demonstrated that an attacker cannot reliably obtain additional information about real patients with help of our generated dataset, which minimizes the concerns for privacy issues.

### 4.2 Limitations

The datasets extracted from the Health Facts database contain many missing values, because not all patients have measurements of all medications/laboratory tests every hour. We performed imputation to obtain fixed-length longitudinal data to fit the model. However, in this process we also eliminated any patterns of the missing data itself, which could contain useful information about patients [49]. While our method generates synthetic data that are similar to the imputed data, it does not have patterns of missing data like the original datasets do.

## 5    Conclusion and Future Work

LongGAN is a new approach to generating synthetic longitudinal EHR data. It can produce synthetic datasets that enable training of machine/deep learning models with comparable predictive performances to those of models trained with real data. For future work, we shall investigate how to combine the transformer [50] architecture with GAN and implement extensions to produce synthetic data on demographics and preserve patterns of missing data. Transformer networks have achieved great success in natural language processing tasks [51, 52] and have been shown to be powerful tools for extracting useful features of sequences [53, 54]. We will also explore other aspects of privacy attack and preservation and differentially private training methods [55, 56], in order to further minimize or eliminate the risk of information leakage.

# References

1. Rothstein, M.A.: Is deidentification sufficient to protect health privacy in research? Am J Bioeth. **10**(9), 3–11 (2010)
2. Foraker, R.E., Yu, S.C., Gupta, A., Michelson, A.P., Pineda Soto, J.A., Colvin, R., et al.: Spot the difference: Comparing results of analyses from real patient data and synthetic derivatives. JAMIA Open. **3**(4), 557–566 (2020)
3. Benaim, A.R., et al.: Analyzing medical research results based on synthetic data and their relation to real data results: Systematic comparison from five observational studies. JMIR Med. Inform. **8**(2), e16492 (2020)
4. Guo, A., Foraker, R.E., MacGregor, R.M., Masood, F.M., Cupps, B.P., Pasque, M.K.: The use of synthetic electronic health record data and deep learning to improve timing of high-risk heart failure surgical intervention by predicting proximity to catastrophic decompensation. Front. Digit. Health **44** (2020)
5. Che, Z., Cheng, Y., Zhai, S., Sun, Z., Liu, Y.: Boosting deep learning risk prediction with generative adversarial networks for electronic health records. In: 2017 IEEE International Conference on Data Mining (ICDM), pp. 787–92 (2017)
6. Walonoski, J.A., Kramer, M., Nichols, J., Quina, A., Moesel, C., Hall, D., et al.: Synthea: an approach, method, and software mechanism for generating synthetic patients and the synthetic electronic health care record. J. Am. Med. Inf. Assoc. JAMIA. **25**, 230–238 (2018)
7. Dube, K., Gallagher, T.: Approach and Method for Generating Realistic Synthetic Electronic Healthcare Records for Secondary Use. In: Gibbons, J., MacCaull, W. (eds.) FHIES 2013. LNCS, vol. 8315, pp. 69–86. Springer, Heidelberg (2014). https://doi.org/10.1007/978-3-642-53956-5_6
8. Goncalves, A., Ray, P., Soper, B., Stevens, J., Coyle, L., Sales, A.P.: Generation and evaluation of synthetic patient data. BMC Med. Res. Method. **20**(1), 1–40 (2020)
9. McLachlan, S., Dube, K., Gallagher, T., Simmonds, J.A., Fenton, N.: Realistic Synthetic Data Generation: The ATEN Framework. In: Cliquet Jr., A., et al. (eds.) BIOSTEC 2018. CCIS, vol. 1024, pp. 497–523. Springer, Cham (2019). https://doi.org/10.1007/978-3-030-29196-9_25
10. Pollack, A.H., Simon, T.D., Snyder, J., Pratt, W.: Creating synthetic patient data to support the design and evaluation of novel health information technology. J. Biomed. Inf. **95**, 103201 (2019)
11. Walonoski, J., et al.: Synthe, novel coronavirus (covid-19) model and synthetic data set. Intell. Based Med. **1**, 100007 (2020)
12. Hochreiter, S., Schmidhuber, J.: Long short-term memory. Neural Comput. **9**, 1735–1780 (1997)
13. Dong X, et al.: Identifying risk of opioid use disorder for patients taking opioid medications with deep learning. arXiv preprint arXiv:201004589 (2020)
14. Dong, X., et al.: Predicting opioid overdose risk of patients with opioid prescriptions using electronic health records based on temporal deep learning. J. Biomed. Inf. **116**, 103725 (2021)
15. Rashidian, S., et al.: Detecting miscoded diabetes diagnosis codes in electronic health records for quality improvement: temporal deep learning approach. JMIR Med. Inform. **8**(12), e22649 (2020)
16. Tao, M., Tang, H., Wu, S., Sebe, N., Wu, F., Jing, X.: Df-gan: deep fusion generative adversarial networks for text-to-image synthesis. ArXiv. abs/2008.05865 (2020)
17. Clark, A., Donahue, J., Simonyan, K.: Adversarial video generation on complex datasets. arXiv: Computer Vision and Pattern Recognition (2019)

18. Engel, J., Agrawal, K.K., Chen, S., Gulrajani, I., Donahue, C., Roberts, A.: Gansynth: adversarial neural audio synthesis. ArXiv; abs/1902.08710 (2019)
19. Goodfellow, I., et al.: Generative adversarial nets. In: NIPS (2014).
20. Choi, E., Biswal, S., Malin, B., Duke, J., Stewart, W., Sun, J.: Generating multi-label discrete electronic health records using generative adversarial networks. ArXiv; abs/1703.06490 (2017)
21. Rashidian, S., et al.: SMOOTH-GAN: towards sharp and smooth synthetic ehr data generation. In: Michalowski, M., Moskovitch, R. (eds.) Artificial Intelligence in Medicine. AIME 2020. Lecture Notes in Computer Science, vol. 12299. Springer, Cham (2020)
22. Esteban, C., Hyland, S.L., Rätsch, G.: Real-valued (medical) time series generation with recurrent conditional GANs. ArXiv. abs/1706.02633 (2017)
23. Yoon, J., Jarrett, D., Schaar, M.V.D.: Time-series generative adversarial networks. In: NeurIPS (2019)
24. Lee, D., Yu, H., Jiang, X., Rogith, D., Gudala, M., Tejani, M., et al.: Generating sequential electronic health records using dual adversarial autoencoder. J. Am. Med. Inform. Assoc. **27**(9), 1411–1419 (2020)
25. Jordon, J., Yoon, J., Schaar, M.V.D.: Pate-gan: generating synthetic data with differential privacy guarantees. In: ICLR (2019)
26. Baowaly, M.K., Lin, C., Liu, C.-L., Chen, K.-T.: Synthesizing electronic health records using improved generative adversarial networks. J. Am. Med. Inform. Assoc. **26**(228), 41 (2019)
27. Yoon, J., Drumright, L.N., Van Der Schaar, M.: Anonymization through data synthesis using generative adversarial networks (ads-gan). IEEE J. Biomed. Health Informatics. **24**(8), 2378–2388
28. Gulrajani, I., Ahmed, F., Arjovsky, M., Dumoulin, V., Courville, A.: Improved training of wasserstein gans. In: NIPS (2017)
29. Nguyen, H.D., Tran, K.P., Thomassey, S., Hamad, M.: Forecasting and anomaly detection approaches using LSTM and LSTM autoencoder techniques with the applications in supply chain management. Int. J. Inf. Manag. **57**, 102282 (2021)
30. Chawla, A., Lee, B., Jacob, P., Fallon, S.: Bidirectional LSTM autoencoder for sequence based anomaly detection in cyber security. Int. J. Simulation: Syst., Sci. Technol. (2019)
31. Wong, T., Luo, Z.: Recurrent auto-encoder model for multidimensional time series representation (2018)
32. Mirza, M, Osindero, S.: Conditional generative adversarial nets. ArXiv. abs/1411.1784 (2014)
33. Al-Shawwa, B., Glynn, E., Hoffman, M.A., Ehsan, Z., Ingram, D.G.: Outpatient health care utilization for sleep disorders in the cerner health facts database. J. Clin. Sleep Med. **17**(2), 203–209 (2021)
34. Petrick, J.L., Nguyen, T., Cook, M.B.: Temporal trends of esophageal disorders by age in the cerner health facts database. Ann. Epidemiol. **26**(2), 151–4.e4 (2016)
35. DeShazo, J.P., Hoffman, M.: A comparison of a multistate inpatient ehr database to the hcup nationwide inpatient sample. BMC Health Services Res. **15**(1), 1–8 (2015)
36. Hripcsak, G., Ryan, P.B., Duke, J.D., Shah, N.H., Park, R.W., Huser, V., et al.: Characterizing treatment pathways at scale using the ohdsi network. Proc Natl Acad Sci U S A. **113**(27), 7329–7336 (2016)
37. Shukla, S.N., Marlin, B.M.: Interpolation-prediction networks for irregularly sampled time series. ArXiv ;abs/1909.07782 (2019)
38. Müller, R., Kornblith, S., Hinton, G.E.: When does label smoothing help? In: NeurIPS (2019)

39. Pedregosa, F., Varoquaux, G., Gramfort, A., Michel, V., Thirion, B., Grisel, O., et al.: Scikit-learn: Machine learning in python. J. Mach. Learn. Res. **12**, 2825–2830 (2011)
40. Abadi, M., et al.: Tensorflow: a system for large-scale machine learning. In: OSDI (2016)
41. Oliphant, T.E.: Guide to NumPy (2015)
42. McKinney, W.: Data structures for statistical computing in python (2010)
43. Virtanen, P., et al.: Scipy 1.0: fundamental algorithms for scientific computing in python. Nat. Method. **17**(3), 261–272 (2020).
44. Matwin, S., Nin, J., Sehatkar, M., Szapiro, T.: A review of attribute disclosure control. In: Navarro-Arribas G., Torra V. (eds.) Advanced Research in Data Privacy. Studies in Computational Intelligence, vol. 567. Springer, Cham (2015)
45. Surendra, H., MohanH, S.: A review of synthetic data generation methods for privacy preserving data publishing. Int. J. Sci. Technol. Res. **6**, 95–101 (2017)
46. Hittmeir, M., Mayer, R., Ekelhart, A.: A baseline for attribute disclosure risk in synthetic data. In: Proceedings of the Tenth ACM Conference on Data and Application Security and Privacy (2020)
47. Stadler, T., Oprisanu, B., Troncoso, C.: Synthetic data - a privacy mirage. ArXiv. abs/2011.07018 (2020)
48. Pascanu, R., Mikolov, T., Bengio, Y.: On the difficulty of training recurrent neural networks. In: ICML (2013)
49. García-Laencina, P.J., Sancho-Gómez, J., Figueiras-Vidal, A.R.: Pattern classification with missing data: A review. Neural Comput. Appl. **19**, 263–282 (2009)
50. Vaswani, A., Shazeer, N., Parmar, N., Uszkoreit, J., Jones, L., Gomez, A.N., et al.: Attention is all you need. ArXiv. abs/1706.03762 (2017)
51. Liu, Y., Ott, M., Goyal, N., Du, J., Joshi, M., Chen, D., et al.: Roberta: a robustly optimized bert pretraining approach. ArXiv. abs/1907.11692 (2019)
52. Devlin, J., Chang, M.W., Lee, K., Toutanova, K.: Bert: pre-training of deep bidirectional transformers for language understanding. In: NAACL-HLT (2019)
53. Choi, K., Hawthorne, C., Simon, I., Dinculescu, M., Engel, J.: Encoding musical style with transformer autoencoders. In: ICML (2020)
54. Fang, L., Zeng, T., Liu, C.C., Bo, L., Dong, W., Chen, C.: Transformer-based conditional variational autoencoder for controllable story generation. ArXiv abs/2101.00828 (2021)
55. Toreini, E., et al.: Technologies for trustworthy machine learning: A survey in a socio-technical context. ArXiv. abs/2007.08911 (2020)
56. Dwork, C., Roth, A.: The algorithmic foundations of differential privacy. Found Trends Theor. Comput. Sci. **9**, 211–407 (2014)

# TRACE: Early Detection of Chronic Kidney Disease Onset with Transformer-Enhanced Feature Embedding

Yu Wang[1] , Ziqiao Guan[1] , Wei Hou[2] , and Fusheng Wang[1,3](✉)

[1] Department of Computer Science, Stony Brook University,
Stony Brook, NY 11794, USA
{yuwang4,ziguan}@cs.stonybrook.edu, fusheng.wang@stonybrook.edu
[2] Department of Family, Population and Preventive Medicine,
Stony Brook University, Stony Brook, NY 11794, USA
wei.hou@stonybrookmedicine.edu
[3] Department of Biomedical Informatics, Stony Brook University,
Stony Brook, NY 11794, USA

**Abstract.** Chronic kidney disease (CKD) has a poor prognosis due to excessive risk factors and comorbidities associated with it. The early detection of CKD faces challenges of *insufficient medical histories of positive patients* and *complicated risk factors*. In this paper, we propose the **TRACE** (Transformer-RNN Autoencoder-enhanced CKD Detector) framework, an end-to-end prediction model using patients' medical history data, to deal with these challenges. **TRACE** presents a comprehensive medical history representation with a novel key component: a Transformer-RNN autoencoder. The autoencoder jointly learns a medical concept embedding via Transformer for each hospital visit, and a latent representation which summarizes a patient's medical history across all the visits. We compared **TRACE** with multiple state-of-the-art methods on a dataset derived from real-world medical records. Our model has achieved 0.5708 AUPRC with a 2.31% relative improvement over the best-performing method. We also validated the clinical meaning of the learned embeddings through visualizations and a case study, showing the potential of **TRACE** to serve as a general disease prediction model.

**Keywords:** Chronic kidney disease prediction · Deep learning · Transformer · Electronic health records

## 1 Introduction

Chronic kidney disease (CKD) is a general term for many heterogeneous diseases that irreversibly alter kidney structure or cause a chronic reduction in kidney function [25]. It is defined by the presence of kidney damage, or decreased kidney function, or both, for a minimum of three months. Diagnosis of CKD is

© Springer Nature Switzerland AG 2021
E. K. Rezig et al. (Eds.): Poly 2021/DMAH 2021, LNCS 12921, pp. 166–182, 2021.
https://doi.org/10.1007/978-3-030-93663-1_13

often made after accidental findings from screening laboratory tests, or when the symptom already becomes severe [42]. According to the US Centers for Disease Control and Prevention, approximately 15% of US adults have CKD, but most people may not feel ill or notice any symptoms until CKD is advanced [7]. Two major causes of CKD are hypertension and diabetes. Kidney failure is the most serious outcome of CKD and severe conditions can only be treated by dialysis and transplantation, which are indications of end-stage kidney disease. CKD is a well-known risk factor for cardiovascular disease and all-cause mortality [2,40]. However, less than 2% of CKD patients finally require renal replacement therapy, because many of them die from cardiovascular causes before end-stage kidney disease can occur [22].

CKD has a poor prognosis due to excessive risk factors and comorbidities associated with it [24]. The early detection of CKD, for health benefits, is an even more challenging task. For the purposes of early detection and control, a promising direction is to regularly monitor risk factors of CKD for high-risk patients. It is also worth trying to focus the screening for CKD on younger, healthier populations, although it is less likely to detect CKD in such cohorts [40]. In short, early detection of CKD faces challenges of *insufficient medical histories of positive patients* and *complicated risk factors* from a data standpoint. This calls for more effective machine learning prediction models to address these issues.

To address the first challenge, we need a prediction model that can *better extract knowledge from the insufficient medical histories*. In recent years, deep learning has emerged as a powerful tool to gain insight into EHR data [10,32,39,43]. Previous studies predicted heart failure onset with recurrent neural networks (RNNs) [16] and the reverse time attention mechanism [14]. These models proposed different ideas for sequence modeling, but they did not perform very well in our experiments. Apart from sequence modeling, we also need a better feature representation for the early detection of CKD onset. This ties in with the second challenge – complicated risk factors.

Given how extensive the risk factors are when assessing a patient's likelihood of having CKD, it is critical to *learn an embedding to measure the latent similarity between these risk factors and CKD*. An embedding maps discrete medical concepts to a continuous latent space and summarizes the interactions between medical concepts. Several models can learn embeddings of medical concepts [12,17,18]. However, these models have yet to make the most of the sequential nature of EHR data because they only learned medical concept embeddings for individual hospital visits. We can use a sequence aggregator, such as RNN or 1-D convolutional neural networks (CNNs), to link a sequence of visits and encode them to a patient-level representation.

Motivated by the challenges and the previous work, we propose the TRACE (Transformer-RNN Autoencoder-enhanced CKD Detector) framework, which combines ideas of both RNN autoencoder and Transformer [18,41]. TRACE jointly learns the Transformer-encoded hidden structure of individual hospital visits while predicting CKD onset with RNN. In this work, we used Cerner Health Facts [21], a large database derived from EHR systems across the US, as our data source. The database includes comprehensive patient-level details of diagnoses, procedures, medications, and laboratory tests. The EHR data are structured data without clinical notes and images. Our features include both medical codes and non-medical code information. We summarize our contributions as follows:

- We propose a Transformer-RNN autoencoder architecture. This autoencoder jointly learns a medical concept embedding via Transformer for individual hospital visits, as well as a patient embedding via an RNN encoder-decoder structure which summarizes the entire medical history of this patient.
- We adopt two pre-training processes to capture proper latent representations for patients' conditions and hospital visit histories respectively. We also demonstrated that TRACE successfully alleviated the aforementioned challenges by incorporating the pre-trained latent representations.

## 2   Related Work

### 2.1   Deep Learning in Healthcare Domain

Deep learning algorithms have become popular approaches for modeling disease progression [11,14,26,27], patient characterization [3,8], and generating synthetic EHR data for research purposes [15].

The most common application of modeling disease progression is predicting disease outcomes. Deep neural networks have very limited power when learning disease trajectories from scratch, sometimes it is necessary to incorporate prior medical knowledge [28,33] or supplement EHR data with inherent hierarchical structure of medical ontologies [13]. Missing value is also a challenge is modeling EHR data. [9] has demonstrated that RNNs are able to capture the long-term dependency in time series and improve prediction performance.

Deep learning models anticipate a large volume of data to achieve satisfactory results, which usually exceeds the capacity of most healthcare facilities. A straightforward solution is to combine EHR data from multiple sources, but data harmonization is a labor-intensive process. [34] recently proposed a representation of EHRs based on the Fast Healthcare Interoperability Resources (FHIR) format for deep learning models without site-specific data harmonization. When working on an imbalanced dataset with insufficient positive samples, data augmentation techniques can benefit training. CONAN [19] incorporated generative adversarial networks (GANs) to create candidate positive and negative samples in rare disease detection. Pre-training and transfer learning [4,20] can also help to solve this problem. G-BERT [38] used the pre-trained hospital visit representations for downstream predictive tasks. [35] trained a CNN on a large global database with biomedical abstracts, and transferred the learned knowledge to predict diagnosis codes for one medical center.

### 2.2   Representation Learning for Medical Concepts

Representation learning algorithms in healthcare domain are mainly borrowed from natural language processing (NLP). The general idea is to encode discrete medical concepts (e.g., medical codes) to one-hot vectors [5] and then apply Word2Vec algorithms [30] to learn embeddings.

For example, Med2Vec [12] utilized skip-gram [31] to learn intra-visit medical code co-occurrences as well as inter-visit sequential information. The generic skip-gram model is based on the assumption that a word can play different roles at different positions in a sentence. However, this assumption doesn't hold for medical codes given their unordered nature. When we adopt NLP algorithms to model medical concepts, we typically apply the algorithms to the feature dimension instead of the temporal dimension, and the order in which these medical concepts occur is ignored.

MiME [17] leveraged the inherent structure of medical codes to learn a multilevel embedding of EHR data, but this model required the EHR data to contain complete structure information between diagnoses and treatments. Recently, GCT [18] has been proposed to solve this problem. GCT learned the graphical structure of EHR data during training and proved that Transformer is a suitable model to learn such structure. Our work was motivated by GCT to use Transformer to encode hospital visits.

## 3  Method

### 3.1  Problem Statement

We formulate this problem as a binary prediction task. Given a patient whose medical history is in the form of a sequence of hospital visits $\mathcal{P} = \{\mathcal{V}_1, \mathcal{V}_2, \cdots, \mathcal{V}_T\}$ in chronological order, where $T \in \mathbb{N}$ is the total number of visits that the patient has. Each visit $\mathcal{V}_t$ ($t \in \{1, 2, \cdots, T\}$) consists of a list of medical codes, clinical observations and other information related to this patient. We want to predict whether the patient will be diagnosed with CKD for the first time in the following visit $\mathcal{V}_{T+1}$.

### 3.2  Vector Representations of EHRs

Figure 1 illustrates the vector representations of a patient's hospital visit history $\mathcal{P}$, which contains both medical codes and non-medical code information. For simplicity, all notations and algorithms in this paper are presented for a single patient unless otherwise specified.

**Medical Code Representations.** Medical codes include diagnosis codes, procedure codes, and medication codes. Medical codes are *the primary features* for our prediction task. We denote the set of medical codes in our EHR data by $\mathcal{C} = \{c_1, c_2, \cdots, c_{|\mathcal{C}|}\}$ with size $|\mathcal{C}|$. All medical codes that occur at a hospital visit $\mathcal{V}_t$ are represented by a multi-hot vector $x_t \in \{0, 1\}^{|\mathcal{C}|}$ where the $i$-th element is 1 if $c_i \in \mathcal{V}_t$.

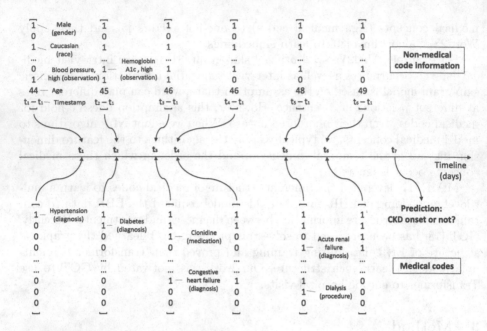

**Fig. 1.** Vector representation of a patient's EHR data. This patient had seven hospital visits at time $\{t_1, t_2, \cdots, t_7\}$. We used the first six visits $\{t_1, \cdots, t_6\}$ to construct input vectors to the model and predicted whether there would be a CKD onset at the seventh visit.

**Non-medical Code Information.** Besides medical codes, we also included the patient's observations (e.g., lab tests, vital signs, etc.), age, race, gender, and the timestamp of visit $\mathcal{V}_t$. Observations are *the secondary features* in our dataset. Let $d_t$ denote the vector representation of the non-medical code information, which is a concatenation of multi-hot vector and numeric values. We will provide details of theses non-medical code features in the "Dataset" section.

### 3.3   Model Architecture of TRACE

In this section, we describe TRACE in detail, with the following components: a patient embedding from a pre-trained Transformer-RNN autoencoder, a medical code history encoder, and a joint attention module. The overall architecture is illustrated in Fig. 2.

**Patient Embedding via Transformer-RNN Autoencoder.** We pre-train a Transformer-RNN autoencoder as a joint feature extractor for both feature embedding and patient embedding. This design adopts a Transformer [18] for computing self-correlation of all features at individual hospital visit level, and a subsequent RNN autoencoder for learning a patient representation by reconstructing the input sequence in an unsupervised fashion.

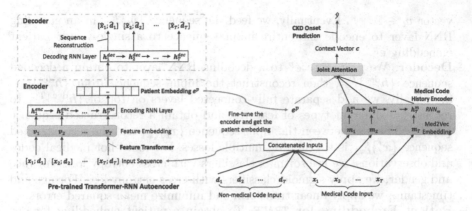

**Fig. 2.** End-to-end structure of TRACE. The model ingests a patient's medical history in the form of two sequences of vectors $\mathcal{X} = \{x_1, x_2, \cdots, x_T\}$ and $\mathcal{D} = \{d_1, d_2, \cdots, d_T\}$, next propagates them to the encoder module of a pre-trained Transformer-RNN autoencoder for a patient embedding, then combines the patient embedding with the patient's medical code history to compute joint attention, and finally outputs a probability score $\hat{y}$.

The autoencoder ingests a sequence of hospital visits in the form of $\{x'_t\}_{t=1}^{T}$ where $x'_t = [x_t; d_t] \in \mathbb{R}^{n \times 1}$ and $n$ is the total number of features. The sequence $\{x'_t\}_{t=1}^{T}$ then runs through an encode-decoder structure to reconstruct itself.

- **Encoder.** We first map each $x'_t$ ($t \in \{1, 2, \cdots, T\}$) to a latent space with a learnable embedding matrix $W_x$ by $Z_t = W_x \odot x'_t \in \mathbb{R}^{n \times d_z}$. This extends the raw input vector $x'_t$ to a *vector array* for the Transformer to process. Since Transformer has a quadratic time and space complexity and is expensive to compute, we downsize the feature dimension from $n$ to $\tilde{n}$ ($\tilde{n} \ll n$) via a linear transform $\tilde{Z}_t = \tilde{W}_z Z_t \in \mathbb{R}^{\tilde{n} \times d_z}$. This improves scalability by reducing the complexity to $\mathcal{O}(\tilde{n}^2)$.
  We learn an embedding for the downsized feature space using a Transformer with one encoder block and a single attention head as follows,

$$X_t = \text{Transformer}(\tilde{Z}_t), \tag{1}$$

where $X_t \in \mathbb{R}^{\tilde{n} \times d_{\text{emb}}}$. Positional encoding is removed from our framework, since the features are not ordered. Let $\tilde{W}_\alpha \in \mathbb{R}^{\tilde{n} \times \tilde{n}}$ denote the learned attention weights for the downsized feature space, we compute attention weights for the *original feature space* by

$$W_\alpha = \tilde{W}_z \tilde{W}_\alpha \tilde{W}_z^\top \tag{2}$$

where $W_\alpha \in \mathbb{R}^{\tilde{n} \times \tilde{n}}$ is the desired attention weights for the original feature space.
To aggregate the embedding of all features occurred at time $t$, we average-pool $X_t$ by the downsized feature dimension to obtain a single embedding

vector $v_t \in \mathbb{R}^{d_{emb}}$. Eventually, we feed the sequence $\{v_t\}_{t=1}^T$ in an encoding RNN layer to encode the entire input sequence to a single-vector patient embedding $e^p$.

- **Decoder.** We propagate $e^p$ to a decoding RNN layer to obtain a decoded sequence $\{h_t^{dec}\}_{t=1}^T$, then reconstruct the input sequence from $\{h_t^{dec}\}_{t=1}^T$. Specifically, we add separate fully-connected layers on top of $\{h_t^{dec}\}_{t=1}^T$ to reconstruct different types of features, and obtain a reconstructed sequence $\{\hat{x}_t'\}_{t=1}^T$. The loss between the input sequence $\{x_t'\}_{t=1}^T$ and the reconstructed sequence $\{\hat{x}_t'\}_{t=1}^T$ is the sum of multiple losses. For multi-hot medical codes and observations, we use softmax classifiers with cross entropy loss. For race and gender, we apply sigmoid classifiers with cross entropy loss. For age and timestamp, we apply linear transform and minimize mean squared errors.
- **Patient Embedding for TRACE.** To obtain a patient embedding for our end-to-end prediction task, we feed the input sequence $\{[x_t; d_t]\}_{t=1}^T$ in the pre-trained encoder and compute the embedding vector $e^p$ for this patient (Fig. 2).

**Medical Code History Encoder.** Considering that medical codes summarize other non-medical code features to some extent, we separately encode the patient's medical code history for information gain in our model.

We first map the discrete medical code inputs $x_t$ to a continuous latent embedding space $m_t$ as follows,

$$m_t = W_m x_t, \tag{3}$$

where $W_m \in \mathbb{R}^{|\mathcal{C}| \times d_m}$ is a word embedding lookup table pre-trained via Med2Vec [12], and $d_m$ is the size of the embedding vector. To encode a sequence of medical codes, we then apply an RNN layer on top of the medical code embedding $m_t$ by

$$h_t^m = \text{RNN}_m(h_{t-1}^m, m_t) \tag{4}$$

where $h_t^m$ is the hidden state of the RNN layer at time $t$.

**Joint Attention.** We want to further have the patient embedding interact with the medical code history. Specifically, we compute interactions between $e^p$ and each $h_t^m$ ($t \in \{1, 2, \cdots, T\}$) as follows,

$$g_t = [e^p; h_t^m], \tag{5}$$

$$\text{score}_t = u^\top \tanh(W_g g_t + b_g), \tag{6}$$

$$\alpha_t = \frac{\exp(\text{score}_t)}{\sum_{t=1}^T \exp(\text{score}_t)}, \tag{7}$$

where $u$ is a learable weight, and $\alpha_t$ is the attention weight assigned to visit $\mathcal{V}_t$. Then we obtain a context vector $c$ for this patient by

$$c = [e^p; \sum_{t=1}^T \alpha_t g_t]. \tag{8}$$

**CKD Onset Prediction.** We use the context vector $c$ to predict the binary label $y \in \{0, 1\}$ as follows,

$$\hat{y} = \sigma(w_y^\top c + b_y), \tag{9}$$

where $\hat{y}$ is the predicted probability score for this patient. The training objective is to use the predicted score $\hat{y}$ and the true label $y$ to minimize the following binary cross entropy loss:

$$\mathcal{L} = -\frac{1}{N} \sum_{j=1}^{N} (y_j \log \hat{y}_j + (1 - y_j) \log(1 - \hat{y}_j)), \tag{10}$$

where $N$ is the total number of patients in our training set.

## 4 Experiments

### 4.1 Dataset

We collected our experimental dataset from two healthcare systems in Cerner Health Facts, each healthcare system comprises multiple healthcare facilities. This is a *case-control study* where negative patients were downsampled through a statistical analysis, such that our model was trained to distinguish positive and negative patients who were similar in terms of age, race and gender.

**Features and Data Preprocessing.** We extracted a patient's diagnosis codes, procedure codes, medication codes, observations, age, race, gender, and admission date for features of each hospital visit. Statistics of the features are available in Table 1.

The raw diagnosis codes, procedure codes and medication codes in Cerner Health Facts are respectively International Classification of Diseases (ICD), Current Procedural Terminology (CPT) and generic drug names. We grouped ICD diagnosis codes by the Clinical Classifications Software (CCS) to obtain higher-level diagnosis codes for experiments, which reduced the number of diagnosis codes from over 69,000 to 275. CKD diagnoses were identified by the CCS codes and were excluded from the feature set. We did not consider hospital visits without any diagnosis codes documented and removed medical codes that appeared in less than 50 hospital visit records.

Apart from medical codes, we also included observations, age, race, gender, and admission date to represent a hospital visit. Observations, race and gender were categorical features encoded to a multi-hot vector (Fig. 1) for a hospital visit. There were 1,261 distinct observations in our feature set. For the admission date of a patient's hospital visit, we converted it to a numeric timestamp by calculating the duration in days from the patient's first visit to this visit. We took the logarithm of numeric features for model inputs.

**Table 1.** Statistics of datasets for our experiments and the pre-training using the Med2Vec model.

|  | Experiments | Med2Vec |
|---|---|---|
| Total # of patients | 147,791 | 1,155,450 |
| # of cases (positives) | 21,113 | N/A |
| # of controls (negatives) | 126,678 | N/A |
| # of patients for training | 110,842 | N/A |
| # of patients for validation | 14,778 | N/A |
| # of patients for testing | 22,171 | N/A |
| Total # of medical codes | 1,679 | 3,884 |
| # of diagnosis codes | 275 | 278 |
| # of procedure codes | 662 | 2,449 |
| # of medication codes | 742 | 1,157 |
| Total # of observations | 1,261 | N/A |
| Total # of races and genders | 10 | N/A |

**Selection of Cases and Controls.** We excluded hospital visits made by non-adult patients because we aimed at predicting CKD onset for adults only. The case/control selection criteria are as follows.

– *Cases (positives)* were patients who had at least one hospital visit prior to CKD onset. The CKD onset was the positive class label for our prediction task.
– *Controls (negatives)* were non-CKD patients who had at least two hospital visits in our dataset. Controls were identified for each case using the propensity score-matching based on logistic regression [36] and the greedy algorithm [6]. Matching variables include age, gender and race. Class labels of control patients came from their latest hospital visit records and were negative labels.

Six controls were selected for each case to match the prevalence of CKD in US adults (i.e., $1/7 \approx 14.29\%$). Eventually, we extracted a total of 147,791 patients for experiments. The dataset was further split into training, validation and test sets in a 75/10/15 ratio. The case/control ratio in each of the training, validation and test sets was the same as the disease prevalence rate in the entire experimental dataset. Table 1 provides details of the study cohort. Since 90% of patients in the dataset had less than 30 hospital visits, we only kept up to 30 most recent hospital visits per patient to improve scalability.

## 4.2    Pre-training for Medical Concepts

There were two types of medical concepts in our dataset: medical codes and observations. We performed two pre-training processes to get proper embeddings for them.

**Independent Pre-training.** We pre-trained embedding weights for *medical codes*[1] using Med2Vec. The dataset for this pre-training task was extracted from 10 healthcare facilities in Cerner Health Facts, not including the two healthcare systems for our experiments. We trained the Med2Vec model on 1,155,450 patients with 15,115,251 hospital visits and obtained pre-trained embedding weights for 3,884 distinct medical codes (Table 1). In our prediction task, we treated medical codes outside the independent pre-training as out-of-vocabulary (OOV) tokens and initialized embedding weights for OOV medical codes with zeros.

**Transformer-Encoded Embedding.** We pre-trained the Transformer-RNN autoencoder on our training set to encode *all features*, where only age, race, gender, and timestamp were not medical concepts (Table 1). This means that the Transformer-encoded feature embedding was a good latent representation of medical concepts. The pre-trained feature embedding was built into TRACE as part of the encoder module for fine-tuning (Fig. 2).

### 4.3  Baseline Models

For comparison, we implemented the following models with $x'_t = [x_t; d_t]$ as the input vector for a hospital visit.

- **Logistic regression (LR).** We counted the occurrences of each medical code and each observation for a patient, all the other features were determined by the patient's last hospital visit in the inputs. A LR model was trained on the resulting vectors.
- **Multi-layer perceptron (MLP).** We used the same approach to construct model inputs as the LR model, but added a fully-connected layer with relu activation between the input layer and the output layer.
- **RNN** and **BiRNN.** We used a fully-connected layer with relu activation to encode inputs and then propagated the resulting vectors to a forward/bidirectional RNN layer. Logistic regression was applied to the last hidden state of the RNN layer to predict CKD onset.
- **RETAIN** [14]. RETAIN model was designed to predicts heart failure onset using backward RNN and two levels of attention weights. We used the same architecture as the RNN baseline, but replaced the RNN layer with the RETAIN module.
- **Dipole** [27]. Dipole model predicts multiple disease outcomes via a bidirectional RNN layer and three different attention mechanisms. We used the same structure as the RNN baseline, but replaced the RNN layer with the Dipole module and trained it using each of the three attention mechanisms, i.e., $Dipole_l$, $Dipole_g$ and $Dipole_c$.

---

[1] We also trained Med2Vec to obtain an embedding for observations, but got very poor results.

**Table 2.** Prediction performance of different models.

| Category | Model | AUPRC | Neg log likelihood |
|---|---|---|---|
| Non- | LR | 0.4527 | 0.3453 |
| sequence | MLP | 0.5359 | 0.3067 |
| CNN | 1-D CNN | 0.5475 | 0.3017 |
| RNN | RNN | 0.5574 | 0.2978 |
| | BiRNN | 0.5510 | 0.2986 |
| | RETAIN | 0.5505 | 0.2986 |
| | Dipole$_l$ | 0.5563 | 0.2969 |
| | Dipole$_g$ | 0.5579 | 0.2994 |
| | Dipole$_c$ | 0.5515 | 0.2962 |
| Ours | **TRACE** | **0.5708** | **0.2929** |

– **1-D CNN.** A modification of AlexNet [23]. We replaced all 2-D convolutional layers with 1-D convolutional layers, which served as a sequence aggregator of individual hospital visits. We computed the mean of AlexNet's outputs across the temporal dimension and applied logistic regression on top of it to generate predictions. The inputs were encoded in the same way as the RNN baseline.

## 4.4    Evaluation Metrics

We measured the model performance on our test set by area under the precision-recall curve (AUPRC). AUPRC can effectively evaluate the fraction of true positives among positive predictions [37], thus it is an appropriate metric when evaluating binary classifiers on imbalanced datasets like ours. In addition to AUPRC, we also calculated negative log likelihood by Eq. 10 to measure the model loss on the test set.

## 4.5    Implementation Details

We implemented all models and calculated all evaluation metrics using Tensor-Flow 2.2.0 [1]. For Med2Vec, we used the code provided by the authors[2]. The dimension of the downsized feature space was $\tilde{n} = 100$. The sizes of all embedding vectors and hidden layers were 128. The dropout rate for the feed-forward layer of Transformer was 0.5. We used the Adadelta optimizer [44] and set the learning rate as 1.0 to match the exact form in the paper. We trained each model for 50 epochs with 100 patients per batch. All experiments were run on a 16 GB NVIDIA Tesla V100 PCIe GPU.

---

[2] https://github.com/mp2893/med2vec

## 4.6    Results

**Prediction Performance.** We evaluated our model and all baselines on the test set. Table 2 shows the AUPRC and negative log likelihood scores of the test set. In general, sequential models (RNNs and 1-D CNN) outperformed non-sequential models (LR and MLP). This is because sequential models were more capable of capturing the underlying patterns in disease trajectories, while non-sequential models only learned from aggregated information of medical histories. In the real-world clinical practice, doctors need to carefully review a patient's medical histories and monitor the patient for a long time to decide whether a chronic disease like CKD can be diagnosed. Occasional occurrences of some symptoms related to CKD are insufficient to support the doctor's decision.

It is noteworthy that all RNN-based baselines demonstrated comparable performance in terms of both metrics, and increased model complexity failed to surpass the simplest RNN model. This seems to indicate that training RNN models from scratch is not suitable for our task. Both RETAIN and Dipole computed attention scores with the outputs of RNN layers. The attention mechanism assigns a score to each hospital visit using the sequential information learned from scratch, which is fine when detecting diseases in their original tasks. However, CKD is quite different because its excessive risk factors could be intertwined. It is hard to determine whether a patient has CKD simply by the existence of several risk factors without extensive prior knowledge.

TRACE successfully alleviated this problem by introducing a pre-trained Transformer-RNN autoencoder. The autoencoder produced a good patient embedding which compressed information in the entire input sequence. With this patient embedding as the prior knowledge, our end-to-end prediction model was able to better discover the correlation between CKD diagnoses and past medical records. TRACE achieved a 2.31% gain in AUPRC compared with the best-performing baseline (i.e., Dipole$_g$).

**Ablation Study.** To understand how each major model component contributed to the overall prediction performance, we compared TRACE with its several variants.

- TRACE_base. This is TRACE without the medical code history encoder and the joint attention. We directly used the fine-tuned patient embedding to get predictions.
- RACE. This is TRACE without Transformer-encoded feature embedding. In the RNN autoencoder, we got a feature embedding through a fully-connected layer with relu activation instead.
- RACE_base. This is RACE without the medical code history encoder and the joint attention. The fine-tuned patient embedding were directly used for getting predictions.

We trained the three variants with the same set of hyperparameters as TRACE. We note the AUPRC scores for the analyses here (Table 3). Overall, pre-trained

Table 3. Ablation study of TRACE.

| Model | AUPRC | Neg log likelihood |
|-------|-------|--------------------|
| RACE_base | 0.5649 | 0.2955 |
| RACE | 0.5631 | 0.2938 |
| TRACE_base | 0.5696 | 0.2937 |
| **TRACE** | **0.5708** | **0.2929** |

RNN autoencoders provided richer patient-level information than raw input features. Even the worst-performing model in Table 3 (i.e., RACE) achieved a 0.93% relative improvement in AUPRC over the best-performing baseline in Table 2 (i.e., Dipole$_g$). Evidently, Transformer has demonstrated its superiority over pure fully-connected layers in encoding medical concepts (RACE vs. TRACE and RACE_base vs. TRACE_base). As we expected, there was slight information gain after adding medical code histories and the joint attention, but the strength was limited (RACE_base vs. RACE and TRACE_base vs. TRACE).

**Patient Embedding Visualization.** Figure 3 plots patient embeddings produced by TRACE and the baselines. We used the t-SNE [29] algorithm for dimensionality reduction. Obviously, TRACE learned a better clustering of positive patients. Given that this is a case-control study, TRACE met our expectation to better distinguish cases and controls who were similar in terms of age, race and gender. In general, positive patients were better clustered in the end-to-end prediction tasks (RACE and TRACE). Patients were more scattered in the autoencoders (Fig. 3b and Fig. 3c) than in the end-to-end prediction models (Fig. 3e and Fig. 3d). Comparing Transformer-RNN autoencoder (Fig. 3b) with the generic RNN autoencoder (Fig. 3c), it is evident that the patient embedding generated by the former is more gathered. This demonstrated the strength of Transformer in encoding features.

**Attention Visualization and Case Study.** We visualize the attention behavior of Transformer in the course of CKD onset prediction. Since TRACE computed self-attention for the downsized feature space $\tilde{Z}_t$, we need to back-propagate to the original feature space by Eq. 2 to get desired attention weights. To improve readability of the visualization, we randomly selected a CKD patient from the test set, who had four hospital visits and at most 20 medical concepts per visit.

Figure 4 illustrates the attention behavior of medical concepts occurred at each hospital visit for the selected patient, which also shows the patient's disease trajectory. This patient had hypertension and diabetes – two major causes of CKD that usually intertwine with other risk factors of CKD. No remarkable attention behavior was present at the first hospital visit. At the second visit, we noticed that esophageal disorders, diabetes and low diastolic blood pressure were mutually attended. At the third visit, the high hemoglobin A1c level and

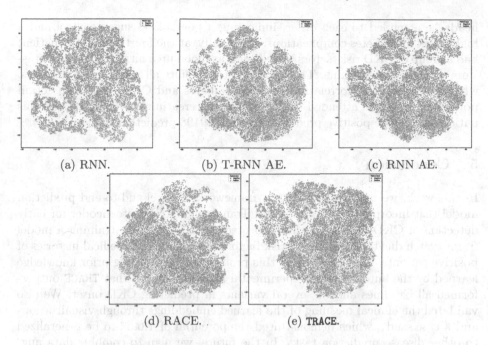

(a) RNN.                (b) T-RNN AE.                (c) RNN AE.

(d) RACE.                (e) TRACE.

**Fig. 3.** Different patient embeddings generated by pre-trained autoencoders and end-to-end prediction models for the test set. T-RNN: Transformer-RNN, AE: autoencoder, orange dot: positive patient, blue dot: negative patient. Dimension reduced via t-SNE. Overall, positive patients were better clustered by RACE and TRACE. Patients were more scattered in the autoencoders than in the end-to-end prediction models. The Transformer-RNN autoencoder produced a more gathered embedding for positive patients than the generic RNN autoencoder. (Color figure online)

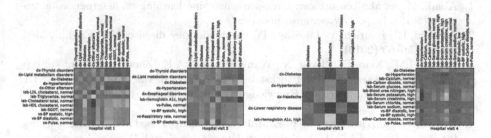

**Fig. 4.** Medical concept attentions produced by TRACE for a CKD patient in the test set. The labels are the medical concepts occurred at each hospital visit. It illustrates how medical concepts on the vertical axis attended to medical concepts on the horizontal axis. "dx-": diagnosis code (medical code), "lab-": lab test (observation), "vs-": vital sign (observation), "other-": observation other than lab test and vital sign, "BP": blood pressure. This patient got a 0.9198 prediction score with four hospital visits as inputs.

headache attended to each other, indicating a poor blood sugar control and a higher risk of diabetes complications. Eventually, at the fourth visit, the patient had a group of CKD risk factors tested, such as blood urea nitrogen, serum potassium and serum creatinine. The abnormal test results all attended to diabetes, which suggested the correlation between diabetes and CKD. The high serum potassium level also attended to the high serum creatinine level. Moreover, this patient got a true positive prediction with a 0.9198 prediction score.

## 5    Conclusion

In this work, we proposed the TRACE framework, a novel end-to-end prediction model that incorporated a pre-trained Transformer-RNN autoencoder for early detection of CKD onset. It is hard to predict CKD onset by training a model from scratch due to the excessive risk factors and insufficient medical histories of positive patients. TRACE alleviated this problem by introducing prior knowledge learned by the autoencoder. Experimental analyses showed that TRACE outperformed all baselines and its several variants in predicting CKD onset. We also validated the clinical meaning of the learned embeddings through visualizations and a case study, which demonstrated the potential of TRACE to be generalized to other disease prediction tasks. In the future, we plan to combine data augmentation techniques like GAN to better address the data insufficiency. We will also adopt more advanced NLP algorithms to train embeddings for patients and features.

## References

1. Abadi, M., et al.: TensorFlow: large-scale machine learning on heterogeneous systems (2015). https://www.tensorflow.org/
2. Abboud, H., Henrich, W.L.: Stage IV chronic kidney disease. New Engl. J. Med. **362**(1), 56–65 (2010)
3. Baytas, I.M., Xiao, C., Zhang, X., Wang, F., Jain, A.K., Zhou, J.: Patient subtyping via time-aware LSTM networks. In: Proceedings of the 23rd ACM SIGKDD International Conference on Knowledge Discovery and Data Mining, pp. 65–74 (2017)
4. Bengio, Y.: Deep learning of representations for unsupervised and transfer learning. In: Proceedings of ICML Workshop on Unsupervised and Transfer Learning, pp. 17–36 (2012)
5. Bengio, Y., Courville, A., Vincent, P.: Representation learning: a review and new perspectives. IEEE Trans. Pattern Anal. Mach. Intell. **35**(8), 1798–1828 (2013)
6. Bergstralh, E., Kosanke, J.: Computerized matching of controls: Section of biostatistics technical report 56. Rochester, MN, Mayo Foundation (1995)
7. CDC: Chronic Kidney Disease in the United States, Atlanta, GA: US Department of Health and Human Services, Centers for Disease Control and Prevention (2019)
8. Che, Z., Kale, D., Li, W., Bahadori, M.T., Liu, Y.: Deep computational phenotyping. In: Proceedings of the 21th ACM SIGKDD International Conference on Knowledge Discovery and Data Mining, pp. 507–516 (2015)

9. Che, Z., Purushotham, S., Cho, K., Sontag, D., Liu, Y.: Recurrent neural networks for multivariate time series with missing values. Sci. Rep. **8**(1), 1–12 (2018)
10. Ching, T., et al.: Opportunities and obstacles for deep learning in biology and medicine. J. R. Soc. Interface **15**(141), 20170387 (2018)
11. Choi, E., Bahadori, M.T., Schuetz, A., Stewart, W.F., Sun, J.: Doctor AI: predicting clinical events via recurrent neural networks. In: Machine Learning for Healthcare Conference, pp. 301–318 (2016)
12. Choi, E., et al.: Multi-layer representation learning for medical concepts. In: Proceedings of the 22nd ACM SIGKDD International Conference on Knowledge Discovery and Data Mining, pp. 1495–1504 (2016)
13. Choi, E., Bahadori, M.T., Song, L., Stewart, W.F., Sun, J.: Gram: graph-based attention model for healthcare representation learning. In: Proceedings of the 23rd ACM SIGKDD International Conference on Knowledge Discovery and Data Mining, pp. 787–795 (2017)
14. Choi, E., Bahadori, M.T., Sun, J., Kulas, J., Schuetz, A., Stewart, W.: RETAIN: an interpretable predictive model for healthcare using reverse time attention mechanism. In: Advances in Neural Information Processing Systems, pp. 3504–3512 (2016)
15. Choi, E., Biswal, S., Malin, B., Duke, J., Stewart, W.F., Sun, J.: Generating multilabel discrete patient records using generative adversarial networks. In: Proceedings of Machine Learning Research, vol. 68, pp. 286–305 (2017)
16. Choi, E., Schuetz, A., Stewart, W.F., Sun, J.: Using recurrent neural network models for early detection of heart failure onset. J. Am. Med. Inform. Assoc. **24**(2), 361–370 (2017)
17. Choi, E., Xiao, C., Stewart, W., Sun, J.: MIME: multilevel medical embedding of electronic health records for predictive healthcare. In: Advances in Neural Information Processing Systems, pp. 4547–4557 (2018)
18. Choi, E., et al.: Learning the graphical structure of electronic health records with graph convolutional transformer. In: Proceedings of the AAAI Conference on Artificial Intelligence, pp. 606–613 (2020)
19. Cui, L., Biswal, S., Glass, L.M., Lever, G., Sun, J., Xiao, C.: CONAN: complementary pattern augmentation for rare disease detection. In: Proceedings of the AAAI Conference on Artificial Intelligence, pp. 614–621 (2020)
20. Dauphin, G.M.Y., et al.: Unsupervised and transfer learning challenge: a deep learning approach. In: Proceedings of ICML Workshop on Unsupervised and Transfer Learning, pp. 97–110 (2012)
21. DeShazo, J.P., Hoffman, M.A.: A comparison of a multistate inpatient EHR database to the HCUP Nationwide inpatient sample. BMC Health Serv. Res. **15**(1), 384 (2015)
22. Keith, D.S., Nichols, G.A., Gullion, C.M., Brown, J.B., Smith, D.H.: Longitudinal follow-up and outcomes among a population with chronic kidney disease in a large managed care organization. Arch. Intern. Med. **164**(6), 659–663 (2004)
23. Krizhevsky, A., Sutskever, I., Hinton, G.E.: ImageNet classification with deep convolutional neural networks. In: Advances in Neural Information Processing Systems, pp. 1097–1105 (2012)
24. Kronenberg, F.: Emerging risk factors and markers of chronic kidney disease progression. Nat. Rev. Nephrol. **5**(12), 677 (2009)
25. Levey, A.S., Coresh, J.: Chronic kidney disease. Lancet **379**(9811), 165–180 (2012)
26. Lipton, Z.C., Kale, D.C., Elkan, C., Wetzel, R.C.: Learning to diagnose with LSTM recurrent neural networks. In: 4th International Conference on Learning Representations (2016)

27. Ma, F., Chitta, R., Zhou, J., You, Q., Sun, T., Gao, J.: Dipole: diagnosis prediction in healthcare via attention-based bidirectional recurrent neural networks. In: Proceedings of the 23rd ACM SIGKDD International Conference on Knowledge Discovery and Data Mining, pp. 1903–1911 (2017)

28. Ma, F., Gao, J., Suo, Q., You, Q., Zhou, J., Zhang, A.: Risk prediction on electronic health records with prior medical knowledge. In: Proceedings of the 24th ACM SIGKDD International Conference on Knowledge Discovery and Data Mining, pp. 1910–1919 (2018)

29. Van der Maaten, L., Hinton, G.: Visualizing data using t-SNE. J. Mach. Learn. Res. **9**, 2579–2605 (2008)

30. Mikolov, T., Chen, K., Corrado, G., Dean, J.: Efficient estimation of word representations in vector space. In: 1st International Conference on Learning Representations (2013)

31. Mikolov, T., Sutskever, I., Chen, K., Corrado, G.S., Dean, J.: Distributed representations of words and phrases and their compositionality. In: Advances in Neural Information Processing Systems, pp. 3111–3119 (2013)

32. Miotto, R., Wang, F., Wang, S., Jiang, X., Dudley, J.T.: Deep learning for healthcare: review, opportunities and challenges. Briefings Bioinform. **19**(6), 1236–1246 (2018)

33. Pham, T., Tran, T., Phung, D., Venkatesh, S.: Predicting healthcare trajectories from medical records: a deep learning approach. J. Biomed. Inform. **69**, 218–229 (2017)

34. Rajkomar, A., et al.: Scalable and accurate deep learning with electronic health records. NPJ Digit. Med. **1**(1), 18 (2018)

35. Rios, A., Kavuluru, R.: Neural transfer learning for assigning diagnosis codes to EMRs. Artif. Intell. Med. **96**, 116–122 (2019)

36. Rosenbaum, P.R., Rubin, D.B.: The central role of the propensity score in observational studies for causal effects. Biometrika **70**(1), 41–55 (1983)

37. Saito, T., Rehmsmeier, M.: The precision-recall plot is more informative than the ROC plot when evaluating binary classifiers on imbalanced datasets. PloS One **10**(3), e0118432 (2015)

38. Shang, J., Ma, T., Xiao, C., Sun, J.: Pre-training of graph augmented Transformers for medication recommendation. In: Proceedings of the Twenty-Eighth International Joint Conference on Artificial Intelligence, pp. 5953–5959 (2019)

39. Shickel, B., Tighe, P.J., Bihorac, A., Rashidi, P.: Deep EHR: a survey of recent advances in deep learning techniques for electronic health record (EHR) analysis. IEEE J. Biomed. Health Inform. **22**(5), 1589–1604 (2017)

40. Tonelli, M., et al.: Chronic kidney disease and mortality risk: a systematic review. J. Am. Soc. Nephrol. **17**(7), 2034–2047 (2006)

41. Vaswani, A., et al.: Attention is all you need. In: Advances in Neural Information Processing Systems, pp. 5998–6008 (2017)

42. Webster, A.C., Nagler, E.V., Morton, R.L., Masson, P.: Chronic kidney disease. Lancet **389**(10075), 1238–1252 (2017)

43. Xiao, C., Choi, E., Sun, J.: Opportunities and challenges in developing deep learning models using electronic health records data: a systematic review. J. Am. Med. Inform. Assoc. **25**(10), 1419–1428 (2018)

44. Zeiler, M.D.: Adadelta: an adaptive learning rate method. arXiv preprint arXiv:1212.5701 (2012)

# Author Index

Printed in the United States
by Baker & Taylor Publisher Services